# SURVIVING IRAQ

# SURVIVING IRAQ
## SOLDIERS' STORIES

### Elise Forbes Tripp

OLIVE
BRANCH
PRESS

An imprint of Interlink Publishing Group, Inc.
**www.interlinkbooks.com**

First published in 2008 by

**OLIVE BRANCH PRESS**
An imprint of Interlink Publishing Group, Inc.
46 Crosby Street, Northampton, Massachusetts 01060
**www.interlinkbooks.com**

Copyright © Elise Forbes Tripp, 2008
Map by Jacob Shemkovitz

**Library of Congress Cataloging-in-Publication Data**
Tripp, Elise Forbes.
Surviving Iraq : soldiers' stories / by Elise Forbes Tripp.—1st ed.
p. cm.
ISBN-13: 978-1-56656-693-3 (pbk.)
1. Iraq War, 2003—Personal narratives, American. 2. United States—
Armed Forces—Iraq—Interviews. I. Title.
DS79.76.T75 2007
956.7044'34092273—dc22
2007026048


*Cover image © AP Wideworld Photos*

Printed and bound in the United States of America

To request our complete 40-page full-color catalog,
please call us toll free at 1-800-238-LINK, visit our
website at www.interlinkbooks.com, or write to
Interlink Publishing
46 Crosby Street, Northampton, MA 01060
e-mail: info@interlinkbooks.com

# CONTENTS

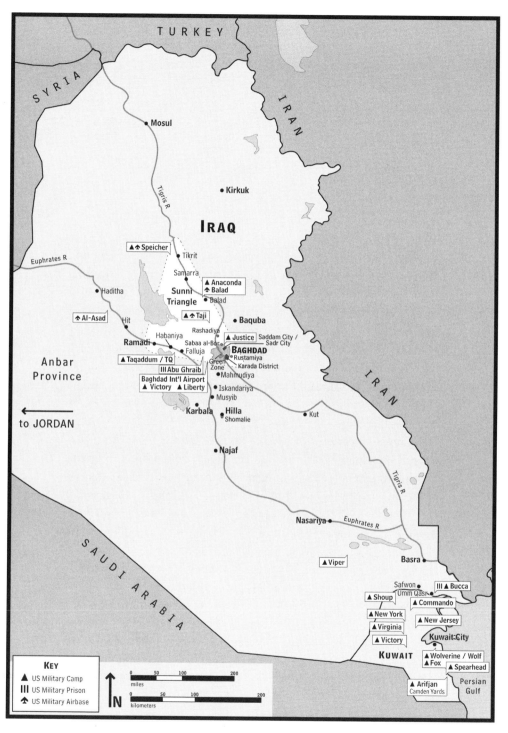

US MILITARY PRESENCE IN IRAQ & KUWAIT

# Preface

# RECORDING AN ORAL HISTORY OF THE IRAQ WAR

*S*urviving Iraq: Soldiers' Stories is a collaborative effort. For seventeen months, I met with veterans of the Iraq war to record these personal stories. I asked each of them to talk about those experiences that meant the most to them, to reflect on their roles in an historic war, and to comment on the war itself. I did not want their stories to be shaped by a set of questions, so what follows is what they chose to record. All interviewees received a copy of the transcript and some corrected, clarified, and added to it. Each narrative conveys an individual veteran's experiences and thoughts without any editorializing. In these stories, the war is in the present—not past—tense, with its history still being written by veterans like these.

The 30 interviews that make up this volume were conducted from the spring of 2005 through the fall of 2006. I had a civilian's view of the war and was unfamiliar with many aspects of the modern US military. My lack of military background, however, had the unintended benefit of having veterans explain to me the paraphernalia of war as they spoke, which in turn makes their stories more accessible to the general reader. The reader will note that I use the general term "soldier" for army soldier, marine, airman, and sailor, just as the term "veteran" applies to all the services.

As I became more familiar with the world of a soldier, I could appreciate why veterans often avoid discussing their war, and do not easily share their stories with civilians. Part of their reluctance comes from their perception of what civilians do and do not want to hear from a veteran. War can widen the military-civilian divide. Some soldiers develop a few typically "military" stories to use as needed. Many civilians either do not know how to ask questions about a soldier's service, or are insensitive. Because, out of uniform, veterans are invisible, they can also choose not to be identified. And yet, while some may not want to be recognized in passing (they do not count the "Support the Troops" decals on cars), they do want their service recognized.

According to the veterans I interviewed, civilians frequently ask how many people they killed in the war. Those that killed resent the insensitivity of the question, and those that did not, the implication that they were any less a soldier. A number of veterans told me that they were glad they did not have to kill anyone. As in all wars, many veterans did not experience actual combat, but rather handled the war's infrastructure—food, fuel, and vehicles.

As I conducted the interviews, it became clear that veterans had many more interesting and reflective things to say than the action- and anecdote-filled war stories they believed civilians wanted to hear. I asked them to speak for the historical record and to reflect on the political, social, and moral experience of war, as well as the enormous impact of engaging in a war. Veterans confirmed that no one comes through war unscathed, unchanged, untouched, unthinking.

I focused on enlisted men and women. Not only are they the most representative group in numbers, but they represent the America where the fate of the Iraq war will be decided. The bottom tier of the military pyramid, where enlisted men and women find themselves, bears the brunt of the fighting. Iraq war fatalities reflect this: through September 2007, 58 percent were from the lower enlisted, 32 percent were non-commissioned officers and ten percent were commissioned officers (Iraq Index, Brookings Institution).

While the annals of war are generally written by officers, enlisted soldiers have just as much significant experience as their superiors and as much to say about it. In their narratives, veterans convey their personal opinions, hoping to be listened to without being judged. I assured them that the project was nonpartisan. All their interviews would be included and no one would be selected or excluded for their views—views that I did not know when I arranged the interviews. If they asked what I *personally* thought about the war, I answered at the end of the interview that I did not think it could be won. Most veterans I spoke to agreed.

Oral history has a cadence that is different from written history. When veterans write their stories they are in command of presentation and language and select their topics with some care. Oral history as I recorded it (without an outline) was extemporaneous—veterans created many of their stories as they talked. In their narratives they shifted in mood and style from clever and funny to thoughtful and candid to philosophical and alienated. They brought up what was most basic: loss, fear, frustration, hope, relief, friendship, and family. The narratives were illuminated by the unspoken language of the eyes and body. I could see that being in a war leaves many people jumpy and worried for some time afterward.

As noted above, when I started an interview, I had no idea if the veteran supported or opposed the war, what they thought of their commander in chief, if they thought their contribution was worthwhile, and whether they felt whole or wounded in some way. Until they told me, I had no information about what had happened to them in Iraq and Kuwait. I recorded the information as it was given, sometimes asking for clarification, but trying to stay out of the way of the story. When I did ask for information on a new topic, my question is bracketed in italics in the text. I doubt that all the details recorded here are historically accurate, for people recreate their roles and change the details of events. While most factual errors in terms, names, or locations have been corrected, the reader should know that some inaccuracies (including those that I did not recognize) undoubtedly remain in the narratives.

I recorded all the interviews one-on-one. While seven veterans living at some distance were taped on the telephone for mutual convenience, I had already met and talked with five of them, leaving only two that I have not yet met in person. The stories are generally in chronological order, moving along with the war. I have, however, grouped the women together to emphasize their new roles in today's armed forces, and to suggest differences in perspective.

Narratives have been significantly edited for length, generally retaining less than half of the original text. I selected passages that were particularly informative, original, unusual, revealing, and expressive. I reduced the length of each narrative so as to include everyone I interviewed, and also to hold the interest of the reader. I did not use ellipsis points for most edits within a topic but used them to indicate major cuts in material and shifts in the story line. To understand the references in the narratives, a chronology of the war, as well as a glossary of military terms, are included in the Appendix. These references are drawn from the narratives themselves and provide readers with relevant background.

I occasionally moved text so as to group together comments on a certain topic and also to make the stories easier to follow. Throughout, I reduced the frequency of filler words such as "and," "like," "stuff," and "whatever." Where I have had to provide a word or change an incorrect or misspoken word, I use brackets; sometimes grammar is standardized for clarification. Some interviewees made their own informational and grammatical corrections, or consulted on ways to clarify the narrative, but most did not choose to revise their narrative. In all cases, I encouraged veterans to use their transcripts wherever and whenever they had the opportunity.

Despite the inclusion of a broad range of veterans by age, sex, branch of service, and time of deployment, interviewing in person favored those who could be recorded in Massachusetts. A number were student veterans who attended the two institutions where I taught as visiting lecturer and adjunct faculty member—the University of Massachusetts at Amherst and Holyoke Community College. Reflecting the demographics of western Massachusetts, I interviewed more Puerto Ricans than African Americans, which happens also to reflect the fact that more Latinos than African Americans are serving and dying (eleven percent vs. nine percent) in this war. The five women I interviewed also reflect the approximate proportion of women in military service. Soldiers in this book grew up in California, Connecticut, the District of Columbia, Kentucky, Illinois, Massachusetts, New Hampshire, New York, Rhode Island, and Virginia; others are naturalized citizens from Puerto Rico, Jamaica, and Portugal.

In any case, it is best not to put labels on the individuals who speak in these pages. Each has a unique story to tell.

# Acknowledgments

I would like to thank my children, Adam Emerson Pachter, a writer of fiction and nonfiction, and Gillian Forbes Pachter, a film director, writer, and producer, for the enormous support and excellent professional advice they each gave. I am most grateful to my husband, Gordon Anderson Tripp, MD, who encouraged and supported me throughout the time I worked on the book, and whose good judgment served the project well.

I also want to note a few facts about my family and war. My mother, Anne Pappenheimer Forbes, MD, was born on 11/11/11—she was seven on the first Armistice Day and eight when her father returned from medical service as a pathologist in World War I. In World War II, my father, William H. Forbes, conducted physiological studies for the armed forces, while his brother, David Forbes, served in the navy. My maternal uncles, Alwin and John Pappenheimer (respectively a biochemist and a physiologist), also joined the war effort as scientists. Yet every one of their male descendants avoided service in Vietnam. And in the next generation, alone among his cousins, my nephew Torry Schoenfeld served in Iraq. War revisits us, generation after generation.

Friends and acquaintances offered me encouragement and practical advice. I am indebted to authors Chris Appy, Madeleine Blais, Abbott (Tom) Gleason, Michael Janeway, William Taubman, Natalie Shorr, Mark Shorr, and editor Richard Todd. Veterans' agents Leo J. Parent, Jr. (Central Franklin County District) and Robert St. George (Holyoke Community College) gave me very good advice on many occasions.

Matt Mitchell, Revan Schendler, and Robert Wilson (Veterans Education Project) all shared their ideas on ways to help veterans be heard. I am most grateful to Professor Robert Meagher

(Hampshire College) who organized the NOSTOI program entitled "Stories of War and Return" in the spring of 2005, from which I learned a great deal.

I am delighted to publish *Surviving Iraq: Soldiers' Stories* with the publisher Michel Moushabeck. Olive Branch Press, and the Interlink Publishing Group, have done a great deal to bring all facets of the Middle East, including the American presence there, to a wider audience. The book benefited a great deal from editor Pamela Thompson's perceptive review, art director Juliana Spear's excellent design, and copy editor Hilary Plum's knowledgeable editing.

# Introduction

# STORIES OF WAR, RETURN, AND LOSS

I conceived the idea for *Surviving Iraq: Soldiers' Stories* when my nephew deployed to Iraq. On January 10, 2003, Arthur H.F. Schoenfeld ("Torry") shipped out as a sergeant in the US Marines' Second Light Armored Reconnaissance Battalion. He sailed, to use the traditional term, on the USS *Kearsage,* which is named for a New Hampshire mountain—a name handed down from ship to ship since the Civil War. His amphibious assault carrier was loaded with aircraft, helicopters, armored vehicles, hovercraft, and almost 2,000 marines. I have a picture of Torry in training. Outfitted for war, his goggles, helmet, radio gear, gun, and vehicle frame one small familiar element in the photograph— his face. I imagined this face among a sea of faces in the hold of a ship, a black-and-white *Time-Life* photograph, something like the invasion of Normandy.

After making camp in Kuwait, he and his battalion invaded Iraq on March 21, 2003, which happened to be the day he was to have ended his four-year commitment to the Marine Corps. He left college and enlisted before there was a war. His first deployment was to Guantánamo Bay, before it became a prison center. He guarded the facility and did some scuba diving. Torry almost missed the Iraq war, but in December 2002, he learned that his discharge would be indefinitely delayed and that he would become part of a massive deployment of troops to the Middle East.

Our family had an electronic link to Torry through dispatches by an embedded reporter. Dennis O'Brien, an ex-marine, wrote for the *Newport News*; sadly, he committed suicide seven months after his five-month assignment. Much of his embedding was on the ship going over, so we learned about cramped quarters, communications bottlenecks, and standing in line. Once, we had wisps of information that suggested that Torry was in Nasariya where Jessica Lynch was captured and freed, and where a number of marines died in "Ambush Alley." It was also where Torry's company took its first—and only—fatality when a soldier grasped a live overhead wire. The whole time he was in Iraq, I tried to imagine Torry as a soldier who could be wounded or worse, but the image was never real.

Torry took part in Task Force Tarawa, part of the marine invasion of Iraq. The name comes from a 1943 battle on a few islets in the Pacific 2,500 miles from Hawaii, where the marines took 3,133 casualties. Counting both US and Japanese losses, 5,680 died or were mortally wounded in 76 hours. Camp Shoup in Kuwait, where marines grouped for the 2003 invasion, is named for Colonel (later General) David M. Shoup, who earned the Medal of Honor for his bravery in the Tarawa battle. Despite the name, Torry's war had little in common with World War II. He came home in June 2003 after a few months in theater. In a nice gesture, when the vessel he was on was diverted to Liberia, his commander used a hovercraft to get him and a few others whose enlistments had also been extended to a ship heading straight home.

Fighting in Iraq did not change Torry's opinion of the war. He deployed and returned a skeptic. He and a number of his mates on shipboard, headed for Iraq in early February 2003, watched Secretary of State Colin Powell deliver his speeches about Iraq's putative weapons of mass destruction to the UN. Some of them found the performance unconvincing. They knew that the world wanted the US to hold off on the war, and they worried that the administration was being reckless. Like most soldiers I interviewed, Torry had a double vision of the war. He was concerned about its purposes and outcome but viewed his own service with pride. To this day, he believes that the initial campaign he fought in was brilliant, but that Washington had no plans for Iraq after the invasion.

———

The war in Iraq is a watershed event for the United States, its allies, the Middle East, and the world. It has a rapidly spreading and compounding impact. The invasion was—as President Bush had promised—a preemptive strike to replace a regime hostile to the United States with a government designed to be an ally in a strategic region. However, the leaders that have replaced Saddam Hussein are functioning within a US occupation—which is likely to compromise their ability to manage their country and the war. Perhaps the Iraqi government will begin to resemble that of South Vietnam 40 years ago, when the US replaced leaders they thought too weak or compromised to help them finish the job.

I was a student when Vietnam became a national issue, and I volunteered to lie under the wheels of a stationary limousine in which Secretary of Defense Robert McNamara was marooned while mobbed by antiwar demonstrators. I took no risk, but he did, because he decided to stand on the vehicle's hood and shout down Harvard undergraduates, screaming that we were too young and too ignorant to know anything about the war. As it turned out, we did, and he didn't.

Donald Rumsfeld, secretary of defense during the first three-and-a-half years of the Iraq war, said famously, "You go to war with the army you have. They're not the army you might want or wish to have at a later time" (Kuwait, December 8, 2004). From my interviews, it seems that many veterans would paraphrase the statement to reflect their own ambivalence: "You go to the war you have. It's not the war you might want or wish to have." Some veterans persistently question their mission, especially as the war gets bloodier and more intractable. While deployed, soldiers look for justification for what they do, yet still wonder what they are fighting for, what the war is really about, if it can be won, and if it is worth it.

The narratives in this book focus on three stages of war, only one of which is combat. To understand soldiers' views, we need to know something about those who enlisted, what they did during their time at war, and what has happened to them since their return home. Most veterans are neither apologists nor pundits, but focus rather on their own enlistment, activation, deployment, and return. Their personal survival during an embedded year without escape is what matters most.

Soldiers start their stories with a variety of reasons why they volunteered to serve in the military, often blaming the "lies" their recruiters told them, which "misled" them into the service. Recruiters benefit from language in the No Child Left Behind Act of 2001 that gives them access to the names, Social Security numbers, addresses, and telephone numbers of all students of enlistment age. Schools must provide this background unless parents know enough to ask them to block the information on their child. Still, recruiters have to work hard to meet their quotas, and the longer the war goes on, the harder it is. One National Guard recruiter complained to me about the obvious—newscasts of the war on TV were having a negative effect on recruitment.

Recruits in the all-volunteer army are primarily high-school graduates from working-class families. In this war, the rural South and rural West are over-represented, and urban American is under-represented. The fewer the opportunities near home, the more attractive the military becomes. Today's enlistees are economic recruits looking for educational benefits for college, a salary, a skill, and a veteran background to help them get jobs. Besides the promise of a college education, they are offered financial "bonuses" to join, sometimes enough for a car. Recruiters are psychologically and socially observant, scanning potential recruits by phone or in the malls, looking for ways to hook them. One told me he always used the line that everyone must have a life plan, which should start with the military. Recruiters also understand that parents can be their adversaries, so one selling point with juniors and seniors in high school is independence from home.

Current incentives used by the military include the service-wide Montgomery GI Bill, offering up to $38,700 (2007 figure) for higher education, to be used within ten years. While in school, a veteran gets a monthly check for tuition and living expenses, which caps at 36 months of college. To receive this stipend, soldiers must have paid in a non-reimbursable $1,200 and been on active duty for three years. The military portrays itself as a school for life, a path to college, and an economic safety net.

The army offers "Enlistment Bonuses of up to $20,000. The Choice of More than 154 Jobs. Up to $70,000 for College, if you Qualify. Up to 100% Tuition Assistance." The air force recruits with a friendly, "Hey senior! It's time to start thinking about your future. Great Education and Training Opportunities. Enrollment at the Fully Accredited Community College of the Air Force." A brochure from the office of the secretary of defense for all branches explains, "You need money for college (we've got up to $50,000 waiting for you)."

The navy approach is: "Dream it. Believe it. Achieve it: Wherever Your Ambition Takes You. You're Capable of Achieving Greatness. We've Got the Financial Capabilities to Help You Get it Done." The Army National Guard invites recruits to "Join America's Team: Belong to Something Greater than Yourself. Serve Your Country Part-Time. Citizen, Soldier, Protector. Hometown Heroes Serving Community and Country Since 1636. Earn up to $30,000 for College." The Air National Guard promises "Cash Bonus. Free Tuition."

The Marine Corps recruits "The Few. The Proud." While the Marine Corps mentions the military activity associated with service more than the other branches, it also tells parents that, "While your son or daughter is on active duty, there will be many opportunities for them to take courses at a college or university level," meaning correspondence and online courses. While these approaches work—as the soldiers' narratives attest—the actual benefits are almost always less than the promises.

All recruits must take the ASVAB, a test that requires English writing and reasoning, basic math skills, and vocational knowledge. The ASVAB can be retaken 30 days after the first failure and every six months thereafter, with a grade of between 31 to 36—depending on the branch of service—out of 99 constituting a passing grade, and below 31 meaning rejection. There are ASVAB preparatory courses available. The requirement of a high-school diploma or the GED (General Educational Development, a high-school equivalency test) can be waived. Middle age is no barrier. Since changes made in 2006, active-duty soldiers and reservists can join up to age 42 and retire with a pension after age 60, or with 20 years' service.

Recruits are often looking for adventure, action, travel, an exciting period in their lives. They are patriotic, often from families who have served in the military. They want to avenge 9/11, which is the first national catastrophe most have experienced. They want to defend the United States and build its lasting security, to fight over there rather than back here. Some also volunteer to fight to end a brutal dictatorship, for a democratic Iraq, to build security in the Middle East, and secure the US access to oil. Some recruits are also looking for a new start. Recruiters ask potential recruits about their record of misdemeanors and felonies, but it is well known that the military will accept a "paper trail" if other criteria are met.

When deployed after their training, soldiers find that the war theater requires tunnel vision, and yet they still have a 360-degree view of the war. They can focus on their immediate surroundings while observing the larger political context. In the field, many prefer to focus on the small rather than the large picture. They substitute an immediate cause, like building a school, for the larger war. On this smaller scale, it is possible to win, make Iraqi friends, save lives. Some choose to focus on the good works Americans perform, which they think are too often ignored by the media.

Soldiers rationalize their war. The battle for Falluja becomes an action in which Iraqi citizens were warned to leave the city before the Americans destroyed it—so that actually, American forces spared them death. But the Americans also destroyed the city because it was a Sunni stronghold, and in retaliation for attacks on US patrols and the killing and public display of the bodies of four contractors. There is also a shift in perception from the offensive to the defensive, from the "Shock and Awe" of the invasion to having to react to an insurgency in which American soldiers are victims. But Americans are fighting insurgents halfway across the globe in a war the US initiated in a country that did not attack them—clearly, an offensive war. Many veterans appreciate that.

What makes fighting this war different from previous ones? There is no single enemy or even *type* of enemy. There is instead a hydra-headed proliferating enemy force that grows new cells and attracts volunteers and mercenaries without regard to national boundaries. The American and coalition forces only briefly conducted a conventional war, defeating the Iraqi army (much weakened by the Gulf War and sanctions) in three weeks. This did not end the war, because President Bush claimed that Iraq was part of the larger global war on terror (GWOT): "The Battle of Iraq is one victory in a war on terror that began on September the 11th, 2001, and still goes on" (May 1, 2003). The strategy of countering terrorism with boots on the ground is the central contradiction of this conflict. Terrorism is a brutal, bloody, and criminal pursuit of an abstraction, not a battlefield enemy.

Wars are generally fought for political objectives and are successful only if these are met. Soldiers are often not sure of the

Iraq war's political purposes. Goals continue to shift, which means soldiers must keep revising why they are there. They view 9/11 as the reason for the war on terror. But there was also the reason given for invading Iraq, as offered to the UN and the world: Saddam Hussein's alleged weapons of mass destruction (WMD). President Bush told sailors on the USS *Lincoln* on May 1, 2003: "No terrorist network will gain weapons of mass destruction from the Iraqi regime, because the regime is no more," a carefully worded inference that the Iraqi regime had had such weapons, although neither UN inspectors nor US forces had found them. Troops left for the war not knowing if they would be attacked with nuclear, biological, or chemical (NBC) weapons, so the earliest arrivals wore protective suits. While weapons of mass destruction were never found in Iraq, the US is now raising concerns about nuclear weapons next door in Iran, raising the same specter of a Middle Eastern country attacking America or selling nuclear technology to terrorists.

Soldiers were told that Saddam Hussein constituted a threat to the United States and many also believed that he bore some responsibility for 9/11—later acknowledged to be untrue, but never forcefully denied. Without that, and without WMD, the rationale for preemptive war became Saddam Hussein himself, his dictatorship, and his attacks on his own citizens. Because Iraqi citizens were seen as oppressed, the American military leadership used the wishful analogy of the liberation of France in 1944 to prepare soldiers for their welcome in Iraq. The liberation period was short, however, and US soldiers now understand that many Iraqis want Americans to go home.

There was no popular uprising against Saddam Hussein in 2003 when he was attacked by the Americans and their global allies. With his defeat, the American–Iraqi (primarily the Shia and Kurdish populations) rationale for cooperation weakened because their common enemy was gone. The American–Iraqi partnership that emerged was not truly a partnership because the two parties were working on different goals: for America, to create a friendly new government; for the Iraqis, to effect social and political realignment, and to settle old scores. Cooperation is only as strong as the weaker partner, so now the US waits for an Iraqi government and army capable of being an ally. Even in an unequal alliance, however, each partner manipulates the other for its own ends, and the stronger power may not get its way.

The soldiers of the American occupation are engaged in fighting a major insurgency that actually started just days into the war. A number of soldiers' narratives mention hostile civilian attitudes and acts during and right after the invasion. US soldiers find the growing insurgency discouraging because it erases progress in rebuilding Iraq; it means there are no safe zones, it is carried out by people often planning to die in the process, and there is no end in sight. Insurgents attack both US occupation forces and the Iraqi government, its infrastructure, police, and army, aiming to get them all to give up. The insurgency is not limited by the availability of Iraqi recruits or funds because it can tap supplies, money, and personnel from outside the country. As this is being written, there is a civil war among Iraqi sects and factions, and the field of battle in Iraq is surrounded by a widening, violent, regional conflict.

The insurgency has also blurred battle lines and zones of occupation, so the war physically engulfs those in support positions. IEDs (improvised explosive devices) and car bombs make traveling or patrolling anywhere in Iraq dangerous. Mortar and rocket attacks make sleeping and eating anywhere in Iraq dangerous. Even Kuwait is not without danger. The number of casualties per soldier in Iraq is low compared to other wars, but it is not decreasing. Rather, as the initial invasion recedes, it grows. These casualties reached more than 3,700 dead and 28,000 wounded by September 2007, eroding support for the war.

One reason given for staying in Iraq is to carry out its physical and political reconstruction, but that goal remains elusive. Rebuilding social and physical infrastructure such as clinics and schools certainly brings great satisfaction to soldiers in the midst of war. Rebuilding political infrastructure is hard, and spreading democracy—another US administration rationale for the war— even harder. Few soldiers believe that Iraq is likely to become a democracy any time soon, if ever. Therefore, most soldiers believe that they are doing what they can in a very limiting political environment, but that Iraqi leaders are not ready or able to take advantage of American help. In addition, it appears that there is no obvious exit from this war, for to leave could bring more chaos and more bloodshed. The US may have planned to make Iraq its

Middle Eastern headquarters, but now it is literally trapped there—in the largest US embassy in the world.

The US occupation also demands some cultural understanding of a region practically unknown to Americans, who make their way in an unfamiliar political and cultural situation, usually without speaking the language. Some American soldiers have daily contact with Iraqis as nationals working for the armed forces, civilians at checkpoints, vendors, enemy prisoners of war, possible insurgents, men, women, and children in whose country Americans have suddenly appeared and are apparently prepared to stay. Soldiers are learning more about Iraq—its customs, the status of women, religious divisions, tribal identities, its merchants and herders. They observe the barter system and corruption and appreciate that these are survival skills. While there, they also operate under extreme weather conditions with temperatures up to 140 degrees, their bottled water often too hot to drink.

Most US soldiers do not demonize all Iraqis by race, religion, or ideology. They do use derogatory language such as "rag-heads," "towel-heads," "hajji," and "Ali Baba." They definitely divide the population into "good guys" and "bad guys," measured by the threat they pose. At the same time, they often report on some positive personal contact and sometimes a real friendship with their translators. John Laneve, a social worker in the Northampton, Massachusetts Veterans' Administration medical center, has processed hundreds of returning veterans: "I can't think of one person that was pejorative about, or demonized, any of the people that they fought against or alongside of." However, there are soldiers who hate Iraqis—they are the reason they are stuck in Iraq. Others may feel sympathy for Iraqis, and choose instead to blame the commander in chief who sent them there.

US soldiers are facing not only a resentful population that has lost almost everything it had, but international brigades from other Muslim countries that are coming to fight with Iraqi sects. Pan-Arab or pan-Muslim brigades are not new in the region, as various Palestinian–Israeli conflicts attest. These fighters face the coalition of the willing, the international military force willing to help the US in Iraq. Yet that coalition has shrunk significantly as governments pull their troops out of an unpopular war, and at the same time, the coalition of Muslims willing to fight in Iraq has grown exponentially. The war no longer has a single target such as Osama bin Laden and al-Qaeda, because those targets have become too dispersed to eradicate. It is a war against all potential enemies in an unrelentingly hostile urban terrain.

This war has other novel features. An unprecedented number of women are enlisting, deploying, and serving. They are also dying. By September 2007, 80 had lost their lives, representing 2.14 percent of total American fatalities. Congress will not permit women in combat situations, or in certain specialties such as the infantry. Still, if you are a female truck driver, an MP, intelligence officer, translator, or anything else, you are risking your life. As the narratives make clear, women support the war effort and take their jobs seriously. Male soldiers, however, often voice their reservations about female colleagues, not only about the strains of living closely together but also about their physical limitations. While disclaiming sexism, most lack professional enthusiasm for women in the service.

Women in the Iraq war go through many of the same adjustments as men, but are much more likely to face assault and rape. In addition, they face the open hostility of male comrades, while also handling sexual pressure because numerically they are at such a premium. There are wives and girlfriends who re-live the war by living with a veteran, and there are wives and girlfriends who themselves need someone to understand what they went through as a soldier. There are the mothers of soldiers, and mothers who leave children behind to be soldiers. There are also single female veterans who have been out of the social loop for years.

US soldiers are now all volunteers, since the draft was discontinued in 1973. Many enlisted men and women thought they would never see war. In the 1990s, President Clinton almost halved the number of active-duty soldiers, and at the same time shifted resources to the Reserves and the state-based National Guard. About 55 percent of the current troops in Iraq are from these two sources—citizens who supplement their income by training one weekend a month and two weeks in the summer. They bring the average age of a soldier in Iraq and Kuwait up significantly. As one veteran said, his reserve unit could be an advertisement for the AARP (American Association of Retired Persons). In some cases, two generations of a family serve together.

Another unusual facet of the Iraq war is that there are significant numbers of soldiers who are not American citizens—both legal and illegal aliens. As the narratives show, there are recruits from around the world, from Poland to the Philippines. The main incentive for these foreign volunteers is the fast-track to citizenship, frequently achieved during their deployment. The US military leadership in Kuwait and Iraq facilitates soldiers' applications for citizenship.

Soldiers in Iraq are 21st-century soldiers. They are facile at war games, familiar with electronic communications, and dependent on an electronic support system even in the battle zone. The Iraq war generation watches movies, videos, plays electronic games, and is adept at technical matters and tactics. Their game-playing has paid off with the high-tech machinery of war. After experience with war games in the arcades, some look forward to playing for real.

E-mail and telephone link soldiers to home throughout their deployment—even daily. One sergeant used to say to his wife, "I have got to go now," without explaining that the background noises were a mortar or rocket attack. She expected that when he signed off to attend to business, he would get right back to her. The military camps are built and provisioned by private contractors with phones, fast food, and sports facilities—a facsimile of hometown America.

Contractors have a high profile in this war, in part because they do much the same work as soldiers but are paid five to ten times as much. Soldiers resent this, of course, although some choose the same option when their tour is up because the salaries are so extraordinarily attractive, especially to young people with low earning power. Some view contractors as mercenaries because they are often ex-soldiers from the Special Forces and other elite groups trained to be effective in security jobs, currently for hire. Such forces are also drawn from a number of countries in the international marketplace.

This is also a war in which the wounded are handled so effectively that they survive horrendous injuries to face a lifetime of limitations. Kevlar helmets and body armor can save the torso and the head, but not the limbs, nor avoid trauma to the brain. In addition, this war appears to have a very high percentage of people acknowledging psychological wounds, something also seen after the Vietnam War.

The narratives that follow reveal that veterans need support for both their physical and psychological wounds. When a soldier returns to the States, getting medical help requires being willing to sign up in a complex and sometimes distrusted system. If soldiers think of re-enlisting, they want a blemish-free evaluation, so both physical and emotional scars are hidden. Laneve, the VA social worker, tells of a group of marines he interviewed:

> I would ask them, "What did you do there, what was your job?" "I am sorry, negative, I can't tell you, sir." "Well, can you tell me where you were?" "Sorry, negative, can't tell you, sir." Sometimes they will come in and say, "I know this is the head shed." A few of them said, "I had no problems over there." "You career military?" "Yes, I am." That explains it to me.

Veterans cannot leave behind in Iraq the internal scars and embedded depression of war. The fragmentation of the mind under extreme pressure is real and should be expected—many psyches will be wounded. Post-traumatic stress disorder (PTSD) is widespread, and in extreme cases there are suicides in the war arena and at home. There are now families of veterans, like the Luceys in the final narrative, trying to reform the VA treatment protocols because the VA failed to prevent their children from committing suicide. Because veterans are claiming PTSD in record numbers, the VA system is trying to stem this tidal wave of claims. The scandal surrounding living conditions and support systems for wounded soldiers at the Walter Reed Medical Center (Washington, DC) which surfaced in early 2007 is symptomatic of a system-wide problem long known to veterans. Even if America abandons this war, veterans will need a well-funded and responsive Department of Veterans Affairs and VA hospital system if they are to be treated effectively.

In these stories we find that soldiers come home with what might be called a mental "chip" that releases fear at sounds (firecrackers like bombs), smells (barbeque like burned flesh), and images (children at play like children run over) implanted by war. War means learning to be on highest alert, so fast driving, defensive seating in a restaurant, and buying guns become the survival techniques that transition soldiers to veterans. They are not all well suited to the home front.

There are also profound moral costs to war. The single event that most soldiers discuss in these narratives, and with the most discomfort, is the abuse by American soldiers of prisoners at Abu Ghraib prison. They understand how it could happen but maintain that it was un-American or atypical. The single most disturbing personal experience soldiers mentioned was that they were told to keep on driving so as not to endanger the convoy, even when children ran in front of their trucks. Soldiers also agonize over the selfishness of survival, over the mortal fear of what having killed will do to them, over the loss of military buddies, and having to leave the "family" of people who understand what they have been through. These losses confirm the permanence of the war experience. The soldier-become-veteran has, to some degree, been transformed.

The idiomatic image of World War II veterans is that of returning heroes. The frequent image of Vietnam veterans is of a soldier coming home only to be abandoned by his government, vilified by his fellow citizens, and pursued by the private demons of his war. Veterans of the Iraq conflict will probably have their own image, neither hero nor outcast. The Iraq war is above all President Bush's war. It is doubtful that veterans will be vilified for fighting in Iraq because the problem was the politicians (American and Iraqi), the political factions, religious leaders, and foreign jihadists. In other words, Iraq will be remembered as a war impossible to win.

What does all of this mean for the returning veteran? American wars of the last century have been approximately a generation apart. There is little continuity, especially as the all-volunteer, economically driven army has replaced the drafted army. The government rewarded World War II soldiers with an education, but this war *entices* recruits with the promise of an education. This is an army of working-class enlistees looking for a way to pay for the next stage of their lives. Citizens ask what they can do for veterans. What veterans need is a sincere welcome home and understanding as they adapt, an education, and jobs. That is what they signed up for. They have just lived one of the greatest stories of their lives, but will be searching for inner peace for some time to come.

> It is an inner struggle. There's this wanting to be in some kind of state that you were in before. You will never, ever, ever be there. Like this army nurse said to me when I was having a bad time when I got back from Iraq. She noticed that I was crying for no reason and she said something to me that I will never forget: "It never goes away. But it gets a little better."
>
> —Scott Palmer, US Army

# ONE

# 9/11 AND THE INVASION OF IRAQ

# JASON RICHARDSON
## Petty Officer 2nd Class, Navy

Nuclear electrician's mate, USS *Truman,* enlisted 1999–2005,
deployed age 21 (November 2002–May 2003,
October 2003–March 2004)
Mediterranean, Persian Gulf

*A "Nuke" on the USS Truman*

*Jason refers to himself throughout his narrative as a "nuke," an intimidating but endearing nickname for someone working on a nuclear reactor. From Princeton, Massachusetts, Jason was sought after as an enlistee since he scored exceptionally well on the ASVAB. He liked the navy, and is currently studying engineering at UMass Amherst. In college he has placed out of a number of high-level courses given his rigorous training and experience with nuclear reactors. In the navy he saw the world through ports of call, and saw the war through the video pictures of the bombing conducted by planes from the deck of his aircraft carrier. Trained before 9/11, Jason was one of what one could call the navy's "first responders." Jason starts his narrative talking about a ship that was not his own, but that was already at sea when 9/11 happened—but then notes, "I know that the first shot of the war was from our cruiser."*

The *Enterprise* was in the Mediterranean on September 11, [2001]. As the captain was watching TV, he saw what was happening [and] immediately ordered the ship to do a 180-degree turn and go back into the Middle East. There are two different ways you can go. For a nuclear carrier, the best way to do it is to go right through the Suez [Canal]. We pay Egypt X amount of dollars to shut it down, it becomes ours, and we send our battle group through it. As the carrier is going through, you can go on each side of the flight deck and look down—and if you would spit or throw a baseball you would hit land. We have our security walking the ship down, we have Egypt's security—basically it's a stand-off for our protection and theirs. Our guns are pointed at *them*, their guns are pointed at *us*, just in case something happens. We can do an entire battle group [in] maybe twelve hours, which is very, very quick.

A battle group—well, now they are called "strike" groups because an admiral wanted to get his name out there by changing something. An aircraft carrier—that's the center piece. You have a couple of destroyers, a couple of cruisers, there *are* submarines—I can't say how many or what type they are—[as] escorts. What else? A tanker to refuel. Even though we're nuclear-powered, our airplanes still use jet fuel. The only way Congress would allow [Admiral] Rickover—the father of nuclear propulsion—to get a reactor was if it was guaranteed to never, ever, have a meltdown. The only way you can do that is to have diesel generators on the ship just in case something happens. We have a back-up with the diesel—the diesel supplies electricity. The reactors are all inherently safe. There will not be an explosion, not on a nuke ship.

[An attack on the ship] is our biggest fear. Where the reactors are placed on the ship, they are in the safest spot. France has the longest-range air-to-sea missile right now, the Exocet, something like a 120-mile range. Iraq had those and Saddam was going to try to use [them] against our ship. I read *Saddam's Secrets* by General Sada. He was in charge of organizing a fleet of 96 MIGs to come after a carrier in the Middle East. And even if one [missile] made it through, that was going to be a success.

But what General Sada knew, because he was American-trained back when we were allies—he learned how to fly in Texas—is if you fire missiles at the carrier we're just going to shut our doors and it's not going to do anything to us, because everything worth hitting is not above the water. So he hits the flight deck, *big deal*. So he hits our two feet of armor, the missile is just going to bounce off.... It was all in the back of our mind: we could go out there and get blown up. If there are missiles or anything coming in besides our own self-defense (because we do have self-defense on the ship besides our airplanes), the other ships know to get in the way of anything. They will sacrifice their ship to save ours.

---

I was in fourth grade when my parents got divorced. When I was growing up, my dad took me to air shows. My grandfather on my mother's side flew airplanes in World War II—he was a captain in the air force. My grandfather on my father's side was a medic over in the European theater. We come from a Republican family, very conservative, my mom not so much, but my father was. When I was in high school, my dad passed away.... My mom remarried, my stepfather [is] very supportive—good guy—*great* guy. My step-grandfather went to Yale under a ROTC scholarship, he was a lieutenant, served on board a submarine. My stepfather said, "Whatever it costs, you are going to go to school, regardless. You can get kicked out of the house or you can go to college or you are going to enlist." That was my ultimatum.

He wanted me to go to college. But then again, he also knew that I was leaning toward the military. "If you want to join, I will talk to your mother about it." She found out I was joining the navy vs. the marines, and then she found out what program I got into—which was the nuclear program. Her first thought—it's a weapon. I'm like, "Mom, no." We do have those, we are trained in nuclear weapons because a weapon and a reactor are very, very similar. That's why we're freaking out about Iran right now. It's so easy to turn a reactor into a weapon—*very, very* simple.

Then I scored really, really high on the ASVAB—99 is a perfect score, I scored a 98. My navy recruiter was blown away that he actually got one of me because it is unheard of for an upper-middle-class white guy to actually enlist out of New England. We've got Ivy League schools everywhere, the money is there. The guy was so happy he snagged me. Even the marine I was talking to was, "Hey, if you qualify for the nuke program, go for it. You can go a lot faster than you will in the marines.".…

I was just an enlisted guy—that's all I was.… My mom signed off on it six months before I graduated high school. October came, [a] guy came and picked me up. "You ready to go?" Shipped off to Great Lakes, Illinois. After boot camp, the Naval Weapons Station, Charleston—the Naval Nuclear Power Training Command in Goose Creek, South Carolina. In Charleston was our first indoc[trination] to two years of the most stringent school I could ever imagine. The campus is beautiful. I lucked out, had my own room—for nukes it's kind of expected. We will tell everyone we are the smartest. Going through the pipeline, going from Charleston until you get to a boat, a lot of guys wash out, attrition rate is huge. We lose a lot of people when it comes to passing the school, a lot do drugs. The navy is the only branch that actually kicks people out for smoking some weed. I was the only person in my division that made it to a ship out of 86 nukes. …

Rickover designed it so it's an enlisted man who controls the reactor, not an officer—because an officer can get corrupted by power. Enlisted guys don't really care about that stuff. The reactor operator, even though he is supervised by an officer, has absolute control. He is the man in charge—or woman, because girls are there, too. If the reactor officer says something wrong, the reactor operator usually starts yelling at the watch officer. It's the only place in the military where you can get away with swearing your mouth off at an officer and not saying "sir" or "ma'am," because we are smarter than them and everyone knows that.

We had six months of nuke school, again down in Charleston. Once you complete that, you go to a real reactor in Ballston Spa, New York, or a moored submarine down in Charleston. I chose to go to New York because I don't like the South. You choose either submarine or carrier—I said because I'm an East Coast guy, anything on the East Coast, and they gave me the *Truman*. I first walked on board August 25, 2001, right before September 11. …

My best friend was a marine, got a ROTC scholarship and was going to MIT, so I was at MIT when September 11 happened. They evacuated MIT. They said, "There's another plane in the air, everyone go." I didn't really know what was going on, so I went to the Prudential Center. I drank the night before, so I was still not really with it. So I went to the Pru and the security guy turned me around. He was like, "A plane just crashed into the World Trade Center, go."

We were all gearing up, we were getting ready to go. We didn't know where yet. A couple of the [Navy] SEALs said we are either going to Afghanistan or Iraq, chances are we are going to Iraq. We hauled ass over there. They said, "Get ready for bombing," because the invasion was going to begin. The *Roosevelt* did twelve hours and we did twelve hours continual bombing for the Shock and Awe. The captain came over the 1-MC, which is the announcing circuit, the night before the invasion. We all saw President Bush make the announcement.... I remember the first shot of the war was from our cruiser. It was a Tomahawk getting shot off. We are talking Iraq. Our ship was not involved in Afghanistan at all—that was the West Coast carriers. We were in the Med[iterranean]. There were already two carriers in the Gulf, two carriers over in Afghanistan. Afghanistan was over fairly soon—we only dealt with Iraq.

So we saw the first shot of the war. We were stocked to the brim with bombs. We could not get bombs fast enough. They even took away half of our galley (where we eat) to assemble bombs. These were laser-guided bombs. They are *very* impressive.... We knew we weren't going to be going nuclear, it wasn't even brought up. The bombs, because we don't want them going off in the ship, you bring them up, you put them together, bolt them onto the jet. It was very interesting watching an F-14 or an F-18 go out fully loaded and come back empty. And then we got to go see the pictures. There was a video produced by our AV department of a lot of the bombings that we did, which the public will never see, but that was a *cool* video. Actually, that was for morale and morale only.... We got most of our news from Fox, satellite TV. It was *very* cool to see something that we were doing was actually making a difference in the battle.

We were there to protect the special ops [operations] guys in the north [of Iraq] because Turkey back-doored us. The army ships [in Turkey] were ready to unload, Turkey said no. And so our Special Forces in the north got screwed by Turkey, so we were out there to protect those guys. I think there were 200 special ops guys in the north before they got reinforced by the infantry, the marines, and maybe 30,000 troops. [Our targets] were individual military targets. Our special ops guys paint lasers on targets. You get a laser—like a regular pen laser, not really that much bigger but a lot more powerful. What happens is: the bomb from the airplane gets a reflection of the laser off of the target—doesn't see the laser itself but gets a reflection—and it focuses in on that and then bombs it.

[*Who focuses the laser?*] That is a Special Forces person, a Navy SEAL, a Force Recon, which is a very specialized marine unit, it *could* be Delta Force, or Army Rangers can do it too, they are all trained at the same place by the same guys. They're a few hundred yards away [from the target], just blending in. A lot of marine snipers can do that too because they blend in very, very well. What they usually do is go in at night, paint the target, leave the laser pointer there, and *get the hell out*. "Paint" means they aim that laser and keep it on the target. Basically, they put it on a tripod and hope it doesn't get caught. We could see the smart-bomb camera going in like you see on the news, we see it just before you guys do. ...

Basically, we did air strikes all day—that went on for four months. We got relieved, the *George Washington* came over and we did the high-five. We go to England, treated like *kings* in England, they *loved* us because they're backing us up, and we loved England. When they found out we were American, "We'll buy you drinks." Then we left England and we hauled butt back to Norfolk where we got a great reception. Carriers always get a good reception. I got good and sunburned that day, but it was worth it. You can see us with the naked eye from space. ...

We called victory but the war wasn't over. [Bush] flew onto the *Lincoln*—which was pretty good for them. We would have liked that, but that's okay. If it was over, we wouldn't have gone back the second time. I stayed on the *Truman*. And this time we knew that we were going to the Middle East, which did not sit well with any of us. We liked the colder water of the Mediterranean, and we didn't like being targets—in the Mediterranean we weren't scared. But in the Middle East it isn't really true.

We get back over there, stayed in the Persian [Gulf] the entire time. We started doing flight ops that night that we got there, started bombing stuff there. Mainly it was the army calling it in, where they are going hunting, where they needed back-up. And we never turned our back completely to Iran, never—we still don't.

There is always something aimed over there. We are always within one fuel tank, well, half a fuel tank because the guy has to get back—we are always within one trip of Iran, too. Just in case.

[*Are you given the reasons for the war?*] As a nuke, we don't need to know. It's not our business. They say we don't kill people, which is *wrong*, because I know due to what we do, really we do—and that is not an issue with any of us. But they keep us in the dark a lot. They don't want us getting a *conscience*. Same with the air force nukes with regard to the weapons, they don't want them getting a conscience either, because with one flick of the wrist, we can shut down the entire battle group. There is one switch that a nuke with a conscience can shut [the reactor] down. We can stop the battle group for days. So they don't want us knowing all.

[*What about calls to patriotism?*] Those are mostly for the marines on board, they get fed that stuff. We are a lot more freethinkers. If I was to categorize a typical nuke, I would say he is pretty moderate. I wouldn't say everyone else on board is a very conservative Republican. Whereas nukes are pretty much moderates, some of them are very liberal, too. They join just to get the college money, but they also understand what happened, they knew why we were out there.

And there were things *we* knew from the SEALs that would come back to the ship and the pictures—we knew that al-Qaeda was in Iraq for a while, we knew Saddam was funneling money to them. So we knew we were doing good. It really boiled down to "we are the good guys, they are the bad guys." On September 11 when they hit the Pentagon, there were a lot of military friends that were killed. There were a lot of people from New York that were on our ship, and they had *no problem* with us being out there. [*But 9/11 was not planned or carried out by Iraq.*] True.

[Iraqis] either have a nuclear weapon or they don't. My friends on the ground found a lot of things. Unfortunately, we didn't shut off the borders in time. Syria and Jordan got a lot of "things." The irony of the whole damn French thing is: every centrifuge we found, every weapon we found (besides Soviet weapons)—at Baghdad airport we found helicopters, helmets—they were all French. Those guys brought back a lot of tools, my friends on the ground would come and ask, what is this? And being a nuke, there was only one reason why that tool was there. And there were traces of uranium, you can feel it, it is still warm, and it gets warm all by itself for a reason. As a nuke, I knew exactly what those were for.

Hans Blix [chief UN weapons monitor]—I am really surprised he didn't find what we found…. I would love to one day either find them or stop looking because they had to have gone somewhere. [Saddam Hussein] used them once, he hated us, he has to have used again. We *think* [he] paid off some Chinese scientists and old Russian astrophysicists. His nuclear capabilities were not quite up to speed. I don't think he would have had a mobile weapon for a while. He would have eventually gotten it because the tools were there—it's only a matter of assembling it…. We got bad info from bad people. Was it the president's fault for believing that info? I'm not going to blame Bush. He is ultimately responsible, but if it was due to bad info you have got to keep on going down the chain until you find that person. I don't think it was a military blunder, because we're not there to make policy. …

I do watch both sides, I watch CNN and Fox. We had an embedded reporter [who] asked why Fox News is on and not CNN, and I go, "Well, maybe you can answer that for me." He goes, "Ted Turner doesn't exactly like the administration, so [CNN] tries to paint you guys in a bad light." And I go, "You know what, that kind of makes sense to me." So that's where I get that CNN doesn't really like us…. [Fox TV's Bill] O'Reilly hit it dead on. There was someone bitching about us being over there, and O'Reilly was like, "How can you say to those men and women over there that we shouldn't be out there and they shouldn't get our full support when they are watching right now." And I shot off an e-mail right then, "Bill, you are right, we *are* watching right now and just keep on telling people we always *are*." …

———

We had 5,000 people on board. We had every different race, every different nationality. Probably the best thing I got out of the navy was dealing with every different type of ethnicity, class, religion. When I was on watch, I had a white guy, black guy, Mexican, white girl, black girl, Mexican girl, it didn't really matter…. I think there are a lot more black males than white males on board and a lot more black females than white females. I know I am going to sound wrong here, but [females] get an easy life. They can really take advantage of the system—and a lot of them do. I knew that all a woman has to do is get pregnant to get off the ship. They get their own sleeping areas, which are better than the guys' areas. They don't have to do as well on the physical test as us. ...

After the first deployment ended they started to pitch for re-enlistment, and we get $45,000 for a two-year re-enlistment—and I turned it down. Once they started giving up on me I started to fill out my college stuff on my second deployment. After I got home, got accepted here [UMass Amherst], and tuition is waived [$1,700] but you have got $7,000 fees to pay. That *beyond* infuriated me. I immediately wrote a nasty letter to [Governor] Mitt [Romney]. I did get a reply, but the fees were still not waived either for reservists or active-duty guys, they were waived for the National Guard. Coming here, I had no financial aid, no nothing. ...

But people around here don't really like us—they want ROTC off the campus, or they want all the recruiters off the campus.... And when they find out I'm a soldier, the first thing they ask is how many people I've killed. "You were over there? Did you kill anyone?" "I'm not answering that! If I did, I did. If I didn't, I didn't." It's not like I go over there, "Oh good, I get a kill count." If I was a marine I would probably deck the guy because one of my friends [did]. The police came and the marine wasn't charged. The punk apologized.... I am *very* against Cindy Sheehan [antiwar activist whose son died in Iraq]. She could be a grieving mother—her son died in combat—that's a big deal. However, her son also re-enlisted. It's not like he was sent over there.... There are ways—you are going to be called a coward—but there are ways to get out of going. The easiest way is to smoke a little weed and you're out—no questions asked.

Now, the guys that were in combat, it does take a long time for them to re-acclimate themselves. A couple of my buddies' fathers are Vietnam vets. They talked with us—how they weren't really debriefed, how they never had any counseling, it wasn't even *available.* When we are coming back we have a psychologist fly on board. I got basically the counseling I needed—which wasn't psychological. It was, how do I deal with finding a job? What's the right way to address a professor? What is the right way to address a boss? I will not continually say, "Yes, sir, yes, sir, yes, sir."

# NATHAN D. HOLLWAY
### Firefighter, Air Force

Enlisted 2000–2004, deployed age 21 (September 2001) Qatar

*Air Support in Qatar*

*Nathan enlisted in the air force as a firefighter. When I met him at Holyoke Community College, he ended his interview with the comment that he wanted to go back to the Middle East as a contractor and make some money. A year and a half later he was in Djibouti working as a civilian. He has traveled with his father and brother to South Africa, seeing the world and having a great time. He is appreciative of his family's support. "With all of my traveling, my parents have been encouraging and helpful along the way and I love them for it." Nathan likes to run 10K road races, and competes in his town's annual St. Patrick's Day race. While stationed in Qatar in support of the war in Afghanistan, he ran in the desert every day. Politically a firm Democrat, he questions the war's prospects. Although he served in OEF, not in OIF, he comments that in Iraq, "I think we could be in over our heads now."*

I enlisted in the military in 2000. ... Then September 11 happened and it caught everybody off guard. I was on duty that day—everyone remembers where they were that day like it was yesterday. It was about 8 o'clock in the morning. I was on the rescue truck and got back to the fire station and all the bay doors in the fire station were closed and that confused everybody because we always have doors open. What's going on? There's a whole bunch of people and we just saw their faces and could tell something has happened, like they've seen a ghost. I remember an older guy—he said an airplane just went into the World Trade Center.

At first we thought that some pilot must have fallen asleep. We are glued to the TV and we saw the second one hit, and we were just confused—it was a terrorist attack.... Everyone had to spend the night in the fire station. All of our lines are secure—no one is allowed to call off base. My mom was worried. She sent a few e-mails and I got to write back to her, "I'm safe, don't worry." Three days after September 11th, our fire station had a meeting with the commander, [who] said, "Out of the 80 firefighters here, eight people are going to have to go. Do I have any volunteers?" Everybody raised their hand—everyone's patriotic now. Me being sort of new in the fire station, I didn't have a good chance of going. ...

I went to work the next day and the fire chief pulled me aside and said, "Airman Hollway, you got all your bags packed?" "Yes, sir." I had no bags packed. I knew I wanted to go, "Yes, sir, my bags are packed," and he said, "Well, get them down here because you're taking Airman K.'s spot." My heart drops, goose bumps, I am twenty years old. "Right on it, sir." I went home and I started packing my bags. I called my mother. Three, four days before I had told her, "The list is out, you have nothing to worry about." She picked up the phone and I'm like, "Hey, how's it going? I got some news for you." She started crying—she knew. "Mom, I have to go, I'll call you as soon as I get a chance." It was by far the hardest thing I ever told my mom. It was horrible.

The next day we left from Shreveport, Louisiana, went to Atlanta, to South Carolina, to Germany, and eventually Qatar. It took us three days to get there. We weren't allowed to leave the plane at all. They served us box lunches—I forgot to pack my toothbrush and toothpaste. Three days on the airplane eating boxed lunches without a toothbrush is by far the worst experience of my life! That was almost *worse* than calling my mom. We finally got to an airbase—there is absolutely *nothing*. No tents, and there's a total of 158 people on this base. Six hours a day you're firefighting, setting up the fire station, getting all the vehicles in order, learning the hydrants of the whole base and the other twelve hours—putting up tents after tents.

The desert to me—it's a totally different place from New England. You step outside the tent, [the heat] is on your forehead and it's a constant headache. But it's also a peaceful place, it's very scenic—it's the first time in my life that I could look out in the distance, see the horizon, see miles and miles and miles. I enjoyed the scenery and that's what kept me sane. People go crazy over there. I was single, people had families that they were missing, the children's birthdays. People are afraid when they come home that their kids are not going to remember who they are. A lot of people attempted suicide over there—I was the EMT, so I was one of the first people on the scene. A lot of people are being sent home because they cannot deal with the desert and being away from home.

Honestly, I enjoyed it. I enjoyed traveling. It's not a tourist destination—not really beaches and barbeques. It's really cool, the scenery is cool. We worked with host-nation people, people from Qatar. And those people are very friendly. Their English is up to a fourth- or fifth-grade level. But they are very interesting and they are interested in us, too. They're firefighters, too. They loved talking to us, we played soccer with them—it was camaraderie, too. They taught us about the Muslim culture. That was a very rewarding thing from the trip.

We were told that we were going to leave after three months. After 90 days, we were awaiting our orders—"Are they here yet?" That's when I started getting tired of the place. I don't care if you are the happiest, most chipper person in the world, you are going to suffer from depression over there. It's a guaranteed thing. It's a very monotonous life. People sleep for twelve hours a day, get up, work twelve hours, go to sleep—a lot of depression. I tried to make the most of it, but it will catch up to you.

They told us, "Most of you will stay between 180 and 360 days." We weren't prepared for this. You're living the same day over and over again—it's like *Groundhog Day*! The second 90 days, people started getting on each others' nerves. You get off work, you're still sleeping in the same tent as the person you are mad at and you go back to work. I remember one kid was suffering from depression—he threatened to commit suicide. He said. "I'm going to do it," and also he pulled a knife on someone. "I said you keep on talking bad about me and I am going to cut you up." He got sent home early. A lot of people, they couldn't hack it. I stuck out the extra 90 days.

Another way I was able to cope with all the depression was I am an avid runner. I ran every day for an hour at full pace. And it's different in the desert. First, it's flat. And you have the heat. Your mind plays games on you. You can run and you can think about anything—it's like you're a philosopher. You can think about the meaning of life, what's just, what's ethical, it's a separation between mind and body. Your body would be moving, your mind would be thinking about something else. That was my therapy. After that I would feel relaxed, it was like meditation for me. ...

I slept on top of a sleeping bag. Sand is in your boots, sand is in your food, sand everywhere—it's a desert. There's constantly snakes going into the tent, rats, camel spiders, which is like a cross breed between a spider and a scorpion. It's the most interesting-looking insect in the world and they can hop four feet high. They're constantly moving around the tent. And of all the bad experiences, there was the great experience of being there, and the good experience of coming home erased all the bad experiences. It was honestly the most adventurous part of my life. ...

My perspective of all this: I was in the area of operations, I was in support of Operation Enduring Freedom. On our base there were F-16s, bombers, our base is also the headquarters of Special Forces—that was their meeting spot and they went to various places for operations. All those bombers dropped bombs on people, killed people, all those fire jets shoot bullets at people. All those Special Forces people do operations and shoot people with their guns. So I am guilty by association if you think about all the killings in the war, the innocent people. Because I was helping out the cause—guilty, almost. That's why I have a more *positive* perspective of the war, more than the marines, than the army, who go in and see the dead bodies after the bombings.

I was walking back from the chow hall. We had gas masks in case of chemical or biological bombs, I had my helmet on, my flak vest, and a higher-ranking firefighter came around the corner and he yelled, "Fire, fire, fire, fire—get back in your tent." Surely, as firefighters, we would be running *toward* the fire—and he was ordering us to get back in our tent. So we were confused and then the alarm started going off. Was it a chemical-bomb fire?

What happened was two individuals charged the front gate in a SUV, they pulled out assault rifles, they started shooting the front gate personnel. One host-nation person from Qatar was also working on the front gate for translation purposes, he was shot in the leg but he didn't die. The air force personnel dispersed, they ran and hid. One airman first-class shot both people, the driver and the other person, shot both people dead. He received awards and decorations for killing those persons who were trying to attack our base. They grabbed the host-nation individual and they brought him to a local hospital with the two dead bodies. ...

When we first got [to the airbase], there were only 158 people. Then we started getting new troops, as long as we're building tents they're finding more new troops to put in these tents. By the time I left, Qatar had over 3,000 people. And that was in 2002. My understanding now is that Qatar could have 5,000–6,000 people. It's the main headquarters for the entire Middle East. Before Qatar, it was Prince Sultan Air Force Base in Saudi Arabia. Saudi Arabia—it's kind of safe—but it's really *not* a safe place.

The emir of Qatar, he loves Americans, he loves President Bush. There are probably a lot of political things I don't know about, he gets a lot of money from our air force, from military people staying there. I guess he gave a lot of land to President Bush—not *gave* it to him, but he said, "You can have it, you can have all your military personnel live there." Also, a lot of our supplies are from the downtown area. We have a lot of rental cars there, big SUVs. Doha [al-Dawha City] was getting a lot of money from the military personnel. So it was beneficial for them, and beneficial for us because we had such a large base over there. ...

My views changed a little bit. When I was in the military, you know how powerful the US military is because of the numbers, because of the technology, the amount of aircraft we have—aircraft wins wars. How easy to take care of Afghanistan, or al-Qaeda. And we thought we would be in and out of Iraq, no problem, because of Desert Storm, in and out, no problem. That was my view when I was in the military. Since I have been out of the military, we are concentrating on Iraq. And Iraq—it's a mess now.

One of my best friends just got back from Iraq, he's in the army. You know we bombed Iraq *so* much, Iraq is in a primitive state right now. It's sad to see because the amount of money Iraq has through oil, even though they don't have the refineries to refine oil, they have the money to bring up the oil. And then the way we knocked down Iraq—my view is that we are going to be there for a long time. It makes you think the purpose of war, it has more bad qualities than good. I think we could be in over our heads now and because we did all this to Iraq, we are obligated to bring Iraq back to modern days, which is very costly for us. It's costly for everyone, taxpayers—I am thinking about myself. They're living in a primitive state right now—it's absolutely horrible for them.

My friend told me this—a lot of people don't have potable water, we've bombed them to a third-world country. My friend had a lot of interaction with Iraqis and he told me that a lot of the younger generation likes the US soldiers because they bring them candy and they help them out. They think the US soldiers are good. But when it comes to teenagers, teenagers are more prone to attack the soldiers, do car bombings and the rock throwing. It's really sad that the world has to act this way. ...

You would get a bad rap if you leave prematurely. You have to have a way for Iraq to bring in income so they can build new buildings and build new roads. My friend said there's more bombed roads and undrivable roads there than you can ever imagine. The government should be building oil refineries so they can bring in more income.

I would say bring Iraq to a level where they are secure and they have a strong government. Because a government is key, laws are key, if the world didn't have laws it would be chaos—Iraq is pretty chaotic right now. I think we will always be there. For instance, we'll always be in Korea since the Korean war, in Saudi Arabia since Desert Storm, and before then, always in Germany. I think we will always be in Iraq.

I have heard a lot of propaganda from the Democrats, and Michael Moore's book—I have read it—[about] President Bush's ties to Saudi Arabians. The purpose for the ties—being staged over there, and having aircraft over there, and military personnel over there helps out in case there's a conflict—say with Iran or with another Middle Eastern country. Instead of taking all that time going from the US to the Middle East, you already have a base over there. Also having good ties over there, it would help us with our relations with Iraq. Another reason for being over there, we bring them a lot of revenue, we purchase a lot of supplies, food, anything from pencils to renting cars—that helps out the Iraqis. Also being stationed over there just in case a terrorist group builds up, we are so close by we could dismantle a terrorist group or help their government, when they do have government, to take action. ...

Being in the military you always hear a lot of people are against war. Even a lot of higher-up generals are saying that we should bring in all our troops and secure the border of the US.... I don't think necessarily the United States, the top officials' views, the president's, the commander in chief's views are always right. I wish we didn't have to bomb places—innocent people dying. And people die for what cause? Things can be talked out. Man can create disaster, man can fix disaster.

My career choices. Later on in life I want to own my own business. In order to make money, you have to have money. I have received a job offer through Wackenhut. It's a contract company that contracts firefighters to Iraq. My parents are against it, but I am seriously considering it. I also have a friend in Halliburton. You know Halliburton—Dick Cheney. If I can get a job lined up through Halliburton either in Uzbekistan, Pakistan, or Saudi Arabia, I'll probably leave before the summer. I definitely think that company is corrupt. It's been in the paper, it's been in the media, the way the military always gives contracts to Halliburton. That's bad, but also for personal gain, they pay firefighters over there for a one-year contract upwards to $120,000—$80,000 is tax-free. Also they put you up in a tent, you stay on a military base, they feed you, there's a place on base where you can buy supplies, toiletries, and stuff. So coming back you can pocket a good $110,000 and only $30,000 is taxable. So for personal gain I thought about going that route. I still want to get my degree, but also go over there, and be a civilian. Still in danger, still supporting the cause—especially if I join Wackenhut and go to Iraq, [I'll] definitely still be in danger.

Halliburton is everywhere. I'm trying to get to Saudi Arabia. My buddy is over there now, he says it is completely safe. The reason I'm doing that is to keep my mother comfortable. I don't want to put her in any worries. She was worried enough when I made that phone call back when I was in Shreveport saying I was going over to the Middle East. I told her the other day when Wackenhut sent me an application in the mail.... It's a great way to pay bills and later in life complete my goals.

# ARTHUR H.F. SCHOENFELD
Sergeant, Marine Corps

Enlisted 1999–2003, deployed age 27 (January–June 2003)
Task Force Tarawa, Nasariya, Kut, Iraq

*The Invasion of Iraq*

*Arthur (Torry) is from Washington, DC. He left college and enlisted in the marines on March 21, 1999. Four years later, to the day, when he should have been discharged, he was in Task Force Tarawa (Second Marine Expeditionary Brigade) advancing to Iraq from Kuwait. A sergeant in a light-armored vehicle recon unit, he commanded a vehicle that he named the "Baghdad Express"—although it never got that far. He fought in Nasariya, watched the Iraqi army melt away, enjoyed the welcome given to American soldiers, but also noticed early signs of disaffection among Iraqis. On discharge, Torry returned to complete his BA in history from the University of North Carolina. In his narrative he comments on his experiences during the invasion, discusses the insurgency, and offers his considered opinion of the war and its planners: "They just really didn't think."*

[While at sea heading for Iraq] we had seen Colin Powell, someone I actually *do* respect in that administration—probably the only one I do—go and do that talk in front of the UN [Security Council, February 5, 2003]. Me and a few of the guys who were watching it couldn't *believe* they were actually going to send us to war over that. His presentation to the UN was just so *flimsy*. I was embarrassed for Colin Powell—a smart guy—having to give that sort of talk to the UN. We weren't really sure if we were going to go or not at the very beginning. I thought it would be foolish to go in from the standpoint of America and alienating the rest of the world. We hadn't counted on the administration being completely run by a bunch of fools, so they went in. I was reading the news we got, how many people were against us going in—the rest of the world, all the UN. I was really surprised that they ended up going in. I was surprised, but I wasn't totally surprised. ...

We went into Iraq the morning of the 21st. We didn't receive any sort of enemy fire—there was no enemy around. I remember the first night we were in Iraq, we were in the middle of the desert seeing the army convoys following the Third Infantry Division. They had all their headlights on and we were trying to be quiet, keep hidden, and the army just kept driving by as if they were driving back in the United States. From the position that we were in the first night, we went and protected a bridge outside Nasiriya for two nights and there we had our first contact with the enemy. They were actually just troops that had deserted and were going home—they came across our positions and got into a firefight with one of our vehicles.

We were fairly well informed on where we were going, but what happens when you go in—very quickly the world becomes a lot, lot smaller. I don't know what's going on with the north of the unit, or what the Third ID is doing—you're concerned about what's going on directly around you. That isn't really an intentional thing they do. You've got to be concerned about what is going on right there and then, not the bigger picture.

We actually got short-wave radios—we could listen to the BBC to figure out what was going on. I remember in Nasiriya, the BBC guy was about a kilometer from us, and it was sort of like watching a sporting event when a commentator [says], "There's another air strike coming in," and the air strike would come in and it's hitting the works over there, and we would watch it. It was kind of odd listening to the radio sometimes, particularly when people all over the world are listening—and it's happening right in front of you. …

[A few days later] an element of the Fedayeen attacked, or they ran into the side of our column, and there was a huge firefight. But meanwhile the front line of the men and officers started shooting the Iraqis and then proceeded to start shooting at us, and one of our vehicles started shooting back at them—[a] friendly firefight where they started calling in mortars and artillery on us. What really happened is that the front lines of engineering units that were firing at the Iraqis—our vehicles came up over an elevated bridge, [and] they started shooting at *our* vehicles.

The lead vehicle should have known it was Americans but didn't, and started shooting at *them*, at which point they started calling in fire on *us*. We started getting fire, our commander started calling, "Hey, we're getting shelled, can you tell us where these shells are coming from?" The lead army figured out that the shells were coming from the American unit shelling us. So that's how they figured out it was friendly fire.

I remember the next morning… thousands of refugees had [fled] the city… to the desert where they had no food or water. Thousands of [these] refugees [were now] coming back into the city. I felt real bad for them because they didn't have much—you know there was nothing we could give them outside the city. There was a major urban conflict going on—they were stuck in the middle. …

We were driving through a lot of towns, at which point the town would come out all excited, very happy that we were there. It kind of reminded me of the scenes you see when they liberated Paris [in 1944]—where the whole town would be out there cheering. What did strike me was that most of the people were very happy that we were there. But you definitely saw a certain number of individuals who really *weren't* very happy about it. They obviously didn't have the wherewithal to do anything to us—but you could tell. So we were not terribly surprised when the insurgency started breaking out because you could definitely tell that there were lots of unhappy people.

When the war started to end, we were up in Kut, in a terrorist base. I remember all the floors had American or Israeli flags [on them] so you would walk over them. All their targets that they used for shooting had the Star of David on them [pictures of Osama bin Laden are sometimes used for target practice by the US military—ed.]. Obviously they had left this place and we knew it was really over in Kut. There were elements of the Fedayeen still in Kut. We were told that there was a little civil war—well, not civil war—going on, the Fedayeen were getting rid of the foreigners. From Kut, we got word that we were actually heading home, which was pretty exciting. We were all really pleased.

One of the things I thought was interesting: of the Islamic states, other than Turkey, Iraq is the most secular. It is completely legal to have alcohol, whereas some of our quote-unquote *allies* are a lot more strict—fundamentally strict Islamic nations. Like [in] Kuwait, you can't buy alcohol, Saudi Arabia I don't think so either. You just have the feeling that Saddam was secular rule, it was not an Islamic-based rule. Not that there weren't lots of Muslims. Most of the women were covered to some degree, but they weren't covered as fully as people in more strict Islamic places. Generally, they would have a scarf on their head. You saw their faces, they would have some sort of shirt and a long skirt. I've seen plenty of Muslim women in the United States far more covered than they were.... The main problem with cultural differences is that we don't speak the language—it's a totally different tongue.... We were lucky. I don't know exactly who they were, but we had a sort of intelligence-gathering vehicle [with] interpreters on it. But that was unusual. They were marines who spoke Arabic. One of them was a flat-out white guy, one was Arab or Pakistani.

[*What about 9/11?*] I didn't really see it fitting into Iraq—I didn't really see it fitting in that much at all. Speaking for myself, I did not see a direct link between 9/11 and that situation.... I think they expected [Iraq] to be a lot easier than the first [Gulf War]. They went in with a lot less troops to do a lot bigger job, expecting it to be a push-over like the first one was. It's the second part of this war that's the problem. I just think they thought that the war was going to be over quickly. Like when George Bush landed on the aircraft carrier [May 2003], they thought the war was pretty much over.

I could go into a fairly long discussion as to why I think we had problems with the war. I just don't think they realized how messed up Iraq was—infrastructure and a lot of stuff. They really didn't look at the bigger picture when they planned for this war, about how it was going to take a long time and how there were problems that we really just didn't know anything about in Iraq itself. I think we did a brilliant job of winning the fighting part of the war, but made *absolutely no* plans for the massive reconstruction program that they need to embark on. Now that there is the insurgency, it's tough to even get that done.

The problem is that people say "the insurgency" and lump it into one big group. It's not. There are a whole lot of different aspects to it. I think a very sizeable proportion is foreigners slipping in, doing the fighting, and that is really problematic because these are guys that are there just to cause problems, disruptions—this is their chance to get at America. I also think there are plenty of Iraqis who are in it for various reasons—their family got killed in a bombing strike, what have you. And there are also elements that are hard-line people from Saddam Hussein['s regime] who just want to see the thing not work out. The problem we have is that we are not able to provide the Iraqi civilians who are on our side enough support so that they feel protected. ...

People get a slightly warped view of the insurgency over here because that's what is interesting to report on. I remember reading an article in *Time* magazine and it was ten pages all about the insurgency. And then a little blurb about how some groups in the US had funded and opened a clinic for [Iraqi] people suffering from post-traumatic stress disorder from having been tortured. CNN [also] spent a long time at that clinic. It was to benefit average people who were affected by Saddam Hussein. CNN spent one 30-second blurb on it. The car bombing that had happened that day, it wasn't a very large one—not to minimize the people who died in it—but it wasn't like that big oil tanker they had a few days ago, [and yet] they did five or six four-minute excerpts on the car bombing. ...

I think in long-term history, it was foolish for us to think that we could go there and say "Iraq, the country." In reality, Iraq was born out of the Treaty of Versailles [in which the remnants of the Ottoman Empire became mandates of England and France with Iraq placed under British control—ed.]. It is just laying there in the desert with different groups that really don't like each other. The way they were kept in line was through fairly harsh authoritarian-type leadership. We will see if they can work it out. I think the main goal of most of the insurgents is to create a situation that makes it impossible for us or the interim Iraqi government to function at all.

Iraqis don't want to feel that they are *occupied*, they want to have *Iraqi* troops, which is why we need to get them working, because they are *Iraqis* doing the job. When we are there providing security, [the Iraqis] working with us are just "running dogs of the white infidels." The *bigger* our presence is, the *worse* it will be for the government, the coalition government or whatever it's called. The *less* they are seen to be our lackeys the *better* it is for them—which is why they need to get the Iraqi army back on its feet.

[That] was one of the capital mistakes Americans made, when they disbanded it. I've forgotten who it was who said the one thing we shouldn't do is disband the Iraqi army. They got a lot of Iraqi generals and higher-ups to accept that they would turn over their units—basically the US was going to keep the Iraqi army around. Then of course the first thing they do was liquidate the Iraqi army. That pissed off a lot of high-ranking Iraqis who had surrendered on the [understanding] that they were going to have a job in the Iraqi army when the war was over. The fact is that a whole lot of people immediately lost their jobs. Now we are trying to build a new army. I don't think they thought it through at all. They just really didn't think. ...

I really just *don't like* George Bush himself—I don't think he is qualified [or] competent. I don't like the top three. I don't like anyone in this administration. There's a bumper sticker, "Gee-haw is not a foreign policy," [but] I think that *is* their attitude. They don't understand about world geopolitics. You remember after September 11—which Iraq had nothing to do with—the good will across the world? They cashed in that good will for personal political gain—and that is a real shame. You remember all the flags at half mast in all the embassies across the world, people giving flowers, telling how they cried? All that good will just liquidated, thrown away, the security act [PATRIOT Act] passed, the Republican agenda. And now we are virtually a pariah. I don't think you can convince a lot of people that the United States needs [their] help right now. We are out for our own gain. I don't think that that is totally the right view that the world has, but it is held because of this administration.

# ANDRÉ M.M. QUEIROGA
## Corporal, Marine Corps

Enlisted 2001–2005, deployed age 20
(January–May 2003; June 2004–March 2005)
First Battalion, Second Marines, Nasariya and Sunni Triangle, Iraq

*President Bush's Plan for Iraq*

*André is a student at Holyoke Community College planning to pursue environmental studies at the University of Massachusetts and perhaps be a game warden. He fulfilled his dreams of being a marine and becoming an American citizen during his two deployments to Iraq. It took André only two months to get his citizenship because he was in the military. He came to the US with his family from Lisbon, Portugal, when he was eight years old. His father had been a "Green Beret" in the Portuguese Army during Portugal's colonial war in Mozambique. In the invasion of Iraq, André was in Nasariya when eighteen marines he knew were killed. He was also there for the now-famous capture of Jessica Lynch, an event he narrates as a contest between the army and the marines to seize the credit for rescuing her. On the war on terrorism: "Terrorism is like bad breath. No matter how many times you brush your teeth, it is always going to come back."*

I graduated from Ludlow High School on June 1, 2001. I joined the marines, left on August 12 of that year, went to boot camp, Parris Island. While I was there 9/11 happened. We got called into a big formation and they let us know that the towers just got hit. "In a year or so, 99 percent of you are going to be in a foreign country fighting some war." So I thought that's cool—we didn't think much about it.... Got assigned to First Battalion, Second Marines, which is an infantry unit.

This is March 2002 now. The stuff with the UN is going on—with President Bush—it never crossed my mind about going to war. [I] went to California that summer for desert training at Twentynine Palms. I got a call from my mom saying, "Your grandfather is in a coma, and your brother and I are going to see him [in Portugal]." I tried to get my papers and my passport to go—they just wouldn't let me go. I had all my paperwork, why can't they let me go?

I go home for Christmas for leave. Then January 3, went back to North Carolina. They said we have eight days, we are going to be on a ship going to Iraq. Then it clicked in my head—*that's* why they didn't let me go. Because at the time I wasn't an American citizen, I was just a resident alien. They were probably thinking, he probably knows about the war and he's going to flee the country to get out of here. I wasn't looking at it like that—I wanted to see my grandfather.

I call my mom and I tell her, "Listen, you know, the war," she starts crying on the phone. "You'll be okay, we'll pray for you." January 11, when I turned twenty, we loaded up the ship, USS *Ponce*. It was a fleet. A fleet means you've got all your infantry units, and then you've got your attachments, your LAVs, your LARs (light-armored reconnaissance units), tanks, artillery, everything went over there by boat. It took us 30 days.

We got to Kuwait on the fifteenth of February, off-loaded the ship, guns loaded, go to our base, base in the middle of nowhere—Camp Shoup. When we went to the base to get supplies, guys were saying, "Where are you staying at?" "Camp Shoup." "Where is that?" "It's the closest base to the border line." "What's that?" "Oh, it's just a pile of dirt." Stayed there from February 15 to about March 17 getting ready. March 19 we got the word—we are crossing over, President Bush is about to give us our orders.

The night before March 21, they said, "War has started." The first city we hit was Nasariya. They call it the Alley of Death [Ambush Alley] where they were supposed to wait to get more reinforcements. They ended up taking Charlie Company and their AAVs (amphibious assault vehicles) through the alley, and got ambushed—and that's when eighteen of my comrades from Charlie Company died. I knew those guys. They weren't in my company but they were in my unit, we trained all the time together. That was on the 23rd. That was a six-hour firefight. Eighteen marines died and 4,800 Iraqis died. They said it was the biggest killing within six hours since the Vietnam War.

So then we regrouped and that stuff with Jessica Lynch happened. She was supposed to go around the city instead of through it—she got halfway through and she turned around. Insurgent Iraqis, terrorists, the [Republican] Guard, whatever— she made a mistake. *Boom*, they invaded the vehicle. [US soldiers] didn't even have their magazines, they didn't have no rounds in the chamber, nothing. They were in condition four, which means guns were not even ready, take it off safety, pull the trigger, there's nothing in the chamber.

So the US girls got taken away, they kept them both alive so they could do things with them. And our unit from intel found out that she was lost out there—they had one of our own. So they started doing recon, going in without being seen or heard, take pictures, get information. They don't go in and save people right away because you don't have enough on them. [Marine recon] got all the intel on her that she was in the hospital, what floor. Three-sixty [degrees], security all around, they were ready to blow in there, but then—"Oh *no*, we are the army, *we* will rescue her, don't go in." So the army ended up going in there and rescuing her. They went in there because they wanted to look good, they didn't want to say the army messed up and the marines had to go in and save the day.

All I know is what I have heard. There's always the true side of the story and after a while it gets broken down—it gets to a rumor, everyone has an opinion of everything. All that mattered is we got her out, she was safe. So all those stories, all the books she can write, the newspapers, articles, it really doesn't matter to the ones that were there. All's what matters is that we got an American out, she was safe. She was injured, and she is alive this day. She's famous now because of that. That's good, more power to her. Maybe it paid off in the end, you know.

But our mission was to take the southern bridge and the northern bridge of Nasariya, which kept the supply route all the way up to Baghdad. And that was where most firefighting was that day. Charlie Company (infantry) finally took over.... Task Force Tarawa was right there. You had First Battalion, Second Marines; Third Battalion, Second Marines; Second Battalion, Eighth Marines—three infantry units. So each has three ground-troop companies, that's nine, and then they have a weapons company, they have the Humvees with the tow missiles on them and the .50 caliber machine guns, so that's another three on that side, so that's twelve right there. Then you have all the supporting units, you've got tanks, you've got LAR, AAVs, you've got artillery.

I was security force. In the back of my seven-ton [truck] were twelve marines, machine guns, bazookas—we call them HP4s, the missile you put on your shoulder and just shoot. And wherever we went, those guys would get out and provide security so transactions can be made. When the front lines—Charlie Company, Alpha, Bravo—found EPWs [enemy prisoners of war] they would give us a call, "We need this vehicle to go up there and extract some EPWs and bring them to that camp so they can get interrogated." We would load them up in my truck and bring them back to wherever a little tent was where they were being interrogated and drop them off. OIF-I [the Marine Corps labels the stages of the war—ed.]—I guard the bridges [in Nasariya]. I had a route: get water to everybody, bring them food—they call it "beans, bullets, and band-aids." Go out, back and forth, always nonstop, March 21 to May 7.

What I noticed was that at the beginning the Iraqi people didn't like us at all. But after a while they started noticing we were there for *their* own good and they started giving us information, giving us intel, and we give them things in return. Then, "You know what, the Americans aren't bad because they are here taking out the bad guys, so they can get into the warehouses and give us the food. They fix our water supply." They would come in hurt or sick, our corpsmen would take care of them, first aid and everything. If they were hurt, we would fly them out to the closest hospital, or even bring them to our own hospitals. A lot of marines didn't like that because, "What is this guy doing here? Are they the ones that shot me?"

After a while they started liking us because they noticed that [the Americans] are not here to take over their country but to take that person out of power so we can live free. They started showing us where they were having their meetings and where they would hide their guns. They started to become more friends. I didn't get too acquainted with the Iraqi people. The first time we were there we didn't have an interpreter. We just knew the few words we knew, body language. Second [deployment], every convoy that left would have an interpreter with them. …

I don't see it as we won. If we won, we wouldn't be over there fighting, we would have ruled. Bush's intent wasn't to go over there to take over the country. We didn't want to go over there and put the American flag and say this is our land. That's why the first time a couple of people got into trouble for having the American flag on their vehicles, waving it, because it seemed to them as if we were trying to invade their country, trying to name that land with our American flag—which wasn't our intent. Our intent was to go there, take that man out of power. Because of the way he mistreated his people, the way he was going with his military, and the way he was going with his country, leading up to more attacks, a greater chance of being able to fight in a nuclear war. And now it's Iran. And pretty soon it will be Syria, if not the other countries around.

May 7, 13:31, I crossed the border into Kuwait. The whole time I didn't bathe, now where is my shower? Man, I hope I don't come back again! When we got to Kuwait Naval Base we turned in ammunition, turned in our rifles, everything. It was like a calm-down point, so we could rest, get back to being normal again. You can't take a marine out of a fight environment and fly him home right away. He's going to get home and be crazy and he's going to bug out. He's got to have time to unwind.

And it was good. In Kuwait they had a pool, gym, they had a track, they had a Subway, a Baskin-Robbins, a Pizza Hut, Arby's. They had computers, stores, a PX, internet, phones, movie night, you could go to the beach. They're giving you back everything that you didn't have in Iraq. And they're taking away the one thing you always treasure, your rifle. You had it all the time with a round ready to go—you don't need that anymore. You can take a shower every day. You get to go walk around and see females. Go to the movies. Go sit down and get a nice tray and fill it up with all the food you want to eat. *That* means everything to a marine.

It's almost like a clinic. The stuff you want so bad that you talk about it—they have all that there, it's like heaven. And then after a while you start getting used to it and it's, "I can't wait to get home." You sleep in tents with A/C, you've got a mattress, you aren't sleeping on the floor in your vehicle, all curled up. There's no incoming mortars, noise, it is nice and peaceful. You don't have to be in full gear all the time, you can walk in shorts and T-shirts. It's stuff that you'd never think you'd be allowed to do in Kuwait when it's only a couple of miles away from the border with Iraq.

You and your best friend were out there, you would be chopping his head off because you were so sick of each other. You were with each other for so long, you knew everything that that person was going to say. You get to Kuwait and you look at him, "I am sorry for yelling at you, I am sorry for screaming at you or punching you in the face." Your relation gets even stronger.... It's not even a friendship, it's more of a brotherhood—it's what you went through together. I would say in another life—not the military and going to combat—they would have been friends, but they wouldn't have been brothers. He leaned on me when he needed someone to lean on, and I leaned on him. You look at it like both of us stared death right in the face and we made it through because of each other. It's a bond forever.

I flew back May 28. ... The first thing I did was close my eyes and take a deep breath, smelled the American air, oxygen, and you're hearing the birds chirping. You open your eyes, you see all the green trees, you see the sky is all beautiful. I am home, finally I made it. Nothing was taking that smile off my face. A couple of marines were there already, they had cell phones, "Do you guys want to use the cell phone to call your family?" "Hey Mom, I'm home already, I touched ground in the States." She's crying on the phone, you're almost crying because she's crying. So that was the best day, seeing the *American* people, *your* people. Seeing women, seeing cars, seeing stores, you're back cracking that first Budweiser beer. It feels good.

I startled easily. It's something that takes a while to get rid of. The first time I got rid of it, but the second time has taken me a little longer. I still shake a lot if I hear bangs or loud noises. I was there a lot longer the second time, and the consequences were a lot different.... You would be driving around the road, *boom*, a bomb would open up the side and if you didn't have armor, you'd be dead. You don't know when it's your time to go. Just looking, feeling, your body senses something. You stop the convoy, you feel it, something natural comes over you—your eyes, all your senses are at their max. When that adrenaline is pumping, you can smell something a mile away, you can see it a mile away. "Stop the car, I can see something up there in a bush." Get a little robot to go out there, put a little C-4, if there is a bomb, they blow it up. That guy, because he is so good at seeing, he saves maybe three or four people's lives.

We were driving every day. I would say that within six-and-a-half months we put on about 40,000–45,000 miles on our vehicles. Contractors, if they went in their own vehicles, they would get blown up. Like they use Ford Excursions, Ford Explorers, they put vests hanging over the door as though that was going to stop something from blowing up on the side of you. After a couple of them went down, they realized they had to start using military vehicles instead of their own vehicles.

I was talking to a couple of them. If you go for Blackwater, a year contract is like $85,000 non-taxable. If you do another contract you get another $85,000. I have a buddy in Kuwait, he is security forces, and he comes home after every four months for ten days—they pay for your trip home.... It is a lot of money, that's what pulls people in. I told every one of my friends and people who ask me, my life is worth more than any money. Even if I'm in Kuwait and it's safer than Iraq, I am not going. Greedy people. ...

The way I analyze things is—Bush is very smart and people don't see his plan. People say we are there for weapons of mass destruction, and there were no weapons found. That's a bunch of bull. Because the first time I was there I have pictures of missiles and stuff and the only thing missing is the chemical agent for being nuclear. He was mistreating his people. After the first Gulf War, Saddam went ahead and built twenty palaces. He had manmade hills to put his palaces on top of. Everything was palaces from gold to white gold to platinum. And every day he said, "You guys have to cook breakfast, lunch, and dinner just in case I stop by the palace. If I don't stop by you are going to throw all that food away." If you fished in his river, he would shoot you, okay?

We *had* to take him out of power. He was not a good leader for those people. But I look at it another way—he could control all those different types of tribes or religions. Look at what is happening now—they are all fighting amongst each other to see who has the power. Saddam was a tyrant and he was actually the only one who could keep all those people under control. Well, in a way he was good and in a way he was bad. We got him out of power, that's a good thing, no more threat.

But if you look on a map, Iraq is the center of the surrounding countries that are major in terrorism. If the United States can control the middle with the help of the UN, you can try to eliminate terrorism. That's Bush's plan. I look at it this way: terrorism is like bad breath. No matter how many times you brush you teeth, it is always going to come back. But his plan is to slow it down so that there will not be as much terrorism as there is in today's world. So if you can control the *middle*, where Iraq stands, you have got Iran, Syria, all the surrounding countries, the Middle East, which are major in terrorism. You get the UN and the surrounding allies around those countries to come from the *outside* to the *inside* and us from the *inside* to the *outside*, you can do away with a lot of terrorism. But not all of it.

Because of those 2,000 lives [lost by November 2005], we don't get other attacks like the Twin Towers. We don't get attacks on Miami, Los Angeles or Chicago, Houston or Dallas. Imagine if we didn't go to war how many more of those attacks would have been done to our cities, how many more lives would have been taken. These lives that are taken now from war, they are military-person lives—they were there for a purpose. I am not saying they were there to die—they were there to fight. In the case of war you have to have casualties on both sides. But we have to look at the ratio: look at *our* casualties compared to *their* casualties. There is no comparison.

We'll never have a draft—I will tell you that. Look at Congress itself—all their sons and grandsons and daughters are all Americans. I think Bush, senators, representatives—they have kids, they have families, they don't want to see their nephew or their daughter or their son go to war, so they are never going to have a draft. Never. Not ever again. No draft. If you *have* a draft, you are forcing people to do what they are unwilling to do.

# RICHARD W. RILEY
Staff Sergeant, Army National Guard

Enlisted 1979–2006, deployed age 44
(December 2002–August 2003)
Camp Arifjan, Kuwait

*Destroying Iraq*

*Rich is 48 years old and works in the pharmacy at UMass Amherst. He was born in Virginia, the sixth in a family of ten children. He is divorced with two daughters, ages 22 and 13. He takes a family-like interest in the young soldiers who serve under him as a staff sergeant in the Massachusetts National Guard-Engineers. He was stationed in Camp Arifjan, a staging area in Kuwait, starting in December 2002—his first deployment to a war zone. His empathy for soldiers is balanced by his antipathy toward the Bush administration and the war in Iraq. "You're going to tell me I'm not patriotic just because I don't believe the way you believe? I am from slave generations. I have been in this country more generations than anyone in my unit has." Rich plans to write his autobiography.*

I have been in the military 27 years and I thank God that I have been fortunate not to serve in front-line combat. I don't know how I would have reacted. I joined in 1978. I am from Virginia in the Chesapeake Bay area. There are no jobs there except for a couple of chicken factories, and I wasn't working *there*. I joined the army when I was seventeen—you didn't have to graduate high school in those days to join the military. So I got out of school and I got my GED in the military…. When I got to Germany, Carter was still president. And when Reagan got in office his first words were, "If the hostages aren't released by the time I am inaugurated into office, we are going into Iran."…

I *knew*, September 11, 2001, I *knew* we were going to be going into Iraq. I *knew* that it was just a matter of time. I *knew* that. I *knew* that President Bush was going to get in off this, I *knew* that. It was a bad move from the start and I will say that it looks worse to me today. We are losing troops on a daily basis, we've got troops screwing up. We've got the majority of the world angry at us. I think it's about oil, I think it's a vendetta. President Bush said himself, "What do you mean 'why do we have to get Saddam?' That man tried to kill my father." Right then and there, people should have said, "Wait a minute, this guy wants to be a vigilante. He wants to go over there and kill this guy—it has got nothing to do with anybody else." The only thing they have done is put that country back into the Stone Age.

It's like they have opened a can of worms, a Pandora's box. There's no turning back now. We can't leave there, we can't leave Afghanistan, we've got North Korea on the rise, we've got Iran on the rise. And the places he wants to do battle—and tell people you can't have nuclear weapons. Who can tell them they can't, when *we* have them, Israel has them, China has them? But I guess we are supposed to be the "responsible" people that have them—Iran is too "irresponsible," North Korea is too "irresponsible." Three-quarters of our military force is in between Iraq, Afghanistan, and Africa. So that leaves 25 percent here. How are you going to fight a war? You can call the North Koreans and Iranians rogue all you want to—Bush is the most rogue person we have. …

I find a lot of GIs getting in trouble speaking what they want to speak. You're not allowed to bad-mouth the commander in chief when you are in the military. I am a *very* outspoken person. I voice my dislike over the war. My commander sat me down and said, "Rich, I can understand what you're saying, but with you saying that and the other guys feeling that—I don't want to hear it anymore." He shut me up right there. I'm a platoon sergeant and I have 23 people under me, and they look up to me to take care of them. I have been in this unit for 23 years, so they listen to me a lot and whatever I say affects them. If I feel negative about this war, these people are going to feel the same way I feel. I would bring the morale down—especially if we get deployed. …

Terrorism—you aren't going to fight it face-to-face. They have attacked our country and [Bush] has put all our lives in danger. I don't think he thought of that. He brings the churches into all of this. It gets scary. I remember the witch hunts in Salem were all about religion. It doesn't take *much* for people to get paranoid. I am a Democrat. I don't know any black Republicans. I had a Kerry/Edwards bumper sticker on my pick-up truck. Someone took a roller with black ink and covered up my bumper sticker. A guy said, "I can't believe you voted for John Kerry, what's your *problem?*" I always complain but I always vote. And I instill in my daughters: when you are old enough to vote, if you *don't* vote—keep your mouth shut.

We're going to be there for the next five, six years. We can't leave. We didn't plan on it, we had no good strategy. It would be so much chaos, it would be a bloodbath…. It is all about oil. From December to the end of February [2003], do you know what the US Army was doing? Guarding oil fields. Because the last time—Desert Storm—the first thing, Saddam set fire to all the oil fields. "You're not going to burn the oil this time!" It's all about *greed*.

Rumsfeld—*warmonger*. Bush—*warmonger*. He never even served in combat and he can send these men to combat. I always said, if you are going to be the president you should *at least* have spent two years in the military—spent some time in a combat zone, like John McCain. *He's* got a better idea of what those guys are doing. I don't think this president belongs in office, he doesn't know how to run a country. How can a man like George Bush win over somebody like John Kerry? That's impossible! I don't think we're that dumb of a country. Something is wrong here—something is *very, very* wrong….

I tell you, they've got the National Guardsmen in a place where they shouldn't be. We don't even train hard enough to go to combat. The Reserves don't even *meet*. They are all elderly guys, they are all older than I am—they're in their fifties. They got in *years* ago, and they're just staying in so they can get at least twenty years. But *now* the president is starting to call everybody back—they called my brother back. My brother's been out of the military for almost forty years!

We have lost to date 1,700 American soldiers [as of mid-2005]—everybody has stopped counting. Remember? "When are we going to get to a thousand?" After a thousand everything calmed down. Almost 2,000 now. And thousands and thousands of Iraqis have been killed, and the children, and the babies. You can't even live there now. You should see that place—destroyed. Everything is blown up. The bombing campaign when the war first started—we destroyed *everything*. Kirkuk, Falluja—we are just blowing stuff away. And we are going to be the ones rebuilding.

People don't realize that even in Kuwait you are in some sort of danger, especially on the base—you would not believe what's going on. There were rapes, there were murders. We built five jail cells—they didn't have any place for prisoners that were committing war crimes. These are all *Americans*. The black guy who converted back to Islam—he killed four people. There's a lot of racism in the military, and him coming from the type of unit that he was in, I could believe some of the stuff he was saying—but you don't just go killing your commander and your first sergeant no matter *how* bad it is....
I remember GIs hot-dogging with 10,000-pound Humvees. Three kids died just out of basic training. One of my best friends died over there. He got run over by a fork-lift—father of three.

The recruiters are lying—they're using scare tactics. You tell a twenty-year-old kid, "You got an appointment with me and if you're not there the cops will have a warrant out for your arrest!" This kid had bipolar—he had just gotten out of a mental hospital and a recruiter talked him into signing [Ohio, September 2004. His parents hid his identity]. Everyone goes in with a vision that they get in and do whatever they want. "I want to go in and be a doctor." "I want to go in and be an MP." "I want to go in and be a dentist." It doesn't *happen* like that. How can you become a medic if you don't have any medic experience?

Let me tell you a little story. Do you know who PFC Jessie Lynch is? They screwed up big time. The commander, he got killed. She was lucky. They took off from Camp Arifjan driving a supply truck. I remember when they left to go north. They were supposed to be going to set up army tents, they got lost in the middle of the desert. When they got lost, they got ambushed. In the heat of the moment confusion sets in, panic sets in. The driver was driving around, they had soldiers in the back, they were bouncing around, and the soldiers got kicked out of the back of it. That's how Jessie Lynch broke her arm. She was lucky, the black girl was lucky, a couple of the kids were lucky.

They tried to lie about it—not the soldiers, but the Pentagon, Rumsfeld—like there was gunfire. She got all her injuries from falling out of the back of the truck—that's when they got captured. The Iraqi doctor was the one who saved her life. It wasn't the First ID [infantry division] breaking down the hospital doors and taking her.... You're wondering why GIs are committing suicide in the desert? You don't hear about that. And you don't hear about the people dying of heatstroke because it is 140 degrees outside. All you hear about is the First ID advancing to the front—not that the soldiers died in Camp Arifjan.

—

I could serve beside a woman, but in combat it would mess with me mentally. It would be like my sister fighting with me. She could be better than me—that is not the point, it would affect me. I think any male that says it would not affect [him] [is] not telling the truth. If you have any morals, or any sense of values, it just has to. You can hear guys say, "Well, they shouldn't be in the military anyway."

I know females in the military that are a hundred times better than a quarter of the males we have in the military. They pay attention more. Their eagerness to learn is twofold a male's. I think it is because they feel they have to accomplish just like the male. I have four females in my unit, and when we were over there I took care of my females. I wouldn't let them go anyplace alone because there were a lot of rapes on the base. I made them do the buddy system, three or four together. They could do things—these women are plumbers, carpenters, they are banging nails right there with us, and the guys are complaining more than they are. ...

Ohio [National Guard] [was] the group that was supposed to take our place. All the leadership was just racist. And they had ten or eleven black kids, they ranked from PFC to E-4, so they had no rank at all—they pretty much had no authority. They talked to these kids like they were dirt. I asked one, "Do you let those guys talk to you like that?" "What are we going to do about it, sergeant?" These kids were depressed, they had *nothing*.... Then one night there was all this shouting in the back hall—"m—f—" that, and "g—d—" that—I have to find out what is going on. There is this E-4 [lower enlisted] and the E-7 [NCO] arguing back and forth. And this black kid was about to hit this sergeant, and I said, "At ease, specialist. Why don't you go in the office while I talk to the NCO?"

I started talking to this guy and he was like, "Don't stick your nose where it don't belong!" I said, "Who the *hell* do you think you are? No wonder you're having such problems with your soldiers—you don't know how to talk to people. You can't talk to people like, 'This is our unit, we do what we want.' No, you don't, because I am going to report you to the colonel tomorrow morning." So I reported him. Things were on an even keel after that, you didn't hear any more bickering.

You know what I've found? We're losing credibility in the world. Nobody likes us any more. They have [had] a hard time with Americans all along, but now we are really "ugly Americans." It's sad. And you know what else gets my goat? We invaded this country to get this man for so-called weapons of mass destruction—which we never found, and he never had them. Meanwhile, thousands and thousands of kids are being slaughtered in Darfur, Sudan, and we are not lifting a hand. We started this war, a lot of lives lost, a lot of money wasted. They blew up some of our towers and they killed 3,000 of our people. We went after the wrong guy anyway.

It's so easy for things to go wrong. Look what happened to those marines [who] killed 24 people [civilians in Haditha, November 2005]. Everyone has been comparing it to My Lai, the Vietnam massacre... there were over 250 people killed in that massacre, women and children and old people. Someone—just like

My Lai—was taking pot shots at those marines and a couple of their buddies got killed. When you see a couple of your buddies get killed, you throw caution to the wind. "We are going to find the bastard that did that." No one has control of you then. I don't think anyone *ordered* Lieutenant Calley to commit those crimes in My Lai. I don't think he had *authority*, I think things got out of hand. I think the higher-ups tried to cover up bad things, but they get out anyway, and when they get out they have got to find a scapegoat. So Lieutenant Calley was the scapegoat for that.

Same thing here. A couple of guys, probably sergeants, are going to get busted for that, no higher-ups are going to take the blame for that. Somebody is firing at you, you have no clue who it is, you try to run, you have got [one] of your men dead. You see the direction the rounds are coming from, you get five GIs, you just break a house down and you start shooting people. You just draw a blank, it's the heat of the moment.... But this marine that's talking, he said he saw some bad stuff, he called his mother and he said he did some bad, bad stuff. I think that he is probably the only one that's going to talk and they're probably shunning him right now—"You are a traitor." You have war, you have people with guns, it's going to happen.... [See Appendix for an update on the Haditha trial.]

It seems that this administration is untouchable. I see that everything they do wrong, they blame on someone else and they get away with it. I just don't know what people are *thinking*. And no one is questioning it. It is ridiculous, and it is very, very *sad*. He has divided the country, every country hates us. Even the Brits that were there with us, they hate us—they hate Tony Blair, too. It's like we're a nation of murderers and bullies—and that is what we are turning out to be. I have found if you are not a flag-waving right-wing person, you are a traitor or you are not American or you don't belong here.... I think [Bush] stole two presidencies because of money, intimidation through voting. That's not America. That sounds like [the] old Russia.

You could talk about the good stuff we are doing all you want to—it doesn't overshadow the bad that is going on. When you are talking about electricity and you are talking about running water, you are talking about schools—you are talking about one or two towns. *Come on,* we just *demolished* Kirkuk, Tikrit, all those places have been destroyed, the whole of Iraq, the Euphrates River is just littered.

When they can get a marine veteran of 32 years, [Representative] Murtha, and try to discredit that man—something is very wrong with that picture. When you get people to come out against what John Kerry did—there is something very wrong with that picture. The only thing I got mad at Senator Kerry about was when they questioned him: "Well, you threw away your medals." He should have said, "Yeah, I threw them away because they weren't *deserved*." It is nobody's business what he did with those. They were his—if he wanted to throw them away, so be it. You can throw away your ribbons.

My people were slaves. I am from slave generations. You're going to tell me I am not patriotic just because I don't believe the way you believe? I have been in this country more generations than anyone in my unit has. I have been in this country eight generations—my great-great-grandfather was a slave. My great-grandfather was a sharecropper. We were poor. We were poor kids on the eastern shore of Virginia.

## PABLO RODRIGUEZ
Technical Sergeant, Air Force Reserve

Enlisted 1984, deployed age 38 (April–June 2003), Najaf,
Baghdad Airport, Iraq

*Guarding Baghdad Airport*

*Pablo is a naturalized American who came to the US at age nine from Santurce, Puerto Rico. He has been a policeman for nineteen years and at the same time he has been in both the Army and the Air Force Reserves. He will be able to retire with twenty years' service in 2010. He is making plans to move to New York and become a musician. His combined family of five girls and a boy are graduates of Smith, Mt. Holyoke, and Amherst Colleges, with the younger ones at Xavier, Hampshire, and Holyoke Community colleges. His companion received her BA from Smith College in May 2007. Pablo was nineteen when he joined the military, with daughters born when he was fifteen and nineteen. "So I went to the active-duty army recruiter and I asked about the [education] benefits, and he says: 'Yes we do…You married?' 'No, but I have two kids.' 'If you want to join the active-duty army, you have to give up custody of your daughters because you can't come in with them.' I said, 'No way, I'm not giving up custody of my daughters.'"*

When this [war] kicked off, I was one of those who was not convinced that we had provided enough proof to say Saddam had the weapons of mass destruction. I wasn't convinced. If I'm telling you that I'm going to your house, and kick you and your husband out of your house because I don't like the way you keep your front yard, I have to go in front of a neighborhood council to prove my reasons why you and your husband should be taken out of your house. I am not going to [tell] you everything because I know you're going to be watching—especially if I've been telling you I'm going to be invading your home, right? So although we had to go in front of the UN, our evidence was not adequate in my view, even though we had to be careful because the Iraqis were watching and listening. ...

I got activated after 9/11.... The rhetoric on Saddam having weapons of mass destruction was becoming more aggressive, the build-up is happening, we are military people, we're going to go to the Middle East. But never did we think we were going to end up in the war. I don't want to sound naïve. The mission of the air force is to support the ground war. So I'm thinking we are going to be in a support role—I was missing the part that this was an *invasion*. In an invasion the rules change—everybody moves forward.

Our first mission was 90 miles south of Baghdad in the middle of nowhere—in a desert. They descended like a MASH unit. The war planners were working under the assumption that the troops going in to take over Baghdad were going to get chemically attacked, gassed, and take casualties. So the war planners said, we are going to put this medical station to remove the wounded, the people who die, to the rear. Obviously, we didn't get chemically attacked and it took seven days for Baghdad to fall. They were planning maybe a month and a half—it took a week and a half.

This is something that blows me away. We didn't have enough people for the area that we had. We were spread really thin. We didn't have radios—the troops were complaining. We had Kevlar, we didn't have communication. We used those K-Mart and Wal-Mart walkie-talkies—they have like a five-mile range. It's not a secure net, someone can listen to our conversation. But we weren't worried too much about that because we knew that the Iraqi military was getting their asses kicked.... And I'm saying to myself, "Here I am in the greatest air force in the world and we've got Mickey Mouse radios in a war!"...

We were in the desert. These people were poor. I have never seen poverty like that in my life. You have families walking around with donkey carts, with wooden wheels right out of ancient times—the mom and the dad barefoot. The ones that were considered to be well off were farmers, they had camels. In the military environment when you're in a defensive posture you're always securing your perimeter. Well, we had to relax that a little bit because the camel farmers would come right through our area of responsibility with their herds grazing, so we would have to drop the weapons and just relax.

A lot of them would talk to us because we would give them water. They seemed to be supportive—but the poverty! We were never under any attack there. Our forces hit the Iraqis so hard that I think what they did is they waited for us to get comfortable, and then they reassessed, they reassembled, and started attacking— which is what is happening now. We were getting intelligence reports that that was exactly what they were planning to do. They were running around like chickens with their heads cut off, we hit them so hard. It was so overwhelming—plus their military was still recovering from the 1991 war.

We moved back to Baghdad to the airport [where] Saddam had a military side and a civilian side. On the military side he had a major castle where the VIP people or he would stay when he was flying somewhere. We would go to the bathroom and see gold-plated faucets, bathtubs. Amazing—marble floors in the airport, tennis courts, swimming pool….

I was never engaged in a firefight. I was in a combat zone—I felt the urgency of it. When we went to Baghdad, [we saw places where] there were bullet holes in the wall. [On] the floor there was the blood from folks, it was dried blood, we could still see where someone had fallen. The airport was littered with bomblets. The air force and the navy dropped bombs, some of those bombs had bomblets. They scatter all over the place, some go off, the duds don't. They do a lot of damage. They call them cluster bombs. The planes were trashed because our troops took the Iraqi planes, removed the engines, took the cockpit, damaged it because they didn't want them to use the planes as weapons. …

I came across a few Iraqis that knew some English. Some would tell me, "I am happy that you guys are here." Others would tell me, "I don't want you guys in my country. He needed to go—Saddam—but now that he is gone I want you to get out of my country." Others didn't want anything to do with us—you had the whole spectrum of Iraqis. I talked to this man and his own opinion was, "Thanks for getting rid of Saddam. I understand you need to be here and we'll both build up this country, get ourselves to a certain level, but then I want you out." I came across another Iraqi and he told this guy, "Thanks for getting rid of Saddam, but get out *now.*" There were those that said: "You're an American—I really don't want to talk to you." That's fine.

I heard from a soldier in the Third ID that towards the end, when it was really evident that we were going to invade the country, Saddam and his people were going to universities and saying, "Hey, you speak English, here is $10,000 for you to join the army." So they were just grabbing people out of the university—"You are now in the military." Giving them a military ID card, Mickey Mouse training, two or three weeks of infantry training, and then, "Here's your uniform, here's your weapon, go out there."

Guarding the airport, they found a huge hangar where they stored the planes full of ammunition. Those missiles that were found were in violation of the treaty that Saddam signed with the UN—the Security Council treaty that said they were not supposed to have a range of more than 100 miles. I guess *technically* those could be considered weapons of mass destruction. There was a lot of stuff that was left unsecured because we didn't have the time or the personnel to secure this site because it is full of ammunition. ...

The Reserves tend to be on the older side. We have a bunch of people who could be members of the AARP! I used to say, "I wish I had a picture of all you guys to send up to AARP. You guys are my role models because when I'm that old I'll still be in the military...." The squad that went from Westover [AF Base, Massachusetts] to Iraq—I think I was one of the oldest ones. I was 38. The rest were younger. When we were hooked up with the active-duty component squad from Dover [AF Base, Delaware] they had a ton of kids. I was one of the fossils.

A lot of [young soldiers] are really mature—these kids were committed. Some of them had the same opinion that I did, they said, "I'm not convinced. I'm going to kick ass," but they were not convinced. They weren't drafted, so they feel they can question the military. But you're in the military—what the hell are you going to do? You're in—you're going to do the job. Obviously, I didn't go to Vietnam, but I think the difference this time around is that people in the military were more aware. Even guys in the army—they would question. I came across a lot of kids that would say, "Fuck this. I'm going to do this and I'm going to get on with college." They felt they were doing their job but they felt they had had enough. Obviously, you can say, I am not convinced that this guy has weapons of mass destruction, but when you join the military—you have to go. If you *don't* go, you will pay the consequences.

I think [Iraq] is going to go back to what it was. We got ourselves into a huge endeavor, a huge challenge—how do you change a country like that overnight? I don't know that we can. I don't think it's ever going to be like what we know ourselves as a democracy. Look at how much time *we* spent coming up with the Constitution. One side of me says I hope they can come up with something to have it more democratic, that the people have more rights and have more say. The women's issue, for example. I have two daughters, my girlfriend has three daughters. Do I want them to have rights? Absolutely. Would I want my kids to be under those conditions in this country? No.

That's why when people ask me about the war, I really don't have an opinion of the war, because I wasn't convinced in the beginning and then I found myself in the middle of it. It's not that I'm confused, but I don't know—it makes me sad. I'm completely torn. Like when they passed that bill a couple of years ago, $87 billion dollars for the troops, one side of me was, "Okay, we need the money, we're at war." Then the other side of me says, "Well, our school system here, right down the street in Holyoke and Springfield. The Latino population—ten kids going, seven drop out of high school."

After the Persian Gulf War, our military was chopped in half. We had what we have now, 50 percent of the assets of the military are the Reserves side of the house and the Guard side of the house. We have civilian soldiers in the war, in the front lines. The Reserves play a huge role. And also women, because there is a controversy that women are not allowed to engage in combat. Security forces are now women, the army has military police that are women. Up to now about 35, 40 women have died [by September 2007, 80 female fatalities, 2.14% of the total—ed.]. Because providing security for a convoy, or driving a fuel truck, and that convoy gets attacked—obviously, they are now on the front lines. I think that's part of equal rights, but the other side of me says we have to protect our women.

Six months ago they passed around a flyer, and they were looking for civilian contractors. They were looking for police officers with at least five years of experience who were full-time police officers, to do training in Iraq—the pay was $107,000 tax-free. And they throw in housing and food. I said to my girlfriend, "You know what, I am really tempted." She said, "No, I don't want you to go back to Iraq. You did your time." I mean—it is a hot topic at home! If you do a year, two years there, you come back with over 200 grand, tax-free. You can go, make a ton of money, come back, and have your house paid off. It's tempting.

My stepson, he's doing anti-recruiting, which I'm not against. I think that they need to have a segment that goes out there and presents the other side. But [in] the same breath, I can tell you that the military for some people is probably the best job. The amount of responsibility, the experience—you can't get any type of civilian job that you won't get there. I still believe for some young man or young woman, you try college and that didn't work for you, sleeping until 1 o'clock in your parents' home—you need to be somewhere. Serving your country.

The bone that I have with it is that recruiters are not telling the kids the mission of each branch. They will be telling you if you come into the marines, the uniform, the money for school, you get travel—but [they're] not telling you the *real* mission of the marines. That it is the ground war, you are going to be in the front, everyone that goes in the marines, you are [an] infantry person first. ...

We're fortunate to have the peace movement in the United States, but I also feel that people who haven't gone to war don't know what war is like. I can tell you that it is hell. I think the military people, they are the real peacemakers. The question becomes, "What's the proper time to use the warrior?" War doesn't have to happen. Whether we agree with this war or not, that is always going to be the key question.... In the [military] indoctrination, they told me about appreciating the veterans, the meaning of being a veteran, having freedom, the effort and the sacrifice that was done by the other generations for us to have freedom. You find yourself there doing it for your country whether you agree with it or not. So I have that appreciation now.

# TWO

# WINNING HEARTS AND MINDS

# PETER GRANATO
## Sergeant, Army Reserve

Enlisted 1996–2005, deployed age 25
(January 2003–March 2004)
Attached to the 800th MP Brigade, Camp Bucca,
Umm Qasr, Basra, Iraq

*The Prisoners of Camp Bucca*

*Peter was an enlisted army reservist from New York and Florida, 1996–2005, serving in Iraq for fourteen months. He had not opposed the war when deployed after 9/11, but became critical during the time he served in Iraq. Peter observed the early months of the coalition forces and also the Coalition Provisional Authority (CPA) under Paul Bremer. He believes that Americans neglected opportunities to work with Iraqi authorities to keep order: "If we tried to win the hearts and minds of people, it was not a good idea to neglect them." Although trained to carry out administrative duties, he served in Camp Bucca [named for a NY fire marshal and army reservist killed in 9/11] as an MP attached to the undisciplined 800th Military Police Brigade, soon to be notorious for its actions in Abu Ghraib prison. Peter has earned an MA in economics while working in the financial field. He supports Iraq veterans running for Congress.*

I am politically moderate [but] being in Iraq turned me against the war. I wasn't initially against it. Seeing some of the things I had seen over there, finding out the truth after coming home about the whole situation and where we are now, turned me against it more than anything. I actually got quite a few perspectives there because I did quite a few different jobs. Now, I wasn't an *officer*—I was actually a junior *enlisted* person. For someone with my low rank, my experience was pretty interesting.

I joined the service in 1996. I was on a pretty bad path—I actually dropped out of high school, got involved with a bad crowd—I did a few stupid things as a kid. In order for my father to take me back into the house, he wanted me to join the service. I went back and took a GED, started going to community college, went into the army reserve.... After 9/11 happened I was outraged—I grew up in the New York–New Jersey area. I was in a patriotic mode. I was blinded by a lot of things. A lot of people were—the media was totally pushing us for the war.

I was expecting to get out in November of 2002. I was called up in December of 2002 on a stop-loss—before I was even called up, I was extended. They don't follow the contract. I didn't get called up until the whole Iraq thing started. I entertained suspicions early on—why Iraq? It didn't really make a lot of sense to me, but I was at a point where I trusted our leadership. December 2002, I was a little disturbed about it, [but] there had to be a reason for it. I wasn't a product of Vietnam, so I didn't realize that your country doesn't always level with [you]. We shipped out the fifth of February [2003].

We were in Camp Arifjan in Kuwait—an American base that was pretty well established. We were pretty surprised—it was in the middle of the desert, there were a good amount of soldiers already there—and this place had Burger Kings and Pizza Huts. That's when it first dawned on me, *holy shit*, there was going to be a war! And also we had so much staging going on and it was like they were talking about "maybe diplomacy" and I'm like, *no*. The staging ground, the preparation, the services—no question that there was going to be something happening here....

They called us to go into Iraq on the 23rd [of March]. They sent a small part of the unit—myself included—just the administrative people. Now, you could question that they sent all the pencil pushers in first before they sent in the military police.

None of us could figure it out. They sent us up north around Nasariya. This was about the time of the Jessica Lynch propaganda…. It wasn't swept for mines and it was pitch black at night. The next day we started to leave—they decided we were going to go all the way down south again. It was up to us to find our way back to where the rest of the unit was. So we really went all the way up north for nothing. [Some units visited the combat zone because being there helped commanding officers get promoted—ed.]

We were assigned to the infamous 800th Military Police Brigade, which if you know anything about the war, you know they are the Abu Ghraib unit. They had no idea what this was about, they were always in revolt, none of them had been in that situation before—they were just totally lost. There were no combat veterans, there were no active-duty people. We ended up [in] a place called Camp Bucca, which is right on the border of Iraq and Kuwait. It was just a prison camp, and there were thousands of Iraqis there… who had not fought [in the war].

We had none of the things that we were trained on for how we were going to set up the camp. They didn't go by any of the protocols that they were supposed to—setting up the administrative line and segregating the prisoners by who was what. There was none of that. Everything that we had learned was out the window. Two or three units of maybe a hundred people were running a camp of about 7,000 prisoners. [In March 2007, there were 13,800 prisoners in Bucca (Iraq Index, Brookings Institution)—ed.] We were working six-to-twelve-to-fifteen-hour shifts in the hot sun. The prisoners—after a couple of months—had gotten so fed up with the whole system there was a lot of fighting going on. There were escapes, there were riots, and people were getting hurt.

After a couple of months, we were given a mission. The town around the camp was Umm Qasr, a port city down in the south of Iraq. The government of the town had collapsed. We arrested all the police and everyone else and they were hanging out at the prison camp. There was no town government or anything. A lot of people don't realize that Iraq was a socialist economy, because to get food people were given food rations, food cards, and now all of a sudden that was gone—there was no government. So they were coming to us for things.

They had given me and three or four other people a mission *inside* the town to be a liaison to the people, and none of us were trained to do any of this stuff. We were supposed to just keep the people away from the [camp] gate. That is a *real impossible* job. Basically, just tell the people to calm down and everything is coming, and tell people who were looking for prisoners if they were in the camp or not. And to give them back property that we had confiscated. We were supposed to do all of this. Now, we were actually out in the town with the people of Umm Qasr. We spent about four or five months out there, meeting people in the town and getting to know what their life was like, suffering *with* them.

I mean, you had people coming to us looking for basic necessities: medical attention, food, clean water, electricity—things that we had no way of providing. There are still things that bother me, such as the helplessness of the people. We had women bringing us babies that were turning blue and green—there was just nothing that you could do. You had to watch people die in front of you, pretty much. That was disturbing. Some of the treatment in the camp was unnerving. And then you find bodies all over the place—they were killing off each other.

[The Americans] totally neglected the towns themselves. Actually, if we tried to win the hearts and minds of people, it was not a good idea to neglect them. That was how we got to feel in regard with how things started to change. About the time we were leaving, you could tell that the people were ticked off [by] the treatment—how we just left them out there to dry. "Oh, just tell everybody it's coming." That was basically the line—"Just tell them it's coming." And nothing ever came. They are probably still waiting for it!

Also, [that was] the first time that I realized that Iraq and 9/11 were two totally different things. The army (the whole time that we were in) was blurring the line. Maybe they weren't specifically coming out and telling people, "We are going to Iraq"—[but] some of them *did*—"We are going to avenge 9/11." That was basically the rallying cry. The army as a whole was saying, you're serving your country because you're getting back [for] what happened on 9/11. But when we got out into the crowd, we started to realize that it was a different mindset between the 9/11-type people, the *al-Qaeda*, as opposed to the *Iraqi*. And I—we—had started to put two and two together because there were people coming in from *outside* of Iraq trying to stir the pot *inside* of Iraq.

They were not very helpful to people who were looking for missing people. There were a lot of Geneva Conventions broken. You were supposed to pay people, you were supposed to allow visitation—they didn't start doing that for many, many months. I didn't quite see any of the Abu Ghraib–type of things that were going on, thank God. I don't think that happened at Bucca. There *were* CIA interrogations, because there were people hanging around the camp that weren't military—nobody knew who the hell they were. They had their own little section of the camp and they would take select people over there. Then we had to leave before they started to do anything. Who knows what they ended up doing.

And there was basically no accountability. It was a free-for-all. There was no leadership—it was a reserve unit, so it was very lax. The officers and the enlisted were drinking together, having parties together. It all ended up eventually in the Taguba report—the major-general who did the investigation [of the Abu Ghraib scandal]. You can find it on some sites on the internet. It tells you about the dysfunctionality of the 800th Military Police battalion. There was no structure in the unit—it was pretty much *whatever* they wanted to do, *whenever* they wanted to do it.

And then, towards the end, they blamed everything on that [Brigadier] General Karpinski, who actually came in in the last four months. I met General Karpinski a couple of times—a very nice woman, very amicable. Very knowledgeable on the military side, I don't know how knowledgeable she was on her mission. She didn't take over the 800th MP Brigade until three months before we left. So it's pretty interesting how they tried to pin the whole thing on her. ...

It's funny, because when you look at all the incidents that have happened, they try to pin the whole thing on a couple of nineteen-year-olds from West Virginia. It happened *five* different places, so.... The whole unit was a breakdown. They had all thought that they were going to be home in six months, so you can only imagine after thirteen months—we never went home. Every time we were supposed to go home, it changed. The unit was strictly bad. The command was lieutenant colonels doing whatever the hell they wanted. They would skip out of the base whenever they could.

They would take their air-conditioned SUVs and go shopping at the malls in Kuwait. They didn't pay much attention to the well-being of the soldiers.

You remember the transition happened while we were there. There wasn't a war anymore. Now it was keeping up with law and order in Iraq—we are getting criminals, petty criminals. You get in a neighborly dispute, your neighbor's dog takes a shit on your lawn, you're mad. You go to tell the American MP that your neighbor is working for this group. The Americans go and raid the house, take the man out of the house and throw him in jail. And this would be a revenge thing—the neighbors would be mad at each other, they had a score to settle, they would tell the American soldiers go take this guy. Probably 20 to 30 percent of the prisoners that we had in the camp were because of that.

I could never figure out who they were interested in—it was like they're just picking names out of a hat. "We'll pick up some of these people." We started to realize some of the people they were picking up didn't belong there. There were cab drivers that made a wrong turn and they ended up at a checkpoint. So what did they do? The marines would put them on a bus and take them down to us [Camp Bucca]. You had a lot of that. We had people who were 85 and who could barely walk—they *blindfolded* them, for Christ's sake. You knew that most of these people lived through shit. Then you had your power-hungry, gung-ho MPs, and then you had no supervision, so you put those things together and what are you going to end up with?

[My title] was admin, but that didn't matter because they had cooks watching prisoners. You remember that Halliburton came in to cook for us after about a month? So the cooks became MPs. No training. They were MPs. That is another thing about the 800th—the whole staff pretty much was MP. It really didn't matter what your title was—you were in the MP unit, you might as well be an MP. The cooks, engineers, they put them all in the [prison] camp.

I didn't realize what was going on at the time, but coming back and reading up on it, there was a point where Ambassador Bremer was not listening to Ayatollah Sistani. He [Bremer] wanted to have elections. And there was a two-week point where I guess Ayatollah Sistani was ticked off and people knew about it, where they were a lot more hostile to us. You could tell that something was not right by the way people looked at you. Of course we had nobody telling us that this was going on. You could actually physically feel the hostility, you could tell when they started having demonstrations.

They [the Shiites] were indebted to that guy, Sistani. If he told them to jump in front of a train, they would. I guess the schmucks who planned this whole thing—or didn't plan it—decided he wasn't important if he wasn't part of the plan. He is actually a moderate cleric from what I have read. Early on, he told [the Shiites] not to attack coalition soldiers and that could explain why areas were okay for the months that we were there.

I think there was a window of opportunity to connect at least with the Shiites where we were, and they blew that opportunity. You can't change an economic system overnight, and that's something that a lot of the people didn't take into account. Especially this ideological government we have in our country. You have a free-market answer to everything. I think that had a big influence over the building of the insurgency. Bremer came in and changed all the laws of the country. All the trade regulations, the financial situation, all the subsidies that the government had given the people—just washed them all out with one stroke of his pen. They totally wanted to try to install a supply-side economic system and use Iraq as an experiment for it.

They had thought that everything would come together overnight. They relied on the Chalabi people, these unreliable exiles—they expected that they would just be able to take charge. *Come on*, you think that the Iraqis are not going to be ticked off that you're going to put some guy [in charge]—first of all, he's a crook, second of all, he hasn't been in this country for 25 years? Then they had thought the economic regulations that Bremer passed would spur foreign investment, which might make sense, but you forget one thing: you need security. No country is going to come in and do foreign investment overnight.

*This* is something that hasn't been reported anywhere. Korea had a little *tiny* contingent of soldiers and quartered them in Umm Qasr guarding the port—I think just because they wanted to be part of the coalition of the willing…. Little by little I'm looking around, there are all these Hyundais driving around all over town. Beat-up Chevrolets, 1970s cars were everywhere—kind of like they have in Cuba, where they fix them and fix them and fix them. You have the same thing there, you have these 1970s Chevies, pick-up trucks and stuff. And all of a sudden you have these 2003, 2004 Hyundai Elantras driving around. What the hell is going on? Where are all those Hyundais coming from? Koreans took over the port—all they are doing is bringing Hyundais into the country. That was their investment. But Bremer, with the trade regulations, allowed them to bring in hundreds of thousands of Hyundais. They flooded the entire country with Hyundais. It's interesting that that kind of stuff never made the news.

Our chaplain was an evangelical and there were a lot of them in our unit also—that's another story, about the proselytizing. It was good versus evil, this is the Crusade, how important Israel was— all he did was indoctrinate the people with these thoughts. The chaplain was definitely, "They are evil, we are good, Jesus wants us to do this." I had never met a chaplain of this persuasion until this thing. He was from the Carolinas—they were importing them from certain parts of the country. All the chaplains that I met on this tour were that type of chaplain.

They believe that the world is going to end soon, so they don't care about global warming. The Israel factor is very important here because the evangelicals are passionately pro-Israel. They have mixed with your Wolfowitzes [Paul Wolfowitz, then deputy secretary of defense], your extreme-right Likud-thinking Americans.... Personally, if I was living in Israel, I would probably *not* want them to stir up a hornet's nest in the Middle East. But apparently the right wing in Israel and the American [pro-]Israelis who are right wing believe that this is a good thing. [*But this has little to do with Iraq.*] No, it doesn't. Apparently, that is part of the reason why they didn't really do very much for the Iraqis! [*Laughter*]

The Iraqis were not devoutly religious prior to this war, believe it or not. Saddam's regime was a *secular* regime. They would have been threatened by Islamic radicals, which is why they kept them at bay—always. This Muqtada al-Sadr—his father was executed by Saddam Hussein. And al-Sadr stayed under the radar for a little while, waited for the right move, and then made his power grab. He was from the radical Iranian faction of the Shiites. Saddam kept the Islamists *down,* we went in and brought the Islamists *up.* Now you pretty much have handed it to the Iranians. I can't imagine people could have been in support of giving the country to Iran.

———

They cut veterans' benefits, and you should see what it's like to go to a VA. It's just a kick in the ass when [the government] can make dividend and capital-gains tax cuts but the VA can't get enough funding. When you actually get cared for, when you get a person, it's great, but getting to the person or the doctor or the specialist—that's the problem. The people who work in the VA are very dedicated, but as far as the *funding* goes, every time you get medication you have a co-pay, it feels like a kick in the ass. The Greatest Generation [World War II] got everything. They had FDR [President Franklin Delano Roosevelt] at the time. As much as people want to compare this schmuck to FDR, it is kind of hard.

Now here is another issue that I want to raise…. Being in the Reserves, and getting out after I did my service, I got no education benefits whatsoever. I pay 100 percent of my tuition. I have $30,000 in loans—in the Reserves you get no portability of your [Montgomery] GI Bill. Once you get out of the service, you lose it, unless you intend to stay in. Obviously, I wasn't going to stay in—I was already being held up longer than I should have [been]. Look at the [Department of] Veterans' Affairs, look at the guy that they put in charge of it. His heart is probably full of coals—a lawyer. … [VA chief Nicholson resigned in July 2007—ed.]

[*Was it hard being out of the military?*] You think, "Wow, when I get home people are going to be totally respectful," but you come to learn after a couple of days of being home, that nobody gives a shit. When I first came home, I had my uniform still on and went out to bars and nobody looked twice. Nobody cared. The only people who actually cared are people when you go out on political campaigns and you talk about it. You try to explain to a bill collector—who cares? At my job, nobody said anything. I ended up losing my job when I got back. …

[*Other things?*] I found myself hoarding water. I went out and bought an AR-15 because I felt weird not having an M-6. You need to be armed in some way. When I went to a restaurant, I would get paranoid if someone was behind me…. When you come home, you go crazy and spend everything you have…. [The military] was interesting—it did a lot for me. Not necessarily *Iraq*, but basic training, when I was on a team, meeting people from all over the country…. It was my first experience of being on my own.

# NATHAN MURPHY
## Lance Corporal, Marine Corps Reserve

Enlisted 2001–2007, deployed age 19
(April–September 2003, September 2004–March 2005)
Motor transport, Kuwait; Camp Taqaddum, Sunni Triangle, Iraq

*To Shoot or Not to Shoot?*

*Nathan is a tall, lanky veteran from Barre, Massachusetts, with a wry sense of humor about himself and his experiences. He wore a broad-brimmed felt hat to our meeting—quite a contrast with the baseball caps I was used to. He attended Northeastern University before being mobilized with the Marine Corps Reserve. His story of recruitment is a cautionary tale of how promises are made to teenagers about college benefits. Nathan remains concerned about the educational benefits that veteran-students receive. At first he found it a challenge to readjust to life as a student at UMass Amherst, but graduated cum laude from the School of Management in May 2007 and then set out for the West. Nathan, who was frequently on convoys during his two tours of duty in Iraq, noted that "We're over there trying to win the hearts and minds and we're just running them off the road. You sit in the desert long enough, you don't care."*

I was a little bit into procrastination as far as the college process goes…. [One day] I was skipping class in the library and my name got called over the intercom—me and this other fellow. Another kid who had graduated a couple of years ago had come back and he had joined the Marine Corps and he needed two names for his recruiter. We said, "Not interested, but we'll give him [our] names if that will make him happy." A couple days later he called me. "Nathan, I hear you're interested in joining the Marine Corps." I said, "To tell you the truth, I'm not really that interested. I want to go to college." And he says, "But Nathan, did you know that marines go to college for *free?*" "*Really?*" That's what I said, and then it was all downhill from there.

January of 2001, I enlisted in the Marine Corps. The night before was the first time I ever drank alcohol. It was kind of like Arlo Guthrie—I wanted to make sure that I felt and looked my best! What happens—you go to your local recruiter station and do a bunch of stuff. They take you to a hotel, you stay the night, and the next morning you go to the military entry processing station. That's where you are processed and that's where they ship you down to the airport.

I graduated on June 9, I had a party on the 10th, on the 11th I was off. I got to Parris Island the 13th…. That graduation week, my recruiter came to my awards night and tells me I'm getting this Marine Corps scholarship award, $50,000 towards school over four years. I'm like, "Great, that's cool," told my Mom, my principal said it was legit—this was a week before boot camp. I was seventeen years old, and I really didn't understand the full implication of making sure it was actually written down. I just trusted the guy.

Fast forward about a year. I'm at Northeastern [University] and I go to register for spring classes and they are all purged [deleted] and I don't have a schedule. What happened was that my mom claimed that we were getting that money from the Marine Corps—so in turn they lowered the amount of financial aid I was getting from the university. And all of a sudden this money isn't there because I was straight lied to. My dad ended up having to spend a good portion of his Christmas bonus, and I had to spend two or three thousand dollars I had saved up—we were in the hole about seven grand. At the time [college] was probably about

$30,000 a year. We were getting about $17,000 a year in financial aid, so my parents were already paying money for me to go there. ...

I am a prime example of the military going after young men and women and taking advantage of them. I think it's despicable. On the other hand, the armed forces have a job to do and part of that job is recruiting. But one thing I always tell people that the Marine Corps has taught me is not to be a sucker. Now a phrase from one of my good friends was, "Believe *none* of what you hear and only *half* of what you see." That's the way it is....

I graduated boot camp September 7, 2001. Four days later, on the 10th, I was hanging out with one of my buddies, and we got good and drunk, [and] wake up the next morning to my mother's phone call. She says, "Turn on the TV"—obviously all this stuff was going down in New York and the Pentagon. I ended up talking to my recruiter, and he told me when I went down there to cover myself just in case—so that my uniform wasn't visible. Because the level of fear at the time in the country was so great that I was a possible military target for any terrorist that might be floating around going from point A to point B....

It was March 17th [2003], St. Paddy's Day, that President Bush gave his speech issuing the 48-hour ultimatum to Saddam Hussein... to disarm, resign, and after that we are going in. All my buddies were already over there in Kuwait. We got to fly on a triple seven [Boeing 777]—best airplane ride I ever had—civilian, your own little TV, every little luxury. They come around and hand you a damp washcloth, steamed—they treated us good.... At first we went to [Camp] Commando, and the people there were like, "We don't know who you are—why you are here." We were just nobodies.... They shipped us to Camp Fox... and *they* were, "We don't know who you guys are." We got a helicopter ride up to Iraq to a place called Camp Viper. This is a sandbowl, it's out in the middle of nowhere—it was the pivotal place in the actual push north. I got into Iraq April 19, 2003. By this time things were pretty much over.... May 1st was the end of major military operations as George W. would say. My *boss*.

The first time when we were in Viper, we saw Iraqis. This is OIF-I—this is stuff that doesn't happen any more. But you stop the convoy, you've got all these Iraqis [who] come up to you trying to sell you all different kinds of stuff. They start with Iraqi money and then they start selling you bayonets, Kevlar, gas masks, booze, whiskey (a favorite—which is stupid because we don't know who these people are). Myself included, we bought that stuff and drank it. My first impression was that these guys are true-born capitalists. They were making a killing out there. Our money was obviously worth a lot more than what they were selling us—some of those guys made some decent loot. When we're driving along, everyone is waving at us, giving us the thumbs up. I've seen little kids waving American flags.

Straight through to September there were people coming out to the roads, waving. Every now and again, you would get the middle finger and they say that some people didn't like us, but for the most part people were pretty friendly. But that's hard to say— just because they are smiling and waving at you doesn't really mean a lot. I know that at that time, most of the country was pretty grateful, I *think*. I talked to a kid that was telling me that Saddam killed his father. He pointed to a scar and said Saddam did it. Obviously not *Saddam*, but while Saddam was in power.

So I would be driving the seven-ton [truck] with one of my buddies with the mail clerk—because the mail clerk had to go with the mail.... We hit the road fast, we weren't stopping for anything. We were passing slow Iraqi vehicles [at] about 45 [mph] and a seven-ton tops off at 66 miles an hour. What would happen is that you would have a slow vehicle and we would just pull up right on their tail. I had one Humvee in front of me and the other three were behind me. So that Humvee would get the guy to pull over— he's got the .50 cal machine gun, faces the gun right down there at the driver and tells him to pull over. They usually pull over and let us all go by. If not, sometimes the guy would pass him and I would pull up and I would get the M-16 out and I'm like, "PULL OVER!" and sometimes you scare them a little bit.

Now sometimes you've got people coming the other way. In Iraq, people just drive like idiots and pass each other all the time. They're coming and you're in the same lane as them, going towards them at 65 miles an hour and they're flashing their lights at you telling you to get out of the way. We would just flash our lights back and say, "Ha, YOU get out of the way." So basically we were running people off of the road at about 65 miles an hour.... we were moving, that was a good time. That was the time where my buddy almost hit the donkey.

This isn't good. We're over there trying to win the hearts and minds and we're just running them off the road. You sit in the desert long enough, you don't care. As a general rule, we don't like people [cutting into] our convoy—there was the threat of someone blowing up a vehicle.... Sometimes you move through busy areas, you lay on the horn, you holler and scream, point your weapons at them. Like, we probably hit a few people. I was on the back of the truck when one of my buddies hit somebody—hit the car. You are driving a big seven-ton truck weaving through traffic, bombing down a busy road at 40 miles an hour. There are people all over the place, donkeys, dogs, kids—it was just intense.

Female marines were in their own tent, a smaller tent, a twenty-person tent. We had three women in our unit, two sergeants and this one lance corporal. One sergeant was someone who I'm comfortable fighting with. She had been on embassy duty, she was hard, you know. The other two weren't as good. It's the general opinion of most men—women just don't do much but cause trouble. Even for one female, they have to have their own tent, their own designated shower. We had guard duty at the shower. They have to have separate things like that, and you can't walk around with your shirt off, officers will get all touchy about it. Second, take me and any of my buddies—we can change a 500-pound LVS [logistics vehicle system] tire. No sweat. One of these girls and her buddies couldn't do that, they couldn't lift the thing, they couldn't lift the *jack*.

[*What would motivate a woman to join the marines?*] That "can-do" feminism attitude. Listen, I'm not sexist. If you've got a female that wants to join the Marine Corps and that is absolutely frigging crazy, *and* can pull her weight—that's cool. If you've got some girl who's just doing it because someone tells her she can, she wants to prove something but she's the size of a twig, this is *serious* business. I've seen a few that can hack it. But most of them don't. Some do. You have got the M2-.50 cal and that thing weighs a ton. If you can't mount it, you shouldn't be operating it—if you can't pick it up and put it on the gun mount. To rack it, you have got to put your weight to that thing—it's a big weapon.

[Women] go through boot camp, then they join the Reserves and they sit around most of the month and they go one weekend a month. And the next thing you know, you're in Iraq after being on Camp Couch for the past two years. The same thing can happen with some men. Some *men* marines are useless, too. Also, when you're in the desert, that breeds a certain amount of tension when there are fifty guys and three girls running around. That can cause all kinds of problems, because people have drives. And that kind of stuff happens. Sometimes it's just two people going back behind the berm and it's no big deal—they're the same rank. But sometimes it is an officer who is *married* doing a lance corporal and getting busted for it, losing his career—she's screwed. I don't know any statistics, but I would say that as many as one out of ten females over there get sent home pregnant. That's a common occurrence.

⎯

September 11, 2003, was the day we left Kuwait, back to the States. Ah, good day. We stopped in Germany, picked up some booze at the PX, got nice and drunk on the way home. All the high rankers were up in first class, and NCOs are in business class, and everyone else is in coach in the back. I got a staff sergeant from my unit, I am hanging out with him up in first class, sipping wine. We went to the cockpit, talking with the pilots and the flight attendants—it was fun. I ended up being in the cockpit when we landed in Pendleton [Marine base in California]—*awesome.*

Being a marine, through the first deployment, weapons of mass destruction, links to al-Qaeda—that's what we went in there believing. We thought it was a *good* thing because we could see the people being happy. Saddam wasn't found yet, but he was getting out. *But,* over that summer of 2003, the number of people getting killed started at once a week, one soldier died, two soldiers died. And it started getting more like every day. By the end of the summer, the death count kept on climbing. Then in April of 2004 was the first thing in Falluja, where they had those four guys [contractors] get tossed around and hung up on a bridge, and we went to Falluja and tore it up a little bit.

[Second] deployment was different. We were at Camp Taqaddum—Camp TQ—it's right near Lake Habaniya, west of

Baghdad, about twelve miles from Falluja, a little bit further from Ramadi. Right between the two cities—two of the most dangerous places in Iraq.... Shortly after we got there, eleven marines in Falluja got killed on the way back to TQ to fly home. We knew this time it was going to be dangerous.... One of my buddies was sent to Najaf—he was driving a fuel truck—and he was just gone, that was that.

The first rocket attack that we had when I was in Camp Taqaddum was towards the end of the day—that's usually when they happen. At dusk, October 12. All of a sudden a rocket landed 500 yards away—I can see this huge explosion with sparks and fire. Someone comes running up for a corpsman and says we've got some marines down. I started up the Humvee that was parked right there by the hut, our corpsman got his stuff and I drove him over there. Driving up I felt it was like an Oliver Stone movie, *Born on the Fourth of July*.

Four people were hit, but I only saw two of them—two marines on the ground. One guy was dead. He had two big holes in his chest. I thought I saw his eyes move, but apparently not— maybe it was an arm twitch. The other guy was just broken all apart. Apparently one guy was able to keep his leg but out of the four guys that were hit, one guy was killed and two other guys for sure lost limbs, either legs or arms. And another corpsman said he went to put a bandage on a leg and he grabbed it and it was just like a big lump of flesh, it was all blown off. So he just put the tourniquet on instead.

We started getting ready for the push to Falluja... we just basically leveled the place.... We have 870 trailers [an LVS with a big trailer]—you can carry heavy equipment gear and stuff—and we had D7 'dozers. And the unit is going to push up to the bridges, build berms, roadblocks, make a hole in a house if you need to!... Two guys ended up dying in an accident—this was on the news. One guy was in one of those 'dozers right by the river and it's dark out, you're operating with no lights—he's got NVGs [night vision goggles] on. I think they were probably taking fire, but he ended up getting rolled into the river and drowning. A guy went in to save him—he ended up drowning, too.

During the day, the push came from the north down into the city. We had air and we had artillery from TQ. It was the most God-awful sound in the world, the explosions, firefights. We had choppers all over the place. Three or four days was the most of it. After a week it was a ghost town. Prior to the battle we dropped leaflets all over the city, thousands of them. That morning we see the Iraqis leaving. On foot, some people are in cars, and they're heading out of town. We see people walking their cows—people are taking what they've got. You see stray dogs and animals running around, freaking out. [The inhabitants] are shooting mortars at us, too....

One interesting thing that happened was I'm right in front of this driveway. I don't know who these people are, but this guy comes out of his house. And he's looking at me down the driveway and I'm like "Whoa!"—I'm staring down the barrel at him. And he's like, "I want to talk with you." And I'm like, "I don't want to talk to you, get out of here, go back to your house." And he takes a step closer, so you have a bunch of guys with M-16s looking at him. One corporal who was in charge [said], "What do you want?" He's like, "I want to talk. I have a question." The corporal asked, "What is it?" "Do we stay or do we go? My family—do we stay or do we go?" We said, "Stay right here." And the guy just said, "Thank you," and went back in his house. This guy is just scared out of his mind. I think he would have known about [the evacuation]. These houses had telephone wires going to them. It was the general consensus they *had* to have known. It was all over CNN. If we want to know what's going on in Falluja, we look at CNN.com because the media knows just as much at that point.

We got back on the road heading back towards TQ, and they exploded an IED and hit the lead vehicle of the convoy. We lost two guys—one of the guys I knew a little bit, the other guy I didn't know so much. We had the wounded in the back of my truck and the guys that got killed were in the back of the Humvee. You never put them together, you know. If you had a broken leg and you just got blown up, you don't want to be looking over at someone that just got killed. I was told that they got hit with RPGs [rocket-propelled grenades] on their way to pick us up but they were armored vehicles. We were light armor—we were just trucks with some armor strapped on.

But while we were waiting for them, this vehicle approaches us. Now according to the rules of engagement for Operation Phantom Fury, after dark, if you see unarmed military-aged men, armed military-aged men, or any vehicle approaching the convoy—take them out. And this vehicle is coming up on us. I swing around and I see it a distance away, comes a little closer, slowed down and saw us and stopped. I don't know if it put its high beams on or whether it was just sitting there checking us out. I don't want to take some vehicle out because I know these people are scared, and he isn't shooting at us yet. Once the IED went off [earlier], I racked the .50 cal just in case stuff went down and that was just a terrifying time because we were sitting ducks there, you know, and I knew [our] guys were down.

So this guy is coming up, it's dark. He stops, I'm aimed in, ready to go, and everybody is aimed in. And the sergeant sees me, *"Don't shoot."* And I'm like, "Do you want me to hit him with the flare?" and he says, "Yeah, hit him with the flare." I pop it, it goes off, the guy goes in reverse. I mean if he had pulled forward instead of going into reverse I probably would have just lit up. I'm *glad*, but you know, after losing two of our guys and given that the rules of engagement were if someone is approaching the convoy—which he *had* done—I'm supposed to light them up.

Two days later... one of my buddies from my actual unit in the States was driving the lead vehicle and the convoy got hit by three IEDs and I'm like, "Oh my God, did my buddy just get killed?" I saw this one [Iraqi] guy going down the road after the explosion. He was unarmed and it's kind of hard to say what distance it was, he was probably close to where the IED went off. It wasn't at night time, but he was suspicious because he was in the area. Some people said I should have taken him out—I didn't. I know that a guy [at the end of the] convoy went through about 300 rounds that day. *Definitely, definitely* killed people. I think he lit up anyone he saw, so that guy may have been killed by him. I don't know.

Between the two experiences I felt a certain amount of guilt for not pulling the trigger. That's a messed-up feeling, because you are questioning—did I do my job? That vehicle—maybe they were scouting us out, maybe they went back and told their buddies about us, and by the time they got back we were gone. Maybe they were just a family. They could have been insurgents. They could have killed some guys later on. I don't know, but the way I see it, my conscience is clean.... I feel fortunate that I didn't have to kill anyone. I didn't the whole deployment.

By this point, obviously, Iraq was a mess... now we're in 2004 going into 2005. Lots of guys take the attitude it's better to fight terrorists over here [Iraq] than on our own soil. But you know what—over here we're not fighting with people who got on the airplane and flew into the towers. The President has come out and said, "I was wrong about the weapons of mass destruction, about the links to al-Qaeda." And my reaction is, "Well, what did he do *that* for?"

At the time when we were in Iraq, it was a good thing that we had liberated this country from Saddam Hussein. He was a bad guy. Of course there's a lot of countries that could use liberation. Somalia is still in anarchy—we were in there back in the '90s. I don't know a huge amount about all the bad guys in the world— the dictators. But I know that Iraq is a country that obviously had a bad leader who was treating his people terribly—but it was more appealing because of oil.

I justified it that we're going in there if maybe there's a chance that this country is going to develop a stable government, and eventually be an example for a new way in the Middle East. Political stability, a bridge between the rest of the world and the Middle East, because there's obviously a huge culture gap. That's a little far-fetched maybe, but it is still a possible outcome of this war. And if this all happens, maybe it was worth it for all these men and women to be killed. I'm not going to lie. My heart does not go out to [Iraqis] as much and that's part of the problems of war. This is creating a whole new racism. We call them hajjis. We don't much care about them. I ran them off the road at 60 [mph]. I would have thought it was a blast to have crushed one of their donkeys into the truck. Other people think it's a blast to light them up. Quite a few have been killed....

I don't know the situation at Abu Ghraib. I don't know exactly what was going on. Being in the desert and being in this war, you've got these prisoners. It isn't just a matter of, "I'm bored, let's see if I can go beat this naked guy and break some bones." You know [what] these people have done. Basically, that is one of the big problems of war, this war, war in general. It happened in Vietnam—you're in a situation where you lose a little bit of humanity. You're trained in violence, in killing, and it becomes natural. It's like things just progress in a really bad way and that's where you get things like Abu Ghraib. You don't want to be in Iraq, you want to be home. People get bored, and they get upset. Some people that are in the military are just sadistic to begin with. That kind of thing can spread.

You know, going back from this time [second deployment] I was *scared* to come back. The first time I told my mom, my dad, everything pretty much. The second time I didn't. I didn't want my mom to have to worry. I said I was fine. When the thing with Falluja comes up, I said we're supporting a unit that's going in—but we're not going in at all. I didn't call them about anything. It's like, "So how was your week?" "Oh, yeah, this week I saw a guy get blown up by a rocket, how was yours?" You form a distance—it's a whole separate mode of personality and being.

So calling home and writing letters home becomes difficult. My ex-girlfriend and I had trouble. I tried to leave a message once on her phone, "I'm sorry I don't want to talk with you, I just want it to be in person." Maybe she could have been more understanding—maybe I could have been better. After a while, she's like, "I am sick of hearing about Iraq. You have been back two months." "*Two months?* I was over there for *six*—do you *know* what I went though over there?" Some people can take their own experiences and they can't understand yours, but they understand *maybe* how you can go through something that can affect you in a way that someone else can't understand. I definitely was torn apart by that deployment.

# ANDREW MCCONNELL
## Master Sergeant, Army

Enlisted 1988, deployed age 34 (April 2003–July 2004)
Baghdad, Musyib, Iskandariya, Iraq

*Reconstruction and Local Politics*

*Andrew is an NCO who teaches ROTC at UMass Amherst and has been in the army twenty years. He is from Illinois, left high school to enlist when he was seventeen, later receiving his GED. He has a strong sense of the army as a second family, sometimes a family that feels closer than the one left at home. He has been married for fourteen years and his wife has been with him through four overseas deployments. When Andrew retires from the army he plans to be a teacher with the Department of Defense school system in Europe. He was not in as much of the invasion as he would have liked or expected to be, due to changes in strategy after Turkey refused to allow US troops to depart from its territory. He dealt daily with Iraqis, and was a close observer of their political culture. He also saw the growth of the insurgency: "The enemy is just as smart as you are… they're adaptive, they're trained, they're different, and this is their home turf.…We have the disadvantage."*

I am Sergeant First Class Andrew McConnell.... My recruiter gave me the option of going to Korea, Panama, or Germany. I served in Coffey Barracks, Ludwigsburg, Germany. I went to Ft. Carson, Colorado with the Fourth ID, then three years in Alaska as an army paratrooper. Then I went back to Germany in Darmstadt. During that tour I went to Bosnia three times. Then recruiting in Houston, Texas—I was there when 9/11 happened.

March 2002, I went back to Germany, in Baumholder. After 9/11 hit, we knew that somewhere, sometime, as a military, we were going to be engaged. Afghanistan was already in play. The year prior to us going into Iraq, we spent a lot of time training for operations in Afghanistan. We were getting a lot of good intelligence from the combat zone on how to deal with al-Qaeda and how they operate. It was a good mixture of us going against conventional forces with armored tanks and artillery, and against more of a guerrilla force.

January 2003 was when we were told we were going to Iraq. Our battle plan was going to be the Third ID and the First Armored Division in the South and the Fourth ID in Turkey. That part changed—the Turkish government decided that they weren't going to allow the Fourth ID to attack from their country. What that did to *us*—they sent the Third ID on their own—and they kind of stole the show from us! Being a combat soldier, that's what we feel like—after being trained year in and year out to go to combat. The Third ID was going to take the main route, which linked up the British force which took the east coast up to Basra. The Third ID was pushing past Basra—the main effort.

The First Armored Division—we were supposed to be on their left flank covering their rear and left as we were pushing up. The Fourth ID—along with a brigade from the 82nd Airborne and a brigade of airborne from Italy—was supposed to be in the north, Kurdistan. They were supposed to push north through Turkey, to take the northern portion of Iraq. We were supposed to cut off any route through Syria and to take care of any desert-oriented troops to the west of Baghdad. The Third ID was supposed to go all the way up to the outskirts of Baghdad and secure it, and the First Armored Division—my division—was supposed to come into and take Baghdad.

Our final push once the Third ID had secured the perimeter, we would have pushed in from that area—that was our battle plan. Third ID was going to secure the Baghdad International Airport like they did and we were then supposed to pass them and start taking the rest of the city, the main presidential palace and to the east. It didn't quite work out that way. We actually got into Kuwait on April 28, 2003, after almost three agonizing weeks of sandstorms and hot weather. We finally moved north—but we didn't quite *roll* north.

The army itself is such a unique organization. Unlike any corporation—even sports teams which are really closely knit—we live together, we eat together, we sleep together, we train together, we go to war together. I think the combination of the closeness in peacetime and in war really makes a bond. Whether you go to war or not, you have to put your life in somebody else's hands—literally, not a figure of speech. That's the bond you have with nobody else in your lifetime—a lot of us don't even have it with spouses. That bond between husband and wife is not as strong as it is between soldier and soldier.

I give [young soldiers] credit for their ingenuity. We call them the Nintendo generation. They play video games, they're always on the computer. Even in the combat zone they brought their computers with them. I think they would sell their weapon before they ever would their laptop! Their mind doesn't focus on sports and the outdoors. In my day I would go camping and my mother would have to drag me inside to eat before it gets dark. Well— these kids live indoors, they can run circles around me on the computer. That's great. That has also led them to a lot of the games that deal with military tactics—all the high-speed, action, violent ones [that] deal with the military. It teaches them to start being adaptive—it's about what you learn by experience. You learn a lot by losing: they're playing that video game and they lose, and they're thinking, how can I do this different to win. I think a lot of it comes back to when they were playing that game they had to make a split-second decision and go with it. There are kids out there that saved lives—obviously they made good decisions. They're also asking *why* do we do it like this, whereas in my generation, you shut up and you do it. ...

They watch *Band of Brothers*, they watch *Saving Private Ryan*, it gives the soldiers a sense of pride in how soldiers in the past have done.... Part of it is the arrogance: We're Americans. We're it. We're the best-trained and the best-equipped army in the world. There are *none* better. And so we're driving down those roads— we're cocky attitude guys now. We were all guilty of this and that got people killed. So we started realizing we really don't have as much reason to be cocky as we thought. Because we take our enemies to the subhuman level—the enemy are animals that just need to be exterminated. You come to realize that the enemy is just as smart as you are. They're smart, they're adaptive, they're trained, they're different, and this is their home turf. Guess what—we have the *disadvantage*. We have to be on our toes.

Unfortunately, we learned that the hard way. For instance, when the Iraqis really started doing the roadside bombs they spent a good six to eight months practicing on us. They weren't trying to do much damage—they were trying to see what worked. They were figuring out our tactics and how we reacted. They created an intelligence network of our capabilities in different areas. So their level of expertise finally grew to the point where they started inflicting 70 percent of the casualties in Iraq due to improvised explosives. It's not even direct fire—they blow us up on the roads.... We were driving in regular soft-skin Humvees so we had no protection—no armor, nothing. We even had plastic doors but took them off. So it was my leg sticking out a foot and a half into the road—that's how we drove around for the first year we were there!

There's a section of the city right south of the Green Zone called Karada, and it's the central marketplace for central Baghdad. We were tasked to patrol and secure that area and keep it free of violence. Baghdad University was in that sector. We made sure that it reopened—we even had a platoon of infantrymen stationed there. We had even lost a soldier there. He was shot in the head while he was getting a Coke from the cafeteria—a handgun. He had taken off his Kevlar. Someone came right behind him and shot him in the back of the head. We forget sometimes that we are in a combat zone and there are people that don't like us.

We had a Christian population. In our area we had a women's Christian hospital as well as a couple of churches that were run by nuns. The nuns were both Iraqi and missionaries. The doctors were all Iraqi Christians. There's a population of about 300,000 Christians in Iraq and a lot of them lived in this neighborhood. So we actually had a platoon stationed right by this hospital 24 hours a day.... There was no tension between local Muslims and Christians.

The average Iraqi is just trying to raise a family, pay their bills, and live a peaceful life. They want a secure environment. I would say 80 percent of the people that I have met were glad that we were there. Eighty percent of *those* said it was time for us to go home. [They liked] getting rid of Saddam and the Baath Party, but by the time my eighteen months was up they said, "It's ready for you guys to leave now, Iraq can take care of Iraq." Of course they didn't understand a lot of the bigger picture, which was that they didn't have a military, a stable police force to handle insurgents, [and] people [are] coming in to cause trouble or make power plays in one of the political parties.

The Arab mindset is so drastically different from the Western mindset. We were trying to throw democracy down their throats. Democracy does not work in Iraq. I can tell you first hand—they don't understand it, they have *no concept* of it, they have never lived it. What they needed was one person in charge to tell them what to do. But we were giving them all these freedoms that they did not know what to *do* with. The Iraqi mindset is the barter system.

Probably within the first couple of months of their being told they could create political parties there were 54 political organizations sprung up overnight. And most of them were headquartered in my sector. There was a political party row! So all these new political parties came up with their agendas—some are crackpot with twelve people and others have thousands of followers. Now, you're telling them, you're in your own country, you decide what needs to be done. Well, with the barter system concept as part of their inherited how they do things, to them that's "I've got to get the best deal for me."

"Do you want to know who the terrorists are? Okay, but what are you going to do for me to get that?" "Well, I'm going to let you keep your freedom and help you with that." "I already have that, you're going to have to do more for me now." So it's always cutting a deal with them. Sometimes it was money, sometimes it was security, sometimes it was, "Hey, I'll tell you who the guys are—you bring your big boss and come to our picnic that we're having," meaning, "Look at me—the Americans are coming to my organization and they're supporting me." Instead, we're going there simply because we want to keep good PR with these people. So we're sitting there and these guys think they're using this to heighten their stature within the community of the political parties.

Their concept of doing this for Iraq—like as a soldier I serve my country—they serve because it's the only way for them to get a job or get their families jobs. We do it for patriotism. Iraqis didn't have patriotism, the reality is that they're trying to get something for them[selves], their organization. Our job was to try to turn 2,000 years of thinking over in a couple of years, to turn them over to a democratic society to understand all the democratic Western ways. They are *not* democratic and they are *not* Western. We are forcing our views and ways on them, not meaning to. We're not being bad guys by doing that. We're simply saying this is what works for us, this is democracy the way we know it—and sometimes we go right over their heads. We use our Western ways of thought with the Iraqis and that's just not rational, you can't do that to them.

A few that I have talked to thought that we were trying to create a puppet government within Iraq to be able to use their oil. But also to gain influence in the region by using Iraqis as our political agenda within the Middle East as the British did before us. And they have a rightful opinion that that is what we're trying to do because that has happened to them in most of their history. But there are a lot of them that asked the question—because they *didn't* know why we were there. Plus as soldiers, we tell them straight up, we're here until you guys figure out how you want to run your lives and then we're leaving. Most of them are tribal. It's not just Sunni and Shia, it's family and the family tribes—it goes back to, "What are you going to do for us?" So they're more concerned about their community. Most of them don't think nationally, they don't think internationally.

We did a lot of work there with rebuilding schools. We paid for the new teachers to come in, we got them textbooks through drives through our families back home, we got them pencils, pens, notebooks. A lot of this was not demand-driven, it was soldiers that wanted to take care. We helped rebuild the hospitals. We even broke some ground because Christian hospitals wouldn't take Muslims and the Muslim hospitals wouldn't take Christians. What we told them was, "If you don't take Muslims, you don't take our money." They took Muslims because they needed the help. The sisters couldn't pay the staff. We would give them generators—I'm not talking about the little ones; I'm talking about million-dollar generators. It wasn't just the Christian hospitals, we gave to Muslim ones as well.

We trained the Iraqi police forces—which we continue to do. When we first got there, they were all Baath Party members, corrupt, it was the Wild West—your family would give money to the police chief. Your son would be in jail… and he could just walk home. Well, we brought international police, our own military police, and we ran a national police academy there. And we put them through *international* law, not just American-style, make sure that we are doing everything internationally. I think it's a four-month course to teach them how to be real police officers.

The infrastructure of Iraq collapsed. A lot of people blame the American military for the looting and rioting and everything else that happened in Iraq. What truly happened was that the infrastructure, every engineer, librarian, banker—whoever made the system work—we expected some of those people to stay in place. Nobody *did*. They were scared because they were Baath Party members. You had to be a Baath Party member to get a job for the government, to go to university. They were being told by *their* propaganda they were going to be executed because they were Baath Party.

Everybody left, so we had no police, no fire, no postal, no bank workers. My first month I spent half my time guarding banks, because we had to keep people from *robbing* them. The electricity was off because there were no engineers left around, the power plant people left, the sewage plant—everybody left. So now we're stuck with the American military, 100,000-plus strong. Not only do we have to secure Iraq, to continue combat operations, but now we've got to *run* it? We were not trained for that. You've got infantry being engineers in the power plants. If you know the difference between AC and DC you get your butt to the power plant. So you have to combine running infrastructure and being a military occupying a country….

You get the insurgents threatening people that work for the Americans, "We're going to kill you." We had an interpreter who had gone home from a shift, shot twice, he survived. We had a maid who was beheaded because she worked for the Americans. More extreme groups thought we were there as an occupation force. We keep saying, "Look, we just got rid of your bad dictator, and now we are trying to rebuild your infrastructure, the police, the military so you can sustain yourself." Well, they're impatient: they want to get on with being an Iraqi in Iraq. I understand Americans being very impatient of being there still as the casualties go up. The problem is—I call it the fast-food age—we want instant gratification. That doesn't happen with a country that has just catastrophically lost its infrastructure. It takes *time*....

We had one year to create an Iraqi infantry company of soldiers. We did it. I was responsible for recruiting and training an Iraqi infantry squad.... They had no regard for the weapons, your lifeline, a part of your body, no sense of time. An Iraqi might just decide not to go to work that day. They simply get docked the pay, they don't get fired. That's the custom.... Not only were we training people, we got into a situation where they were backing us up, I had to make sure they knew how to fire their weapons or they would shoot my own people.... We turned out some really stellar Iraqi soldiers. I tell you, when I left there I was very satisfied with my squad.

We had a couple female of Iraqis that volunteered—some were trying to be a sergeant and a lieutenant. They were Christians—the Christians in Iraq have a little bit more of a modernized sense about women, compared to the Muslims. Some of [the men] refused [to] salute the female lieutenant because she was a woman. You go to a bank—one side is for men and one side is for women. Men will not wait in line with women—two separate lines, although they wait for the same person to serve them. I actually ran a bank for about a month—I learned that.

What I call "insurgent" is someone who is a non-Iraqi that has come from another country and who has come to Iraq simply to gain the experience and prestige of fighting Americans. Iraqis that still fight are what we call terrorists. I hate to use that word because to me they're not *terrorists*. We look back at our own revolution— we didn't consider ourselves terrorists, but the British did. For lack of any other word, terrorists are Iraqis who are fundamentally diehard patriots: "Americans have no business in Iraq and Iraqis will take care of Iraqi business."… Most of the violence we dealt with the first year was Iraqi against Iraqi—tribal and Shia–Sunni violence…. I think that a lot of the Iraqis are finally understanding that they have freedom. I think that someone had to come from the outside and do that.

I still personally don't think a democracy is going to work in Iraq. You can't change 1,500 years of history in five. I think it's going to turn into a civil war before that happens. I think that there will be internal strife—at the very least they need a prime minister or even a dictator, somebody who is just not as bad as Saddam and the Baath Party were. They need a single, central figure. A president with Congress and the Senate—the division of power will not work in Iraq. The Arab mindset and the Western world mindset are just two totally different things.

—

August 7, 2003, in Karada, an American Humvee was ambushed downtown in our sector. One soldier was killed, four others wounded. My Bradley and my company commander's Bradley took off—I was there in about fifteen minutes. And when I arrived on the scene there were over 150 reporters. Which tells me either they were forewarned or they were really close—for them to have gotten that knowledge and gotten there before me?

We initially surrounded the building but we had a hard time because so many reporters were getting in our way. I can't even get a clear shot because the reporters are standing in front of me either looking to get a picture of me or trying to get a better angle on the building. To where I had to say to a group of them, "If you step in front of me again I'm going to shoot your legs." When they heard my selector switch—my weapon go from safety to semi-automatic—they got the hint that I wasn't kidding.

More and more reporters kept showing up—still photo, video—and we couldn't keep our line of sight. On the other hand, it's going to be a big deal if these reporters get shot. It's at the point where they are going to endanger ordinary soldiers' lives—they're on their own. There was one guy who was a French reporter. I usually don't think we're going to get along since they were not among the [coalition of the] willing, but he came up and said there was an Iraqi family in the building next to it, the woman was too scared to come out…. That's when I grabbed one of my soldiers, ran across the street with this reporter who spoke Arabic. We were able to coax the family out.

The problem is that a lot of Americans don't understand the reasons why we are there because they don't research it, they take word of mouth. "We're there for oil." *Really?* How many barrels of oil have we gotten out of Iraq yet? *Zero.* We are not getting oil from Iraq. I know because I have gone to the pipelines when they have been blown up by their own people. [The Associated Press reported that as of July 22, 2007, production was 2.06 million barrels per day compared to pre-war production of 2.58 million per day. While Sgt. McConnell was deployed, monthly income from oil rose from $200 million to $1.4 billion (Brookings Index)—ed.]. I think there's a lot of ignorance as far as people understanding *why* we are there, *who* put us there, and the *true* reason…. Call your congressman, call your senator. They agreed to it. Yet we're always the ones that get blamed for it.

American soldiers make mistakes. Abu Ghraib was a good example of that. But those mistakes also get found out—and they're punished. Most of those people are in prison for three years, one of them is up for 25 years. We find military members who break the law, we punish them. We don't just follow the US law, we follow the Uniform Code of Military Justice. We have a higher standard and we take pride in the fact that most of us do…. Just because we train and put on a uniform doesn't change our basic integrity and moral values. We teach those in the military. But if you didn't have them to start, you're never going to.

# DAVID VACCHI
Lieutenant Colonel, Army

Commissioned 1989, deployed age 36
(September 2002–March 2004)
Kuwait; Kirkuk, Tikrit, Taji, Husseinia, Iraq

*An Officer's View of the War*

*Lieutenant Colonel David Vacchi has a presence on the UMass Amherst campus. This is not just because he heads the ROTC program there and in the surrounding area, but because he has chosen to teach a course and speak in public about the war. Dialogue is important to him. Both his parents were teachers in Rhode Island and his brother is a professor of music at the University of Oregon. He attended Purdue University on an army ROTC scholarship, and plans to stay in the army beyond his twenty years. He is married with two children. He spent a lot of time during his tour working with local Iraqi authorities. "How can you not deal with the Iraqi people? That's what it's all about."*

I [was in] Fort Hood, Texas, Fourth ID and… the call came down for a temporary assignment for someone to go to Kuwait and serve on a joint task force for consequence management. Consequence management is responding to weapons of mass destruction attacks. I was deployed to Kuwait and I was the US Embassy liaison—one of the spokespeople for the joint task force. The joint task force was created in the event that Saddam were to attack anybody in the region with any kind of weapon of mass destruction.

So I take it a little bit personally when people get into, "Saddam didn't have weapons of mass destruction." Okay, we wouldn't have spent tens of millions of dollars creating this task force if that wasn't the case—or at least if no one could have told any differently. You just go over and over again in your head—Saddam wouldn't be that *stupid* to actually use weapons of mass destruction. My conclusion was that… he probably is not going to attack anybody right now with weapons of mass destruction because we would obliterate the very *country* of Iraq. That was my misgiving. But again—as a good soldier—when that decision is made to go in, you stop asking questions and making your point and now you make the best of it.

So in early April of 2003, I switched back with the Fourth ID and joined them in Kuwait in anticipation of the big march north. The Fourth ID was that division that was stuck in Turkey in ports—we were supposed to come in [to Iraq] from the north. You heard all this discussion about how the weapons of mass destruction may have escaped though Iran or Syria or some place through the north…. And the Fourth ID's inability to come in from Turkey and put the lid on the jar is what allowed that to happen. …

The Fourth ID had to drive back around and come in through Kuwait…. The 17th of April, I was with the lead elements of the Fourth ID—we followed in behind the Third ID and the First Marine Expeditionary Force [MEF]. The Third ID was moving up the west side through Nasariya and Karbala and they merged in Baghdad. And the Third ID secured Baghdad while the marines continued forward and took Tikrit, which is Saddam's hometown. [The] Fourth ID came in behind. …

There were some starving families just as we came across the border into Iraq. You could tell right away—they were waving, thumbs up. They were glad to see us—they figured that the long wait was over, I guess. And then the other thing that we saw was there is a big religious [pilgrimage] of the Shia. They go to Karbala and Najaf about this time every year. Previous to 2003, the Shia were not permitted to do that for 25 years by Saddam. And so they were out—a lot of them in bare feet—walking on hot pavement to walk the two or three hundred miles to get to Karbala, to finally participate in this religious event.

We had to go east toward the Iranian border. There was a very well-equipped military force, the Mujahidin-e Khalq, Iranian exiles.… The history of the Fourth ID will talk about how General Odierno went to accept the capitulation. We didn't know if they were going to say piss off or they were actually going to capitulate. It was one of those movie things, General Odierno went with his cigar. We had artillery, aircraft, attack helicopters, everything was ready—we were going to annihilate this force if it didn't go well. The risk was General Odierno was going to be right in the middle of it. If he dropped his cigar—and of course there's guys with binoculars and helicopters—that was the cue to start this massive attack. Everyone was holding their breath. He would have had five, seven minutes to hop in his Humvee or tank and get out as fast as he can. I'm glad he didn't have to do that, because they capitulated.…

[Kirkuk] was the first time that I had exposure to a large number of local Iraqis. In Kirkuk you have a third Kurds, a third Shia, and a third Sunni, and you would think that of all spots, this is where the Iraqi civil war is going to happen. And that's where I learned that Iraqis are Iraqis. Everybody makes this big deal out of Sunnis and Shias—civil war and all this business. [Iraqis said], "There's not going to be a civil war." "Well, how do you know?" "Well, would there be a civil war in America because Lutherans or Episcopalians are different from Catholics?" And of course the obvious answer is, "That's asinine!" "Well, that's the difference between Sunnis and Shias." So this idea that there's going to be a civil war is just preposterous.… I'm kind of putting myself out on a limb on that.

I remember we had some hardcore part of Saddam's upper administration Sunnis in my area, and I asked them, "Have you had any problem with the Shias?" "No." I asked the Shia, "Do you have any problem with those Sunnis over there?" "Well, no. Sometimes their sons, they get into a little bit of trouble, they are all part of Rashadiya—our town over here." As I was leaving Iraq finally at the end of 2004, I called a unification lunch. Sunnis and Shia, senior members from all over the area, all the way from Baquba—were together eating. Nobody seemed to be talking about their religious affiliations. It's not an issue. And so this whole idea of a civil war infuriates me—the wasted energy. And you have people out there saying, "Oh, we're in a civil war now."

It's *sectarian* violence. It's people who lose perspective over a political issue and become violent. Everyone is making an issue out of it—this portion of Sunni government and this portion of Shia government, this portion of Kurds—and we are exacerbating the issue by highlighting that. But it's just a matter of people who feel that their needs and concerns are not being addressed and they're lashing out. It's becoming tit for tat—who remembers who threw the first stone in the Israeli–Palestinian issue? They've been fighting each other for 5,000 years and they're going to keep fighting each other for the next 5,000. We're at the beginning of that in Iraq, and it has got to *stop*. And that's the reason we have got to get this government set.

The majority of the violence has now focused Iraqi on Iraqi—or insurgents against Iraqis. I'm convinced that this Shia mosque that was destroyed in Samarra—the insurgents did that because they knew that Shia militant groups would seek reprisals against the Sunnis and that would create the unrest. Because the agenda of the terrorists—they don't care what is going on in Iraq as long as it's unstable.

Why didn't George Bush [senior] go into Iraq and remove Saddam back then [1991]? Who is going to be in charge now? At least back then they knew that the mess that we're in now is the same mess that would have happened fifteen years ago had we gone in then. Because Saddam, like him or hate him, he was a known quantity. It was *unpleasant*, but it was *stable*. The natural human inclination would be to want to remove someone who so blatantly treats people so poorly. Yet, when we have gone and *done* that there are consequences, and we are *in* the consequences. I think that we're doing a fair job, but none of the *good* news from Iraq is getting published in the media—which is a tough thing… Young [soldiers] want to see some of the good news in the media so they can say "I contributed to that, I was part of that."…

After Kirkuk we moved back down to Taji Airbase, which is just north of Baghdad. The senior commander in Taji was one of the worst guys I've ever seen, and so I will read to you from my personal diary from Iraq. At the time, I was a civil affairs officer, helping the rebuilding—which was also gratifying.

> Colonel Stramara took off for Tikrit today—I can't even explain what a burden is lifted off of Taji when he is gone. He is the worst leader I have ever experienced in the Army…. 23 June, 2003. Got my ass chewed again today….. Colonel Stramara threatened my career if I risk soldiers' lives again. What risk…? Who is going to threaten his career when he risks soldiers' lives? He told me to slow down. When are we ever going to do something that will get us out of this country?

The other one was [Lieutenant] Colonel Al West. And of course Colonel West is the guy that made some media—he was supposedly getting intelligence from an Iraqi policeman who had turned bad. He fired his pistol by the side of the prisoner's head. It was a big court-martial case back in 2003. And of course you had O'Reilly on [Fox] TV that was coming to his defense, "You got to do whatever you got to do to get this intelligence." Well, I have a bit of a different take. …

I worked with Colonel West a little bit when I was a civil-affairs officer at Taji and he did a pretty good job of trying to stabilize the area of Sabaa al-Bor…. Colonel West had gotten—amazingly—in June of 2003, sheikhs and commoners together on the same City Council. Like the House of Lords and the House of Commons, it was a pretty impressive accomplishment. Because really all these people have their issues and they need to come together for the City Council. He was rebuilding the police station.

The danger of being in these interpersonal situations as a civil-affairs officer or in the engagement arena of war is that you could become too emotionally invested in what's going on. And Colonel West heard a rumor that someone wanted to assassinate him—somebody from the police department. He took this Iraqi policeman who he arrested—chief of police—and he was threatening "action" to get him to tell what the information was. And his final bluff was to put the guy's head down by one of these clearing barrels and he fired his weapon into the clearing barrel. Strictly speaking, that's not a violation of the Geneva Convention, but *holy crap*!

This Colonel Stramara had created an environment in which a senior leader—who had nineteen-plus years in the Army—is going to do something that *stupid* to get information that's not even there. There was no information to be had. Right now there's this group of people in the army—you have to generalize to make a point—that have 20 to 30 years running the army, and as a generation in the army those people are bad. They aren't evil, they're just bad at what they do. Because they grew up in a time— post–Vietnam War—[when] it was a *shrinking* force, and then it was an *under-resourced* force in the early '80s. And so what they learned was the way to succeed is to backstab everybody, to make your buddy look bad. ...

And the other tactic of choice among these guys is to be overbearing, unreasonable, and to be a screamer. Just pound your fist on the desk. They're not all like that.... You're either like that and you succeed, or you're not like that and you hit a glass ceiling. Stramara was—is—one of those guys. Oh, by the way, he's the only full-bird colonel in the Fourth ID at that time *not* to get promoted to one-star general. One time he had a thirteen-year-old in jail for over two weeks. I was just pleading with him, "Let the kid go home or let him go to school." "Oh, he has information, and if he doesn't have information then when his father comes in to get him we will arrest his father to get information from his father." What do you think you are *accomplishing*?

[Colonel West] lapses for just a minute because Colonel Stramara is not going to want to hear you didn't get intelligence from this guy. So the only thing you can do is go over the edge— in my opinion—fire a round, this guy is going to wet his pants after that happens anyway. No information comes forward because there's no information. Then you can at least go to the boss and say, "I didn't get anything from him, I fired a round by the side of the guy's head." And so there was a court-martial and he was allowed to retire.... Of course the people who were defending him said, "You have to do what you have to do to get the intelligence." No, you *don't*. The only thing that has kept [the] reputation of the United States is the times when we are *beyond* reproach. When we are *within* reproach, people are going to get us and we are going to lose credibility. So you have to take the high road.

In my area I had a lot of powerful sheikhs…. They're going to be there long after we are gone. If they die, then their son is the next sheikh anyway. So the perpetuation of the family and the lineage is going to be there. So *really*, the only way to succeed is to have a buy-in from the local leaders. And if you have a democratic election that the people support, then you've got to support the local leaders even if the guy in charge is a little shady. Over in Rashadiya—where everything is run by the sheikhs—sheikhs have *got* to be running the place. If they want to have their sons in the Iraqi National Guard, you've got to have their sons drawing a paycheck, because nobody had a job back then. …

There was an interesting case regarding the *smagh*, the Arab male headdress—we call it the "towel" sometimes. This question of respect came up early in the war as we began random traffic stops—there was this issue in the 82nd Airborne and the USMC. They would take [Iraqis] out of their cars and they would smack it off their head, they would remove it so you could see if there was a bomb under there. It's idiotic. It is ignorance of customs, and disrespect.

Word of mouth spreads very quickly in Iraq, much better than cell phones or TV. Now we have the coalition out here—knocking the *smagh* off. You would meet these sheikhs, and you would want to have these agreements, "We want to make sure we have your support for the election." And he says, "All I worry about is the respect of my people." "What are you talking about?" "When you stop people at a traffic stop, we understand that you're looking for bombs. We don't mind if you search the car, [but] don't touch the women, and don't knock the *smagh* off the head."

———

According to our own doctrine, you fight wars and then there is something after a war which is diplomatic—the State Department, the secretary of state. I think that during that public affairs disaster on the aircraft carrier when it said, "Mission accomplished"—you know, Bush didn't approve that, it was some public affairs officer [and] I think he got fired for doing that—but major ground operations were over at that point. That was the point where in my understanding of our doctrine, the secretary of state and the State Department should have taken over in Iraq and the Department of Defense should have become the supporting agency. The Department of Defense runs wars, they don't run diplomacy—the Department of State runs diplomacy…. *Clearly* by now, the secretary of state should be calling the shots over there and it's not happening. This is what diplomats do. It is not what soldiers do. Soldiers kill people and break things. We don't nation-build, we don't do occupations well.

We thought fifteen years ago Saddam being in charge was the lesser of two evils. We didn't know what the alternative was, but at least it was a known quantity and it was quasi-stable. Saddam being in charge in 2003 also was not the *issue*. The issue was Saddam as an older Iraqi man in his seventies couldn't have but ten more years left in him. He's going to die of natural causes. The worst thing to have happen is his two absolutely lunatic sons take over that country. It would have been only a matter of weeks or months before they went back and tried to annex Kuwait again and they would probably start the Iran–Iraq War again. …

When they captured Saddam, there was celebration— everybody was happy. Two months before that, Uday and Qusay were killed in Mosul, and the celebration was so violent that we cancelled all security patrols because of all the shooting, in all different directions, because they were so happy that those two sons were dead. They were both psychopaths—between the two of them they were the right and left hand of evil—for sure.

# BENJAMIN FLANDERS
Sergeant, Army National Guard

Enlisted 1998, deployed age 26
(March 2004–February 2005)
MP, Camp Anaconda, Balad, Iraq

*Who Are the Insurgents?*

*Ben joined the Army National Guard as an infantryman in the Tenth Mountain Division from New Hampshire. The day he was to get out of the service, he left for a year in Iraq, where he served as military police. He is married and lives in Danvers, Massachusetts. Ben received his BA from Gordon College and is a graduate student in mathematics at Boston College. He follows the war closely, reads widely, and is a careful observer of the multifaceted insurgency. He has been interviewed on TV, for books, given speeches, as well as lobbied in Washington. He finds Americans do not really follow what happens in Iraq. "We're not a global society—we could care less what's going on in the world—even for places like Iraq where people are dying, are fighting, governments are trying to get established." He is also preparing to become a second lieutenant in ROTC. Ben wants to continue to serve his country, "Something I'm very compelled to do," possibly pursuing a career in government.*

How I started. I was graduating high school and I had been to three different high schools at that point because of family situations— divorce. So I was very disillusioned by just being a high-school student, and I started taking stock of myself and thinking, I'm a pretty smart guy, but what had I *done?* I think I wanted to challenge myself. I say "I think," because I have *no idea* why I joined the military. Well, a friend of mine was playing the trumpet in the army band for New Hampshire and he said, "Try it—it's money for college."...

So I take this aptitude test in the army, and I score really high. They say you can do anything you want, and [my recruiter] mentioned mountain infantry. They do rock climbing and ice climbing, skiing and cross-country skiing, and snowshoeing, along with the whole infantry training. I said I might want to do that because that seems to be the steepest challenge that the National Guard can give me. I think he was trying to give me pause. "You can do anything you want—are you sure you want to do this?"

I could very much imagine my father saying to me, "Are you really *sure* that you want to do this?" And I say, "Yeah, I'll show the old man," so I decided to do infantry training.... It's weird, because if you had said the word "infantry" to me before I signed up for the army I wouldn't even have known what it means. It's an old Roman word. I would think of WWII—the guy with the backpack and the shovel sticking out, the helmet, him charging with the bayonet on. Generally, that guy is also the infantry guy. But to try and look at it from the outside, all you can do is talk to the recruiter—and he doesn't tell you about the military—he's telling you about *signing up* for the military.

When you sign up for the army they say, "Okay, great, here's your bus ticket, here's your plane ticket, you'll be gone from these dates." I didn't have a concept of me being *gone.* My mom was getting very nervous about this, I couldn't see why, and everyone was saying, "Gosh, I don't see why you are doing this." I didn't understand until deployment what the absence is all about.... But it did intrigue me that you're getting on a bus and they're taking you away from home and you're going to go do something. I had no idea what it was, but I wanted to do it anyway....

Infantry is a lot of brute, not so much brain. When I look back, I didn't ever regret choosing it. Infantry skills—there's nothing comparable to that. You could say "police officer," but police officer is more like law enforcement, it's not destructive. "Civil servant"— they're supposed to aid society, whereas infantry is supposed to bring it down. They say "firefighters," "paramedics," because the adrenaline is the same. You have the same sense that you are charging something, or getting shot at as a soldier, running into a burning building. It was the manhood sort of thing, it was a test, it was a measure of *me*.

In the army, they realized with Somalia that the battlefield was not just going to be in the woods [like] Gettysburg—wide open space. People are going to run into civilian settings. Our training started to gear toward MOUT, military operations in urban terrain. There was a strange focus on that and I think they were really scared because of the Somalia incident [in Mogadishu, 1993]. We lost eighteen Rangers and Special Forces there. We go to this piddly little (in their opinion) third-world, African, poor nation that has internal strife, a bunch of rebels, guys with guns and no military training…. A lot of civilian deaths. We killed 1,600 of them. So I think they realized that people are going to be taking the fight to urban settings…. It's so easy [for them] to defend the city, so easy [for them] to fend off an attack. We were training for a kind of SWAT [team]—people really got gung-ho. So we were a bit disappointed that we got relegated to this lowly military police. …

They put you in bases out in the middle of nowhere in Kuwait. We ship in all our accommodations, water, food, tents, generators, the post office, the finance…. These civilian contract companies were like, "Well, you guys ever thought of putting in a phone trailer? We have Green Bean Café—lattés, donuts, you guys want *that*?" We finally landed in Iraq on March 27, 2004, and we left February 16, 2005. We had left [the US] the day I was supposed to get out of the army. I was basically stopped-lossed for the whole year. …

Our term meshed really well with the March timeline because that got us through the elections…. We actually shut down operations around the transition of authority June 30, 2004. Bremer transferred his authority over to an interim government, which then gave way to democratic elections in January [2005]. So January 30, we pulled back and we let the Iraqi people do their thing. We stayed off the roads….

The strategy of the insurgents was that they regarded the police force as collaborators with the infidel government. So they're targets and they're *easy* targets because we try to distance ourselves from them. Because the police system in Iraq—assuming there was no insurgency that has infiltrated the police—is still corrupt. It's more tribal, "Hey, I'll scratch your back, you scratch mine." Because we can't tell who the good guys are, the *real* good guys, the bad guys—we distance ourselves. When we push them away from our military establishments, we push them out to the public where the insurgents can get to them so easily.

They [insurgents] killed 127 people. It was a long line of police recruits standing outside a physician's office trying to get a physical for their job. They rolled a car bomb right up to them—*boom*—there you go. Where was their protection? The insurgents are targeting them because it's so easy to. I'm trying to think about *who* these insurgents are and what they want to accomplish. Recently, Sunni clerics issued a fatwa or an edict saying to the Sunnis—you have to join the security force. These insurgents are against the Iraqi people, which is something I knew, because [of] when you roll on a bunch of guys that are beheaded and just look like regular civilians. You have Samarra, Baquba, which sandwiched us—those were pretty bad cities. In Baquba, they found ten civilians shot execution-style in body bags.

And of course we say that's terrible, but it's more important to ask *why*, why do they do it? It's because they are terrorizing them. The insurgents can control the will of the people very easily. They do it [in] towns [which] don't have enough anti-US sentiment, or they start to collaborate, or there is not enough support for the insurgency. Behead a couple of civilians and put them right in the downtown square or right on the main road for everyone to see. That's how they do things…. The textbook definition of terrorist attack: they attack innocents and randomly take the life of a civilian in the hopes that it causes uncertainty in the minds of the people about the current government. Which is like what September 11 was—"Ha ha, look at this, look what *we* can do." I can see a lot of purposes but one of them is to instill uncertainty in us.

There are so many different groups. It's the former Republican Guard members. Yes, it's also terrorists who have infiltrated from Jordan. It's also former Baath Party members. It's also those loyal to al-Sadr, who is a Shiite. It's people who are loyal to al-Zarkawi, who is with al-Qaeda, a Sunni. It's people who are disgruntled about an accidental death we may have caused. The *mujahideen*. We're fighting a mixed bag of characters. They're making it look like Americans are bad, or that they're vulnerable, or we don't protect them as well as we should. They also do that by targeting the police and the security force. They also target government officials and they target innocent civilians. Some people assume their agenda is that we are occupying Iraq and that they want us out, just like Vietnam. Maybe. But then why do they attack their own people?

Then you look to all those innocent, innocent lives lost and you say—"What were they trying to accomplish there?" If it was just about the military and it was just about the US in there, then they would only target us. But they don't—they are totally trying to undermine the process by which Iraq reconstitutes itself democratically. These people are fanatical—I think they want al-Zarkawi in change and not Jalal Talabani, the new elected president. They want al-Sadr in charge or they want theocracy. They are an insurgent group, which means—dictionary, textbook definition—a group of people who are going against the established government, but they haven't really organized themselves so we can't call them a militia and we can't call them rebels.

For instance, our own country was founded on insurgency. Well, not *really*, because we had things we were trying to push—no taxation without representation, we want the British out of here, we want our independence, we want a militia. Insurgency is *like* a revolution but without the organization, so it's the fighting without the agenda. These aren't like Vietnam—the communists saying, "Well, we have a better way of life for the country, so thank you very much, get out of here...." There is none of that in the insurgency. It's just fighting, it's just violence. That's it.

My theory is that when we took down Saddam we inherited a sociological disorder of the people and that is two primary things. One is that they have learned that violence works, it gets things done—that's how Saddam got things done, he was very heavy-handed with his people. If you don't like the guy, you kill him and all of his family. They were oppressed. The second result of Saddam was the ability of the majority of Iraqis to be silenced. In a town, if you execute one guy and all of his family, that will keep the rest of the village quiet. It's very easy to hold the Iraqi system in a state of fear. If you're not the oppressor, then you're the oppressed. They are very familiar with that, so they are very unlikely to give up information about the insurgents.

We have to answer the question of how are we going to deal with [the insurgency]. We can't ask ourselves how can we completely get *rid* of it because that won't happen. It would be very quixotic to say we're going to stay until all the insurgents are gone or are won over. They're against the democracy, the freedoms we gave Iraq. Just as much as those freedoms aren't going away and we don't wish to see the Iraqi system oppressed again—well, the insurgency is not going to go away, not any time soon.... But *we* leave when they can deal with the insurgency and they can deal with their crime. We get to that point when *they* have a security force that can deal with that. When *they* have their police and when *they* have their army who are trained and equipped and aren't as vulnerable as they are now. When *they* can take care of it, then we can step out. ...

Why is it a contentious relationship for us being there? The Islamic world doesn't like occupiers. They are sick of it—colonized, and fighting and all that business. Iraq wants its *pride* back, just as you are the owner of your house, you make the decisions.... They want foreigners gone. That's the pride of the Arabic world, the Arabic countries. They want national independence.... We have this human *intelligence* barrier, we have this *language* barrier, we have this *cultural* barrier—which are not going to make the Americans effective at rooting out these [insurgents].... May 23, [2003], Paul Bremer said. "No more Iraq police, no more Iraq army." In my opinion, a huge mistake. ...

We said to the Iraq people, "Don't worry, you can rely on us." The most popular comment from the Iraqis, "You guys put a man on the *moon*?! We have been doing this society thing for thousands of years and you come in and you think you can do it better? And you think that all of your Western beliefs, your Western ways of doing business, police work, and government and all that is so much superior to ours and here it is crumbling right before our eyes? You think we're going to trust you now?"

This really got me thinking of putting this short, tumultuous, and important history of Iraq into its proper historical sequence.

What led to this? When I walked in, day one in Iraq, the day we started operations, we were going into these ambushes like we've never seen before. You could say there must have been an insurgency that had galvanized itself and that's what we were fighting in April [2004]. Where did this insurgency come from? We're fighting the insurgents—these people who have their own visions, their supplies, fighting us—how did this happen? Well, we really played into that—we really provided a situation where people can be pissed off. We left the Iraqis without power over the winter and so when the springtime comes and there is a huge troop rotation and we're having housing units pass in front of them, box-loads of food, all up and down the highway and limiting their travel. No wonder.

—

The draft is a really interesting concept because it would compel everybody to think about [the war], which I think is what led to protests about the Vietnam War. The draft would gravely affect young people because they would be the people drafted. But it would also affect much more importantly society's understanding, society's grasp of the conflict, grasp of the challenges, and also it would hold our leaders accountable a lot more.

That's my bottom line. How are the American people being educated? How are they choosing to be educated? Does everyone read the New York Times, in-depth reports? No. In general what I see is that people are choosing, like myself, to watch ABC, NBC, CBS, CNN.com, Fox News, and they're not that interested in the war. We're not a global society, we could care less about what is going on in the world, we could care less even for places like Iraq where every day is a very important day. People are dying, are fighting, governments are trying to get established. It's important. It is so important, but people—how are they educating themselves?

# SOLOMON BLACK
Sergeant, Marine Corps

Enlisted 2001–2005, deployed age 19
(February–October 2003, July 2004–February 2005)
Anbar Province, Haditha, Falluja, Iraq

*Fighting in Haditha and Falluja*

*Sol served as a combat engineer. He is from Marblehead, Massachusetts, and an undergraduate political science major at UMass Amherst. He speaks in public with an ease and assurance that conveys "marine." He is proud of his service, and notes that "I was awarded the Navy Achievement Medal, the combat 'V,' for actions as an engineer team leader, Third Platoon, Charlie Company, First Battalion, Eighth Marines, attached to the First Marine Division. It was for me and my team of engineers, under machine gunfire, to blow up a weapons cache in Falluja." Sol also recounts a different kind of personal episode reflecting Middle East politics. "We had an interpreter named Ahmed. One day [I say], 'I'm Jewish.' 'You are not Jewish. You shouldn't tell people you are Jewish.' 'Like, do you have a problem with Jewish people?' 'No, of course not,' and then I used to catch this guy— I could feel his eyes upon me."*

High school was never my best of days. Towards the end of my junior year I was getting ready to go to college but I just hated it— the last thing I want to do is push myself through four more years of it. So I started looking at the military and the Marine Corps just jumped out at me because they are "badassed motherfuckers." I talked to the marines—I told them I wanted to work with explosives. So I took my test and I scored high enough on it—89— that I could choose any job I wanted to. I'm not dumb by any means. If you get anything below a 30 you don't get into the military. If you get 30–45 or 50 you don't have much choice—postal clerk or a cook, or the guy who carries the bottom of the mortar base plate....

Beginning in 2003, everyone starts talking about the Iraq war before we're going to leave. We float around the ocean—they started sending people to Kuwait. Are we going to get left out? And sure enough, we get orders for Iraq on the boat, right off Kuwait. It's not like we believed in the cause whatsoever, it's just that we trained our asses off to go out there and do our job and we want to do it. We want a chance to prove ourselves. So we're all riled up—we're waiting for the marines to take Baghdad.

I was on the USS *Iwo Jima*, which is a helicopter landing craft.... We're sitting, restless, smoking cigarettes, eating food, watching the news. We started watching the movie *Band of Brothers*. And one day we got three-quarters through the mini-series—every day we would get together in the lounge and we would watch one of the episodes. Our master sergeant, big bodybuilder, Puerto Rican guy, been in the Marine Corps like 25 years, "We ain't watching this shit today, we going to *Iraq*."...

—

[My] second tour was gruesome, it was bad, a lot of deaths, a lot of violence, a lot of long nights, a lot of missions—a grueling seven-and-a-half months. We started out in Haditha. [We found] high-explosive bombs, napalm bombs, weapons. But no weapons of mass destruction, no chemicals—we didn't deal with any of that stuff.... [On] patrol, we would blow the front door[s] in, in the middle of the night.... A lot of people we were grabbing were well off, rich people. One sign—they have hard wooden doors. That was one of the small status symbols. They would have a higher gate around their house. And you did use a big explosive usually to get through their gate, but that was a last resort.

Like if we *knew* there was a serious badass guy there—all right—we would blow in the gate, we would kick in the front door. We used a shotgun a lot for breaching—buckshot will shoot through anything. Any military-aged male, you get him blindfolded and cuffed, all the women get separated and put in one room. We would search the house, all the military-aged men get brought back for military interrogation.

Or we get the soft hit. We've got some intel, this guy was supposed to come by and tell us some stuff but got scared. An interpreter [says], "Open the door," and we knock like twenty minutes and they don't open, that means we use a sledgehammer. Or a shotgun. Explosives cause a real ruckus—explosives were usually secondary until we got to Falluja. Then we just blew everything up. They didn't have a chance there. [*How do you tell who to get?*] We use informants—that's the safety thing. Thank God there's a sergeant and a corporal in the marines so it's never in my hands—let *him* tell you where to go.

The worst is [that] in Falluja we would be walking with our street patrol and we would look down and see wires. Wherever you see wires, there is a bomb somewhere. You would look and there would be mines, rockets, here, there, IEDs, and it's all wired together and all they have to do is touch it to a car battery. They would use anything possible—a garage door opener, cell phones, walkie-talkies. The easiest way—the most basic way—that a lot of them did it is you have the wire, use an electric blasting cap, then tape it into the fuse well of an artillery round, then touch the other end of the wire to a car battery—*boom*—just like that. ...

They sent us to a small town called Kharma about fifteen miles outside of Falluja. I guess after Falluja a lot of the insurgents ran out to Kharma. There we did SASO missions—this is what we trained for before we went to Iraq—security and stability operations. It's a word that when we got to Falluja got thrown out the window—pretty much shoot anything that moves. Pretty much you have the authority to do whatever you want in Falluja as long as you consult with one rank higher—*very, very* liberal rules of engagement [ROE]. Like before we went in there the

Judge Advocate [attorney in charge of legal administration] sat down and said, "These are the rules—there haven't been ROEs this liberal since Vietnam."

My battalion alone killed 900 insurgents [in the November 2004 attack on Falluja]. There were a lot there. People were giving [inaccurate] reports, like lots of civilians were getting killed in Falluja. That city was empty. We dropped leaflets and anyone who was anyone [got out]. It wasn't like in New Orleans, where people were too poor to get out, or too lazy to get out, or people were stubborn. People knew some shit was going to go down and they left. Throughout the entire city—I pushed from the complete southern part of Falluja to the complete northern end of Falluja—I saw three civilian families. And what they do is they hang white flags all over their house—they stay inside. If they won't leave their house, we go in there and we search their house. "All right, guys, stay inside, be safe and don't mess with the military or you'll be killed."

When we were in Falluja we did a lot of explosive breaching on doors. You go through a door and there's a guy on the other side with a gun, poking his head around the corner. *Boom, boom, boom*, you're dead. So you run up to a door, you slap on a quarter-stick of C-4—which a lot of people thought was overkill. You train here in the States on a plywood door—you get over there and it's like an inch-and-a-half steel door, stainless-steel doors, solid, thick. So over there you use that to overcome, that's what we do—we're marines. We're putting quarter-sticks, sometimes half-sticks of C-4 on the door. *Boom.*

Every window in the house will go out. You have twenty seconds for the smoke and dust to clear. You go in. If there *are* insurgents in the house, the shock will get them—it all matters where they're sitting. If they're in that room where the door goes off, the residual over-pressure should kill them. Sometimes the explosion will blow the door across the room where it will stick into a wall. Insurgents got smart and they started adapting to that. They would barricade themselves in the last room in the house and use the front door as a hallway. The last one to use the door would kick over a desk, maybe sand bags. You would throw that in, *boom*, they would hear you go into one room. Nothing. They would hear you go into another room. Nothing. That third room—your guard is down, you think that the house is empty—that's when they get you.

When I was in Iraq, there were a lot of foreign fighters. I was in Falluja—85 percent were foreign fighters. I'm not going to say 85 percent, but the *vast* majority. They all have fake IDs and they would be interrogated by the interpreters. Our interpreters are from all over the world, too. If they have an ID from Jordan, the Jordanian interpreter translates for the intelligence guy. The Jordanian interpreters can tell in two seconds that he is from Saudi Arabia. One guy we got [said], "Oh, I live here." One of our interpreters was from Falluja and he said, "Really, where did you go to school?" "Oh, I attended school, it was an affluent district where everyone goes to school." "Where is the soccer field?" Pretty much, this guy was full of shit.

We were seeing Chechnyans, the ones that are fighting the Russians. Chechnyan snipers killed two of our best friends. They're soldiers for hire. They're crazy, they're radicals, they are Islamic. They grew up in a warrior culture. The Marine Corps is what we consider a warrior culture, but we start at eighteen. Chechnyans start with a gun in their hands. They are *warriors*. They are definitely the most worthy of adversaries....

You go to Iraq, the country is in turmoil, it's awful. When it starts getting nasty, there's no place for politics. It was 9/11 on a lot of people's minds. I tried to change that. Everybody I met it was like, "These guys came to our country." "Let's stop right here. *No, they didn't.* But we're here. End of story. Do what you have to do, we are getting home alive."...

I've always been a leader, ever since I can remember, even before I joined the military. It just comes naturally to me—you attack, I step up and figure out a way to handle it. I may not be right 100 percent of the time, but I'm always ready to step up and do something. I was this close to re-enlisting, [but] the last thing I want to do in life is for me to get killed.... [But] it was that I was *really* good at my job—everyone liked me in my unit. I never got complaints—I always got complimented—it seemed like I had found my niche. At the same time, I didn't like being away from loved ones. I almost died, having five friends die in Iraq. And I just thought I would be more productive in society....

I grew up in a middle-class family, my mom is highly educated, my dad went to Tufts [University]. And my mom's a diehard liberal. I'm like, "These fucking towel heads, they're all the same…." [But isn't that like] you're telling me because I'm *Jewish* I'm like the crazy radicals who sit on top of the kibbutz, who firebomb the Israeli policemen who try to remove them? No. We have a friend Amadu from Gambia and we love him. When I got back from Iraq my mom said, "Amadu is going to come over for Passover." I got really upset, "You're going to fucking disrespect the house like that, Mom?" And she said, "You don't understand. You aren't Muslim…." I felt like such an asshole for saying something like that to my mom.

You build up this animosity—you try not to. When I'm over here, these things don't bother me at all. When you're over there you have interpreters and we had people that work on the bases. You can trust them as far as you can throw them. You can't trust a lot of these Iraqis. We had an interpreter named Ahmed. One day we're talking to each other and [I say] "I'm Jewish." [He says], "You are not Jewish. You shouldn't tell people you are Jewish." "Like, do you have a problem with Jewish people?" "No, of course not," and then I used to catch this guy, I could feel his eyes upon me.

These Iraqi police were trained for missions in the city—very specific—like they were all mapped out. We would go to this mosque and Red Team is going to penetrate through here. These guys are trained by some serious *machers*, they have ex-CIA, Delta Force mercenaries training them. And one of them disappeared with maps and plans the night of the Falluja assault. We had combined forces—we were pushing over behind the combined Iraqi Special Forces and police. We were doing all the fighting until we get to the mosques. These Americans—who aren't really on the books as being Americans—are leading these Iraqi guys and they go in and the Iraqis are in charge of the mosques. That's their stuff, we don't want to disrespect anything, we don't want a picture of us shooting down the head of a mosque. Like, those things happen. That's all I have to say about that.

I look at Abu Ghraib—it was people getting bored. I know that sounds sick and tormented but you've got these army guys sitting in a jail, they've got nothing to do. They're reservists, they say, "Let's torture these guys." I know it sounds awful but there's a lot of people in the military that who aren't that smart. They get bored easily, instead of picking up a book, writing a letter, playing poker—they decided it was a good idea to strip them naked and torture them.

I don't see what happened as having anything to do with the marines. People are like, "Oh, the general should have known." Yes and no. The general *shouldn't* have known because it's not the general's job to check up on that. It's someone else's job to check up and report to someone who reports to someone who reports to the general. I'm not one to lobby for officers at all, but there are some officers out there that are great leaders. It's all about the chain of command. I don't think the general should take the fall for that unless it's going on under his nose. That's like saying that the chancellor of this school is responsible if one guy goes out and stabs somebody—[because] he runs the show. [But] *reacting appropriately*— without question. I don't know much about it. I don't want to talk about it.

We flew civilian—getting home took four days.... We stopped in Germany for a couple of hours, stretch your legs, get something to eat, use the bathroom. And from there we went to Bangor [Maine]. Bangor is really great—all the old marines come out waving flags. And they have cell phones and they hand them out so you can use them to call your family and tell them you're home. I almost cried. They had a little bar there too, and everyone had one beer just because they had to....

I think about war a lot more now than I ever did before—but it doesn't follow me. That's why people stay in the Marine Corps, because a lot of people go home, get a job as a construction worker—that just doesn't do it for them. That's what I've been feeling a lot of lately. I won't say *emptiness*, but it doesn't feel like I'm doing anything significant. When I woke up in the morning over there, I woke up three of my guys, I grabbed two mine detectors, grabbed two satchels of C-4, grabbed four two-minute systems, and went to blow up some mines. *Damn*, I was doing something—I was saving people's lives. I wake up here, I go to class, write a paper, lift some weights. I've tried community service, but it doesn't put others' lives in your hands.

This month is the anniversary of Falluja. I had a bunch of friends who died and it also happens to be that the 2,000th death [of US soldiers] will be at the beginning of the month [November 2005]. And I felt like shit for three or four days. I was thinking about all this stuff going on—what do I do? Little me over here at University of Massachusetts—what am I doing? I don't have stripes on my vest, I don't have a helmet on my head, I don't have the C-4 in my hand, I'm not over there doing it—and I feel like I owe these guys that. I was depressed for a couple of days—just down and out—*not* in a good mood. I don't want to hang out. I want to sit in my room and watch TV. I want to think.

What I did was call up a bunch of my old friends from the marines and we talked about it. I have those friends in the marines—we used to go on road trips and we used to go out and drink beer and go to the beach and try to pick up women. Go play basketball. Set off landmines, blow things up—all sorts of crazy stuff. Then at the same time, we just sit down, have a cup of coffee, ask about college. "College isn't good." "College is good, how's it going for you?" I said, "Not bad."…

When you get back from Iraq and you hug your girlfriend, and you sit down and tell your friends and your family these stories, they look at you like, "Wow, you did that!" I went over there. I did my job. I brought all my guys home alive. And I'm *not* crazy! Life is good. I wouldn't say I'm *not* the same. But no one *is* the same after combat.

# THREE

## BOOTS ON THE GROUND

# BENJAMIN SHRIBER
Specialist, Army Reserve

Enlisted 2002–2006, deployed age 19
(April 2003–March 2004)
Kuwait

*Stuck in Kuwait*

*Ben served in the Army Reserve at the beginning of the war, staying in Kuwait for his eleven-month deployment. He spoke about how different wars inspire different commitments, and rated the Iraq war low by those standards. He would have preferred to fight in a war like World War II, Darfur (to control the genocide), or Afghanistan. Morale in Kuwait during the early months of the war was often low because soldiers did not feel useful to the war effort. Ben recounts the reason he thinks he was "stuck" in Kuwait: his commander apparently fell asleep in a general's meeting, and lost his chance to get a promotion by taking his troops to Iraq. In his narrative, Ben usually refers to the US president without using his name, but the context makes his references clear. At the time Ben spoke, he was still in the Army Reserve.*

Afghanistan was going on when I joined and I really wasn't against going to Afghanistan. Then when the Iraq war started I didn't really like the idea, but I wasn't going to try to get out of it. Did what I had to do. We trained with the Seabees—carpentry and masonry. I guess that was kind of fitting because my dad does remodeling houses, kitchens, bathrooms, additions. They say there are hundreds of opportunities within the army, but when you get to the MEPS center, it's only what they have available. Two hundred and twelve jobs I think they have—not all 212 are available, unless if you went active you might get all 212.

They offered me chemical, and I said that sounds *wonderful*, dealing with deadly nerve agents—where do I sign? No, I didn't say that, even though it was a good bonus. There's a bonus on the jobs they need most, jobs that are understaffed. Carpentry, masonry had a $5,000 bonus. They have a kicker, which is basically an addition to the [Montgomery] GI Bill—everyone gets the GI Bill. Benefits are part of the reason why I signed up, but it wasn't the complete reason. If I was completely against the military—no matter what benefits they were offering—I wouldn't have signed.

I think it was just that I needed some structure—that's why most people join. Some of the people in the military that are the best soldiers are people who used to be in gangs, committed crimes, people who had rough backgrounds. Some people just come straight from the farm in the Midwest to sign up. Whatever people's motives are, overall, people are there for the same reason, to be a part of something. ...

They called us up Friday, February 9, 2003. After two months waiting around there, they started the invasion. I never went to Iraq—we went close, but we were in Kuwait. Eleven months. There would be weeks where you would have nothing to do. Sit around and watch movies. They would find "creative" ways to fill our time. Guard duty on towers that are not even on the perimeter—basically a guard tower *within* the perimeter. It was almost insulting to have to do guard duty there because we knew it was fucking *pointless*. There were a lot of jobs that they had us do that were complete bullshit.

There was one job that we had—to put a half a mile of nine-inch PVC on the ground for a helicopter wash rack and we hooked up the water supply. The plumber told the officer getting materials that we shouldn't use glue because in the heat the glue would melt, so we had to use rubber gaskets. And sure enough, he used the glue and we had all kinds of leaks in it, we had to pull it all up, put different pipes back down with heavy gaskets. It was stupid things like that that just drove me nuts. Have us spend a couple extra weeks on a project just because someone wanted to use cheap materials. Most of the jobs, you would just feel like it was pointless—it just sucks.

I met people from the area, mostly third-country nationals—from Egypt, India, Bangladesh, Sri Lanka, Philippines—people who were poor who came to Kuwait for jobs. There are plenty of jobs in Kuwait because [Kuwaitis] don't want to do the menial jobs. The Kuwaitis are snobs. You see them at the malls, decked out in expensive clothes. They were just spoiled little brats—the kids especially. Same thing with the Saudis. I've read things about Saudi Arabian society. They have way too much money and way too much free time on their hands. So what are they going to do? They spend it in arrogant and lavish ways. And now we're finding that you have all these oil-rich Arabs and they start looking towards terrorism and terrorist groups. They don't care if they're giving up their wealth for Allah. Something that was almost *predictable*....

I always wondered what they were thinking. I don't know if they hate me or love me. I think they know deep down that the Kuwaitis wouldn't have that kind of money if we weren't protecting them. We saved their ass when Saddam invaded. Saudis too—and I don't even think they want to admit it. To us, the Saudis are a boy-toy, they play us constantly and we play them too. It's a weird little love triangle you have going on in the Middle East, between Israel and the Saudis [and us].

I think the main reason we didn't go to Iraq actually was an accident, because we were slotted to go up there and work in the middle of Iraq. Our battalion commander, there were rumors that he fell asleep in a general's meeting—that wouldn't surprise me. For a guy who was all gung-ho about going in there, doing whatever needs to be done, telling us we are good to go to Iraq—and he falls asleep. I think one of the generals got slightly pissed off: "You're so ready to go, why don't you just stay here in Kuwait—how do you like *that*?" And to officers, everything is a career move for them. To not be allowed to go into Iraq, when all this action is going on, is almost heartbreaking for them. It's like the athlete who can't go to the semifinals. ...

The way I see it, the war was bullshit. It was poorly planned and poorly pitched. I mean they really didn't do a very good job of pitching the war to the UN or to Congress. But Congress just rolled over and did whatever he said because, you know, we're having a war on terrorism. Personally—I am against the war. But that doesn't really excuse me from my duties as of now. I really don't feel like doing much of what I'm told to do, mainly because I'm against it.

If it was Afghanistan, I think it would be different. A soldier is not supposed to have feelings or supposed to have opinions on what is going on. Someone who really makes a great soldier is someone who puts their feelings in the back seat, their opinions, their thoughts. It's not just for the big picture, it's not just for going to war or not going to war. It's also about the little things, like when you're told you have to build an air-conditioning rack for someone higher up. We had to build A/C racks for some officers. They had us sweeping streets one time. Someone who really had that mentality when told to sweep the streets would just do it because they're told to do it. I know people like that and I don't quite understand how they tick. And I don't think they understand how I tick either. They tell me that constantly. "What the hell is wrong with you?"

I was kind of excited about making some decent money, [but] you really can't put such a small amount of money in front of logic. I should have thought about this before I signed up—you can't be jumping into things that are dangerous and possibly life-threatening without considering is the money even worth it. That's why some people seem so naïve to me. "Oh, but think of the money you'll make!" I'm like, "No. Don't think of the *money* you make, think about what you are actually going to *do*."

The money isn't really that good if you think about it. It *is* good when you make $40,000 tax-free—for a kid my age that's good—but to me $40,000 is not that much. Not something you would be volunteering to go for, jumping through hoops for. I know some people who have volunteered to go back because they think it's such a good deal. [Contractors] are putting the money in the forefront, the first thing they're thinking about when they're going over there.

They're not thinking that they can be blindfolded with an AK stuck in their mouth….

World War II, you would have wanted to be there just for the cause. I think if there was a World War II happening today, it would be easier to want to be a part of. If there was genocide occurring somewhere—there *is* Darfur, you have people dying. If we were tasked to go in there it would be kind of scary, but you wouldn't feel, "Fuck, I'm doing this for the administration's business buddies who are going to make all kinds of money." You would think you're going to help those people.

Bush is trying to put the humanitarian face on the whole thing when really the whole thing is a scheme to make money. It's not a *scheme*, but if you look at all the contractors over there, they're all his good friends. They are *qualified* for the job, they're not just putting people who don't belong there. Halliburton is one of the most qualified companies to do it, but it just seems fishy that Cheney was the president [CEO] beforehand. It's so blatantly obvious, it's amazing that it's not more out there—because people don't realize. I can't even believe he was re-elected.

You remember when [Bush] found out 9/11 happened, when they went in and told him, he was reading a children's book upside down. [Some perceive the footage this way—ed.] It was in that movie *Fahrenheit 9/11*. I know most of that is biased, picking and choosing, but they did show a clip of him with the book in his hand upside down. And he's sitting there like an idiot. You never really know what is going on in his head. He's a strange one.

[*What explanations were you given for the war?*] There is no explanation. Politics and the military are separate. They don't explain to you why you're there. They just tell you this is where we're going, and this is what we're doing. Anything else that is discussed is discussed on a personal basis. People would talk nonstop about everything. Not just about politics—about war, about people, there was nothing to do *but* sit around. The first tent I lived in, all they did was argue—they got a high off of arguing with each other. I would sit there and I would play video games just to be away from it all. Luckily, I had my laptop the whole time so I was preoccupied watching movies….

One kid did tattoos over there—he was a tattoo artist. He had all his equipment set up. He did one for me. He must have made a lot of money because he charged a couple of hundred sometimes. Tattoos are expensive, but he also had a monopoly. We would have people coming in from Iraq—word got around you could get tattoos in Kuwait. They couldn't get tattoos in Iraq. People up and down Iraq, Kuwait, people were coming from all over once they heard about it. Our leadership looked the other way because they figured it would keep people happy.

We had a landmine go off in the camp. Someone brought it back from up north. They had it in a gym locker and they were wrestling and they bumped it. Someone got injured pretty badly—it was pretty stupid. People did stupid things like that. Camp itself—the monotony of it is mind-numbing. You've got Pizza Hut, you've got Subway, a coffee shop—if you want to splurge on a night on the town, that's what you get. We spent a lot of time in the gym to kill time, kill the boredom. There was the internet, but you have to wait in line—the same with the phone. A lot of the stuff didn't get set up until a few months in. Camp Arifjan—when we first got there it was open, you could drive anywhere. Slowly, you would see improvements, and the next thing you know you have street signs!...

You get citizenship a lot easier if you're in the military. You have people from a lot of countries. We had Samoans and a unit from Hawaii, Puerto Rico. The unit that replaced us was from Puerto Rico, pretty much only spoke Spanish—which was kind of annoying for the Americans that were attached to it. They recruit Hispanic, black, white, they don't even care. There's a lot of everybody. Definitely the ratio for race in the army doesn't match the ratio in society.

That's one of the few opportunities if you're living in a city like Springfield [Massachusetts]—there's not too many job opportunities out there. Outsourcing and other things have caused our economy to just be garbage. So what are you going to do? You can flip burgers at Burger King or you could go join the army and "Be All You Can Be." What do you think someone is going to take when they realize they could have their own car, they could have a place to stay, they can have all the things they've wanted—and if they stay at Burger King they aren't going to get that. So it's pretty much simple mathematics. Same goes for me.

[*How do people treat you as a veteran?*] I like it, I hate it at the same time. Sometimes people will try and kiss your ass. They may respect your service a lot, but I've heard it a million times. That's why I tell my mom not to bring up shit about the army in front of people. I will be in front of some stranger, someone she doesn't know, someone I don't know. She'll be talking and I'll say, "I'm 21 and in college," and they will ask why. "I was working," and she will have to put in, "He was in the army." It's like, "God damn it, Mom, here come the questions." She knows she gets on my nerves, too. It's not her, it's me, really—I just can't stand that stuff.

I hate fielding questions—everyone has the same frigging questions. It's like I should have a tape recorder and play them the answers to the questions that I know they're going to ask. "It's awesome. What did you guys *do* up there?" "Did you kill anybody?" "Are you in the army or are you in the Reserves?" I understand that not everyone is going to understand how it works—it took me a while before I understood everything completely. It's like if Einstein had to answer simple multiplication every fucking day when he tutored kids, he would probably go out of his mind! [Other college students] are so oblivious and apathetic. They don't seem to understand what I'm talking about, or understand the gravity of it. ...

One of the things I had trouble with was that we were over there working for the whole year—they're paying us 40 grand and up. The lowest-paid [army] people are getting low thirties, to over $120,000 for some of the officers. Then you have the Brown and Root guys [contractors] getting $100,000 a year, and they're doing the jobs that we could be doing. A lot of the jobs are tasked out— they give some out to Brown and Root, some to other contractors. Then they have the rest go to us, the engineers. What we were doing was the silly shit, build a guard shack, build this crap, and *they* would be doing the massive projects which we definitely could have handled—some of them. They're taking all this money from taxpayers while we're sitting here collecting tax money, too. ...

[*What was the high point for you?*] When I got alcohol in the mail! That was pretty cool, because I went six months without it. The biggest slap in the face was that the reason we couldn't have alcohol wasn't that we have live ammunition and guns lying around everywhere, it's because we want to respect the Kuwaiti laws. We're here for them, so we don't want to be offending them. It's *outrageous*. If we're here because we save their ass, we save their country, the least Kuwait could do is tell us it is perfectly all right for you guys to have alcohol here, on *our* base. Maybe the Kuwaitis didn't say we couldn't have it, or maybe we just decided to appease them anyways. We decided not to "insult" them by bringing alcohol into their country, because we were already on a limb by using them as a jump-off point.

[In Iraq] they have a black market for anything. You could buy explosives if you wanted to. People bought steroids, people bought drugs—you could get anything in Iraq. I'm sure if you wanted a kilo of heroin you could find it. That's the kind of place it is, because it's lawless. The military doesn't care about drugs—they're more concerned about weaponry.

—

I don't know if Muslims are *inherently* out of their minds, but it seems to me that almost every Muslim country is about out of its fucking mind. Lebanon, Egypt, Syria, they are all out of their *fucking skulls*. Where on earth do people burn fucking shit over a *cartoon* other than in Muslim lands? I hate to put them all in the same category because I know there are some very educated, sophisticated Muslims that are taking a bad rap. What you see is crowds of people in Pakistan, and all over, just screaming and burning stuff. It's a Danish newspaper—who the hell *cares*? [This refers to Muslim outrage over cartoons depicting the Prophet Mohammed in a Danish newspaper, September 30, 2005—ed.]

I'm sure that some Christians would be pissed if they were making fun of Jesus. But how many times in *Family Guy* have you seen Jesus depicted as something comical? We're just talking a cartoonish depiction! You don't see the Christian right—and the Christian right is pretty nuts, too—but they are not burning [stuff]. It's a whole different world. Maybe it's just that they feel that they aren't being heard, and they want to become more vocal. Maybe they don't really have a platform other than to congregate in the streets and they know the news cameras will be there.

# NICHOLAS A. MORTON
### Sergeant, Army Reserve

Enlisted 2002, deployed age 20
(September 2004–June 2005)
Baghdad, Iraq

*Pulling Security in Baghdad*

*Nick is from the small town of Merrimac, Massachusetts. Both his grandfathers served in the navy in World War II. An intense and energized young man, he received a scholarship to Milton Academy, a leading prep school in Massachusetts. When he graduated in 2001, instead of college or the service academies, he decided to enlist in the Army Reserve, and was on active duty in Baghdad. He has taken advantage of the military's advanced training, and credits the army for the many opportunities it has offered him. "The great thing about the army is that the army doesn't care who you were or what you did before you joined the army. So you can join the army and turn your life around." Nick is currently in the ROTC program at the University of Maryland and plans to graduate in 2010. A Democrat, he is very skeptical about the aims of the Iraq war.*

I went to Milton Academy. Everyone goes to college right from there. If you join the service, you're going to a service academy— you're not going to enlist, [but] I ended up joining in March of 2002. I got put on active duty in July '04. We got to Baghdad on September 24. My MOS is civil affairs—we're supposed to be the ones engaging Iraqi civilians, trying to develop reconstruction projects, trying to do passive intelligence-gathering. I graduated first in my class when I was in AIT [advanced individual training]. I didn't do anything close to what my training was for—I was in a civil affairs unit, [but] our mission was to provide PSD [personal security] for the battalion commander. Take him wherever he wanted to go, provide convoy escort for the guys from the embassy. Sometimes we were bringing around State Department guys, other shady characters in civilian clothes, foreign nationals. ...

A lot of people think that US soldiers go over there and it's a full-blown war—it's really *not*. It's very dangerous—don't get me wrong. But at the same time, if someone invaded my country—I don't care if it was the Pope himself invades my country—I'm going to be pissed. I'm going to start at least throwing rocks at him, maybe bullets. I can understand where they're coming from.... You try not to think about it. It's just not worth it to think about the bigger picture while you're over there.

When you come home on leave and you get back for good— that's when you start wondering, you put everything together. Iraq—it's a country in a mess. There are a lot of good Iraqis out there, there're a lot of bad Iraqis out there. We did interact with a lot of Iraqis—my friend Sergeant M., she's an Arabic linguist, so we communicated. We used to go to Baghdad City Hall, take these majors and colonels, they would meet with their Iraqi counterparts. We would just sit down in the parking lot and pull security and look out for bad guys. It's a highly guarded area, there's a lot of Iraqi police. We would always talk to them, joke around with them, kind of schmooze. The Iraqi police and the Iraqi National Guard—they all love us. I think they kind of look up to us. ...

There was one lady [a street vendor] selling little plaques that had engravings. One was George Bush and the other was Saddam Hussein. "George Bush, George Bush," she was trying to sell that during our elections. I said, "No, I don't like George Bush," and she's like, "Who do you like? John Kerry?" Oh yeah, she knew!

You would be driving and you would see a bunch of mud huts with satellite dishes on them for TV. They have cell phones now—it's called *Iraqna*. All the young guys will pull out their cell phones, play American rap songs that are popular on their ring tones. And they're taking pictures with their camera phones. It's *crazy*.

Some of our team's mission was to train. "Let's take the Iraqi police out to the range and teach them how to shoot someone." We ran it like a US military range. "Okay, get on the firing line, go ahead and ensure your weapon is on safe," and they didn't even know where "safe" *is* on their weapon—all they know is how to make it shoot! We told them to fire one round first—these guys [are] like *brrrrr*. We have weapons discipline in the US military— you carry your weapon at the low ready, you keep your finger off the trigger, you keep it on safe until you actually engage targets. These guys walk around with their finger on the trigger, the gun over their shoulder—pointing it at their buddy behind them! One guy was carrying it like a baseball bat, holding it by the barrel, he had it up on his shoulder. One guy was holding it upside down, with the magazine [up].

The sooner we get them trained, the sooner we can get the hell out of there. In the Iraqi National Guard they don't have basic training. They will get a bunch of recruits—like in [our] Revolutionary War days—and they will form a regiment right there. That's probably the only job with any job security over there—Iraqi National Guard or Iraqi police. A lot of them start in for the paycheck. When they do recruitment they'll say, "We need 50 new police officers," and 400 people show up. These guys will be 50 years old trying out with 18, 20-year-old kids. They *really* want those jobs.

They say that the Iraqi police and National Guard are infiltrated by the insurgents. A terrorist is not really a military term—it's more like a value judgment. Insurgents—that's the bad guys in Iraq. AIF—Anti-Iraqi Forces—are against the progress of Iraq. That encompasses insurgents, common criminals, and then full-blown terrorists. An insurgent is fighting *for* something, like a revolutionary. Terrorists are just trying to cause mayhem and destruction. Which ultimately they're both doing—so are the criminals.

We had an interpreter who was a great guy, an Iraqi national. He was in Saddam's army for nine years and eight of those years he was deployed to the Iran–Iraq War. He absolutely *hated* Saddam.

He was a really good guy. I trust that guy with my life. He said these are all Syrians that are blowing things up. The border with Syria—all the borders in Iraq—are like sieves. You can double the amount of US soldiers and double the amount of Iraqi soldiers and put them all around the border and they would still be a mile apart from each other. Especially open desert—it's not like a forest where you can't drive your car through. All these guys can get jeeps or off-road vehicles.

There are a lot of different groups of insurgents. The most threatening guy in Baghdad was Muqtada al-Sadr, a Shiite cleric who would spend time between Sadr City (which is a Shiite slum) and Najaf in the south. He was our problem because he had the Mahdi army—religious fighters very loyal to him, [who] would do whatever he wanted. The US military made deals with him, and during the elections they let him run because by letting him run they put him out there in a larger pool. He was marginalized—he didn't get any support. I guess that was a wake-up call for him. You now have Mahdi army guys like a civilian patrol that works with the Iraqi police and with US forces.

You definitely have your homegrown insurgents in Iraq, a really big problem at the beginning of the war. The Fedayeen was basically the Iraqi military and Saddam loyalists, who, just as soon as the Americans came in, threw off their uniforms and went and sat in their house and let the Americans drive by. Then they put on black ski masks and started shooting at them from behind. Fedayeen forces are definitely cut down a lot now. Saddam loyalists are not such a big force.

Probably the biggest force would be the AMZ, Abu al-Zarkawi [later killed by US soldiers—ed.] and his people. The thing about a movement like Zarkawi's, or al-Qaeda in general—that's a pan-Islamic movement. Muslims don't see the world like we see the world. Not just extremist Muslims—Muslims in general. The way we see the world is the nation-state, sovereignty, and international relations. You pull out your fifth-grade map with different colored countries, nice clean lines in between them. For Muslims, all Muslims are your brothers. In the border cities in Jordan, they accept either Saudi currency or Jordanian currency. People drive cars that have Saudi license plates on them. You know that that border doesn't *exist*.

Al-Qaeda is a very small minority of extremists. Fifteen of the nineteen September 11 hijackers were Saudi Arabian—Osama bin Laden was Saudi Arabian. Saudi Arabia has its own very radical sects of Islam that the government tries to keep a hold on. These kingdoms and these monarchies in the Middle East that are friendly with the US like Jordan and Saudi Arabia don't want these extremists to take over just as much as we don't want them to. These extremists have a view of world life as jihad—they will bring the jihad wherever they need to go. So in Afghanistan when the Taliban was fighting the Russians, you had fighters from Jordan and Saudi Arabia going to Afghanistan to fight, so I don't see why they wouldn't come to Iraq.

The only way you can know if someone is an insurgent or not is if they're shooting at you, or if you already have them identified through intel. A lot of those "cordon and search" missions are to locate key personnel. Through intelligence-gathering by US military and other organizations, [we] get an idea of what kinds of terror cells operate in that area. They will talk to every different leader of the town or area they're in and find out who is this terrorist leader or insurgent leader, who are his captains. They will try to locate him, then intel will designate what house you're going to hit and "cordon and search." You're trying to get the guy, you're not trying to *kill* him. You want to grab him so you can get more intel—see if you can get his friends and his friends' friends.

They really don't do that anymore because it doesn't help at all—and it really makes the Iraqi people mad. The only time they will do a "cordon and search" is if they have active intelligence or if they keep hearing rumors that these guys are operating out of this house, this block, or this area is really bad, and that's when they will hit it. As a US soldier you're not an intel guy, you don't know what the guys look like that you are looking for. You go in—you restrain everyone and detain everybody in the house. Then the intel guys come, identify who they want to take with them for questioning. As a soldier it is impossible to tell who is an insurgent and who is not. If someone shoots at you, you shoot back. ...

Definitely, their elections on January 30, 2005 were a major step, and everyone knew that—Americans and Iraqis alike.... It was like waking up in a different country. By noontime most people had voted, and I realized how much of a joke elections are here in the

THREE: BOOTS ON THE GROUND

States. Election day—nobody cares. There, because of security, they basically shut everything down for two days before and two days after elections. On election day itself, no civilian traffic was allowed within the city of Baghdad. The only vehicles allowed to move were US vehicles, coalition vehicles, and Iraqi security forces.

So imagine all the streets are shut down, all the businesses are shut down, school is closed. It's like a giant block party, Mardi Gras. Everybody was out, old men, old women, young kids. Everyone is holding up their finger, all the people who voted. It got to a point where we had to have people dismount from our vehicles and walk in front because we didn't want to hit anybody because they were running in front of vehicles and waving. So we were moving up five miles an hour on the main road which we would normally do at 40 miles an hour. It was so *surreal*—it was like being in a different country. All the Iraqis were so happy, they were cheering.

I always changed my security posture depending on what the situation is. Usually I would have one hand on my .50 cal and I would have one hand on my rifle, my M-4. So we're driving down the street and everyone was happy, so I just let my machine gun sit—but I'm still holding my rifle—and I'm waving with my other hand. There was this group of really old men sitting there and they're waving at me and I'm waving at them. And the guy motions like he is holding a gun and saying, "Put it down," like you don't need that anymore. I still had it real close, I just set it down on the turret so they couldn't see it, and they started clapping and waving. It's something I will never forget. It was like their first free election in God knows how long.

City Hall never got attacked, all these vehicle attacks, all these other places, City Hall never got attacked. One thing that everyone assumed was that the mayor of Baghdad was corrupt—he was in with the insurgents. The tribal system—Saddam tried to stamp it out—it still holds clout. We worked very closely with the sheikh who our interpreter also worked for. The interpreter was getting paid by us and getting paid by the sheikh. And the sheikh would tell major pieces of intelligence that would always turn out to be true.

I was talking to our interpreter and I said, "The sheikh is a powerful man." He said to me, "Yeah, why do you think he knows so much about what the insurgents are doing? There was a group of insurgents that threatened my life, they tried to kill me many times. I go to the sheikh and I said they are threatening to kill me. He will take care of it. So the next week I see that those same insurgents are meeting and having tea with the sheikh!" So there are a lot of guys who are just playing both sides because the only guys that can *survive* are the guys that play both sides. If you are all [pro-] American, you're going to get whacked by the insurgents, assassinated. If you are all insurgent, you're going to get whacked by the Americans or apprehended by them. Iraqi rulers who will succeed will play both sides because they're smart. ...

I'm sure it will be like Japan or Germany after World War II. I'm sure we will be there for the next fifteen years, with a much diminished force, hopefully—just with military advisers. And I'm sure they will keep a couple of units over there to train the guys. I'm sure there will be a lot of airbases over there—we'll keep those. The mission when we got there was reconstruction and rebuild, fight the insurgency. When we left, the mission was train Iraqi security forces, build up the government, get the hell out of there.

I'm a Democrat, I don't like Bush at all. I don't think the Iraq war is justified at all. First it was for weapons of mass destruction, now the pitch is we're bringing these guys democracy. It's supposed to be a noble cause. If you want a noble cause, we should have 130,000 soldiers in Sudan right now preventing genocide. *That* would be a much more noble cause.

People don't realize that we *can't* leave now. It's not like in Vietnam where one side is going to easily win, and then there will be stability in the country. If we were to leave now, there is a high probability that the country would fracture into three parts, the Kurds, the Sunnis, and the Shiites—the north, the middle, and the south. There would be civil war and it would be lawless and it would just be a hotbed for terrorism, like Afghanistan was under the Taliban. We can't leave now.

I might go back to Baghdad. I've applied to a couple of those security companies—Kellogg, Brown and Root. You have modern-day mercenaries over there, about 30,000 strong. There was a really good article about it in the March '05 *Foreign Affairs*, about private military in Iraq and Afghanistan. You can go on the

Department of State website and you can pull up a list of all the private security contractors that are working in Iraq—200 companies. All these guys are former Special Operations soldiers, former British SAS, former American Special Forces, Army Rangers, Navy SEALs. It's definitely a gray area. I knew guys over there. They said, "When you get out, call up our company, we always need more people. We do the exact same job as you, [but] we get paid fifteen times as much." I mean, these guys are making $240,000 a year. It's only the first $80,000 that's tax-free, but you're still making $240,000 a year....

If you're a Special Forces soldier, a highly trained killing machine (amongst other things), you're very good with weapons and security, you get out of the US military after twenty years, you can start a whole other career.... A Special Forces guy will go and form his own company. There will be five or six guys, they will say, "I was Special Forces, I was fifth group" (Special Forces is divided into groups—there are seven or eight of them). So you have all these guys from fifth group [who] will make their own company, and all these guys from seventh group will own another security company. There was a bunch of guys from third group that founded their own security company and the headquarters was in Romania, because of the taxes. So if you were searching the Department of State website you would see this Romanian security company—but it's all Americans....

I met a lot of guys, they don't like the States, they just really *enjoy* war. Adrenaline is a drug, you know. It's probably the hottest drug going right now. You get out there and you get like, "Ahhh." Nothing registers and it's all on a very primal level. You don't think about stuff until days or weeks later. You see grenades falling down from above and you just swerve and avoid them—"Whoa, that was close!" Someone is shooting you, you just duck and shoot back, it doesn't register until much, much later.

—

I thought I was totally normal when I came home. I thought everything was hunky-dory. I was telling some story about how we were fighting this kid, kicking him around my buddy's house. And my dad is like, "You know, it just seems you've been wound a lot tighter since you got back from Iraq." And I'm [like], "I've been wound a lot tighter?!" And I was like, "Maybe it's *good* to be wound tighter!" For maybe about two months after I got back, I was wound tighter.

Soldiers are the worst when it comes to disposable income—you will just *blow* it…. Every time you lay down some ridiculous amount of money for something stupid, it makes you feel better. I spent $25,000 in three months, but I did spend $8,000 or $9,000 on tuition, so I didn't exactly blow that. I did buy a couple of guns, so that is $1,000 or $1,500 right there. I didn't buy a new truck—I bought that when we got out of basic training. I spent my money on good times.

So we got back from Iraq and you're used to having a gun. I had never fired a gun in the civilian world before I bought my guns when I got back from Iraq. Especially the first couple of weeks, you feel nervous going to the store without a gun. We used to carry edged weapons [knives] on us all the time before we got our guns. We were down in North Carolina demobilizing. We all go to the gun store three days after we got back from Iraq. Technically, my military orders give me residency in North Carolina, and you don't need a permit for a shotgun in North Carolina—you can buy rifles and shotguns all day long. They do a background check and you have to fill out a form and that goes into the system, but you can do it right there.

So I bought a nice little tactical shotgun. And my buddy—it was pretty funny—he says, "That ain't no *hunting* shotgun, buddy. That's a *'what-the-fuck-are-you-doing-in-my-house?'* shotgun." He went over the top and bought an M-4—a rifle that we carry over there, a shorter version of the M-16. And then he bought an ACOG (advanced combat optical gun-sight) and he set it up exactly the same as we had in Iraq. An M-4 cost him $900 for the rifle and $1,600 for the scope. My shotgun was only $400.

Our battalion commander says, "Hey, what did you guys do today?" "Sir, we had a blast. We went down to the gun store and bought some guns, went on the range, blasted some rounds." Our battalion commander looks at us. "Let me get this straight. You're trying to decompress and readjust from Iraq and you go into the gun store and buy guns and go shooting. Great, guys, real fucking great! Glad to see that!"

I got my class A license for a concealed weapon. As soon as I got that, my girlfriend (at the time) said, "You should buy a pistol." She likes the gun thing. So I bought a nice little pistol, which is actually only for military or law enforcement. So now I have my two guns—that pistol was $700—I had to buy a holster and ammo, so it was all-told $1,000. It was good because I have a job as an armed guard now. I was reading the classified ads for armed guards—I need a job where I can carry a gun. When I called up: "Do you have a class A license to carry a concealed weapon?" "Yes." "Do you have your own pistol?" "Yes." "Do you have any experience?" "Well, I just got back from *Iraq*." "Okay, great, when can you start?" That was the interview.

—

When I was in basic training, the guy that slept next to me—he's a great guy, a real good guy. He was 26, he had his BS in finance— he was a financial analyst. He was making $100,000–$120,000 a year before 9/11 happened. He said, "Screw it, I am joining the military." He came from a military family, he was from the South, he was educated, he had always had this nagging feeling he should have joined the military. He was going to officer-candidate school, officer basic course with the infantry, platoon leader, and then he was going right to airborne school. He was going to ranger school, and then Special Forces. You have this real stand-up guy—just joined the military out of the blue.

The guy that slept above, he was 22. He was a good kid and he was from Houston. I said to him, "What did you do before you joined the army?" And he said, "I worked at Walgreen's as a photo tech ten hours a week." And I was like, "Ten hours a week, how do you make any money?" And he was like, "Actually, I sell Ecstasy in night clubs…. But my mom was getting kind of upset, all these drugs, so I figured I'd try to go straight. Do something good for myself." Two different types of people—we're all on the same team.

There was a kid across the bay from us and his name was Pablo. He had an emaciated face, bug eyes, big toothy grin—real goofy kid. Someone goes, "Pablo, what did you do before you joined the army?" He goes, "I smoked a lot of crack." Oh *really*, I couldn't tell by looking at you! The great thing about the army is that the army doesn't care who you were or what you did before you joined the army. They don't care unless there is a paper trail. If you have a couple of felonies that are on the books, they might care about that, depending on what it is, they will probably still let you in. So you can join the army and turn your life around if your life is going bad.

That is obviously why the army has a disproportionate number of poor people from lower-income parts of America. It's a good way to get started off in life, to establish a base for yourself.... The army is a meritocracy, aside from the whole dichotomy between enlisted and officers. But they're pushing a lot more programs called "green to gold" where you can be enlisted for four or five years and then they will pay for you to go to college, do ROTC, get your degree, and then become an officer. The whole idea of a division between officers and enlisted is archaic. There's no need for it anymore because the noncommissioned officer corps in the army is so strong. I'm a noncommissioned officer and the NCO motto is "backbone of the army."

# JEFFREY PEDDAR
## Corporal, Marine Corps Reserve

Enlisted 2002–2010 (expected), deployed age 19
(August 2004–February 2005)
al-Asad Airbase, Iraq

*Working on al-Asad Airbase*

*Jeff is a tall, blond marine reservist who operated heavy machinery in Iraq. He portrays the novelties and frustrations of service as he experienced them in the war zone, including fond memories of the puppies his unit cared for. He spoke frankly about the issue of women in the army: "Say I got shot on the battlefield like back in Vietnam, and someone had to carry me out of the jungle. Would a woman really be able to pick me up over their shoulder, and run with me on their back?" Now at UMass Amherst, he has built up a business providing personal training at a health club, an avocation he took up while in the war arena. As a personal trainer, he is able to help pay his way through college. He is in the School of Management earning a business degree and he plans to be a businessman and entrepreneur. He expects to graduate in 2009.*

I signed up for the marines when I was seventeen at the beginning of my senior year at Newton South High School. I was thinking about the whole college thing. Of course I'm going to go to college and get a degree, but if I'm going for a job, why would someone accept me over [others]? So I went to the military. It took me a few weeks to convince myself. I signed up in the reserve because this was just as a supplement to college. Little did I know, the stuff that the recruiters tell you isn't entirely accurate, like, "Oh, you're in college, you'll be able to tell your unit that and they won't send you overseas."

So the recruiter came over, it took a couple of weeks to convince my mom, we finally got her. I sprang it on her, she tried to convince me not to—she threatened not to [sign]. I told her, "It's *my* decision, I'm not going to talk to you if you don't. You're affecting my life, this is not your call to make, it's mine." Granted I was seventeen at the time—I still had a lot of growing up to do. I told my dad—he lives in Georgia. My folks have been divorced a long time. He didn't really want me to, but he's going to support me whatever I decide to do. ...

There were only a handful of options that the recruiter said. I found out now that there are more options and sign-up bonuses that no one tells you about until later on [when] you find out that all these other guys get hooked up with them. I kind of missed out on that. I chose the heavy equipment operator for my MOS. The way I looked at it, it was either that or I could be military police, I could be infantry, or I could be crash, fire, rescue. Heavy equipment—I have all this experience for when I'm outside of the marines, free training that's extremely valuable. ...

We were the first reserve marine support squadron to deploy.... We took a civilian airline over to Kuwait [August 2004]. It was ungodly hot. I was the only one [who] bought one of those mini two-dollar fans from CVS [drug store] and that was great. I used it for a day and then I threw it out—you get used to sweating. The next day, we took a C-130 [to Iraq]. We had our flak jackets and Kevlar on and our rifles and everything. We had no idea what to expect. We thought we might get shot at in the air flying over—none of us had ever been there before. We got off the plane and I remember the base—it was like going to high school for the first time, or middle school. You go there and look at the school and it looks *humongous*. Once you're actually on the base—I know the base like the back of my hand. It was al-Asad Airbase, a hundred miles west of Baghdad.

Within a day or two of being there all of a sudden we heard, *boom*! We were in the chow hall, it was lunch time. You don't know what to expect, you hear this really loud boom, and we could see the explosion. We were like, "Shit, what do we *do*?" Everyone is freaking out. In the chow hall they told us to hide under the plastic table, everyone got down. If there's a direct hit, what's a plastic table going to do to provide cover?

We were still living in tents, there was no protection, we just had HESCO barriers there. You fill it with sand, it has the netting and chicken wire, it stands up, they're eight feet tall. There's protection if something hits it, the shrapnel is not going to go straight through it. The mortar round is designed so maybe it makes a little bend where the impact is, but everything goes *outwards*. Whereas a bomb, it explodes, everything goes up. [Mortar] is not a big explosion like blowing up the ground, it just shoots the shrapnel everywhere and it pierces into everything.

We saw [Iraqis] all the time, working in the chow hall, driving around the base, the clean-up crew. We were the escort [for] the shit trucks, the water trucks. Sometimes they would put you at the ECP, the entry control point at the gate. First thing in the morning when a truck comes, you check out their IDs, you check out their truck and you escort them on the compound so they never are by themselves. Keep an eye on them, escort them out again. We just stood around and watched them as they did their jobs.

One guy—[the Iraqis] found out he was working for the Americans [contractors]. I was following him, and he came back one day and he had been beaten up a little bit. They broke his CD player. I had an extra one that someone had given me at the beginning, so I gave him that. He was appreciative. A lot of the guys hated Saddam. They would say, "Boo, Saddam." Somehow they were able to communicate. I couldn't understand any Arabic—I had no idea what they were saying.

The people working on base definitely wanted to help us— appreciated it. Some of them were TCNs [third-country nationals] from other countries that came up with these contracting companies, like out of Jordan. They were promised this good-paying job and they're getting everything taken care of. There would be eight, ten of them, and these little poor persons—they would have ten in a tent, the same tent we would have four in. They would share one bathroom and these guys would work twelve-plus hours, every single day. It was like *slave* labor—they were paid next to nothing. The civilians that worked on the base, from KBR [Kellogg, Brown, and Root] contracting company, would tip the Iraqi guys to clean their rooms. I knew one guy who was driving a shit truck. He would drain out the cesspool, suck up all our stuff, and he was getting a dollar a day for that. He didn't get paid, he told me, for the first three months. A lot of them had nothing to do with us—they're contracted. We had no regulation on what happens with them.

The KBR company—they pay great I hear, they take care of their [American] employees. The civilians are under no obligation to stay there. If they change their minds and want out, they can leave that same day or the next flight out. They will get paid for the time that they were there. One guy was on security and he was making $30,000 a *month*, just for doing the same security [as the soldiers]. There would be a convoy and KBR is supposed to supply their own security. So these guys would be security officers for them. If something happened, obviously the marines are going to respond. It's the same thing as being an infantry guy, having to respond to a situation. And this guy was being paid $30,000 every month!

What I was getting paid—I was getting money toward housing, I was paying rent back home and then your basic pay. It ended up being $1,700 every two weeks total, so $3,400 a month… for lance corporal pay over there. It wasn't a significant amount and then we got extra, so it ended up overall a little over $30,000 [a year]. And while you're there it's tax-free.

Someone had a dog and it had puppies, so we had two puppies in our lot, and that was a huge morale booster. The guys loved them. We had night operators and day operators—we rotated with them so there was always someone taking care of them. If you're sitting around doing nothing, play with the puppies, it cheers you up a bit. And our officers, our higher-ups, said we were not allowed to have them. It was just a little hypocritical because there was a female officer and she had cats out there, she had gotten them out there. She was able to send them home, I guess just because she was an officer. We had to give up our puppies. They weren't bothering anyone, they were *adorable.*

Our sergeant major was a woman, the woman in charge. She was awful! We're not talking about her. She was not well-liked. Believe me, I am not sexist. [The women in the unit] are hit on all the time—the guys are away for such a long time. There are a lot of horny guys, they're going to flirt and whatnot. Guys will hit on girls they would not typically be interested in. I guess it was good for the girls—some of the girls must have loved it. They were the center of attention oftentimes.

In terms of work, a lot of the guys did not believe that women should be there. Granted that there's equal opportunity, and you aren't supposed to say stuff. Women cannot physically do everything that men can do. I'm not being sexist or anything. From a personal trainer's perspective, I train a lot of women, all ages, and women just don't build muscle the same way, they are designed for childbirth and other things. I'm very supportive of women athletes, but strength-wise, they don't build muscle the same way guys do. Say I got shot on the battlefield like back in Vietnam and someone had to carry me out of the jungle. Would a woman really be able to pick me up over their shoulder, and run with me on their back? Because I know that I can carry another guy—I've done it in training. Just *size*-wise, they just don't have the same abilities and strength.

I felt bad, there were two females in the combat engineers' section. They pulled their weight, they worked hard, they were in shape. But if they were moving heavy stuff, sheets of plywood— these things are as big as the girls. I mean, they're still picking it up [but] it's heavy and it's awkward—guys are picking it up, no problem. The girls are struggling and no one is helping them out— they're just sitting watching, laughing a little. They have no sympathy—it has got to be tough on them. They get the crummy end of everything. And they bug me being over there because they are an inconvenience for us. We weren't allowed outside with our shirts off because there were women around. You can't use certain bathrooms just because women are around. It sucks for us.

[*Why does a woman go into the military?*] To prove she can do the same things that guys can do. It's also an accomplishment that there is no difference. I'm all for her going over there, she's putting her life on the line the same as us, she's doing her job like everyone else is. I mean, in general, I don't believe that women really belong in the military, in the combat aspect of it. Certain stuff is very physically demanding—in our heavy-equipment platoon we don't have a single female. There are female mechanics and that's great. That's a job that's more suitable—something hands-on that does not require a huge amount of strength. The only reason I see women doing it for the most part is just the challenge because it's a *marine* boot camp. The army, pretty much anyone who goes in gets through it. They don't make it that excruciatingly difficult.

The base we were on was one of Saddam's most developed airbases. When we took it over it was smallish, and now we have completely rebuilt it. We have all these facilities there, everything is running, it is a fully sufficient base…. Now you aren't really fighting [their army]—now it's just terrorists. Us being there is a reason that this is still going on. The Americans went there and now the Americans *can't* just pull out unless they completely destroy everything they have built—that is the only way we could get out.

[*Can we pass these bases on to the Iraqi military?*] No, because then there is potential for them to use them against us. How can they prove that they are faithful to the US? They *can't*, they could change their mind in a split second, they could have weapons development. If we can build bombs on the base, they can certainly build bombs on the base. All they need is the extra parts and in those countries there always seems to be a means to get the supplies that they need. There is a limitless supply of AK-47s in that area.

Now we have a permanent military presence in the Middle East. We have all these bases established. Say there's a conflict in Iran—we can mobilize from Iraq. They are going to turn that into another Okinawa. There was a conflict in Okinawa [Japan] and now we have a huge base there. What purpose would it serve to do everything that we've done in Iraq and just abandon it? That's what happened with Desert Storm. There is no enemy that we're fighting anymore, we're fighting quote-unquote terrorists. We don't have a specific person we're looking for; you don't know who is going to attack you. You're just driving down the street and someone has a bomb strapped to their chest. You have no idea who you are fighting.

Sometimes it is an actual terrorist. They use little kids sometimes. I've heard stories from my friends where there will be a little kid and someone will bribe him with candy to stand in the middle of the road to stop the convoy so they can ambush the convoy. And they are given orders that they're not stopping for anything. So they will run over a little kid and they *still* will get ambushed. Now a little kid has to die. At the beginning they used to stop and they would get ambushed and lose marines. Now they got wise and the orders are to stop for nothing. Kids are sympathetic—they don't want to kill a little kid.

[The attacks] might be reduced, but there's always going to be someone who doesn't like Americans and there's always going to be someone who has access to weapons. You can see us being there is not stopping terrorism in the United States. It is causing *more* terrorism in the Middle East. What they gained is instilling fear in Americans. They accomplished their goal, because now Americans don't feel as safe as they used to. That was their intention—they caused *chaos*. George Bush just took advantage of the American people.

―

You are so excited to see your family and get back to your life. I had an issue with my girlfriend when I was gone—that was over. It's difficult when you can't always call home. Something will happen and you want to discuss it and work it out, and it is a *complete* feeling of helplessness. You have no say in anything. Basically, someone back home says this is how it is—that is how it is. I tried to call at least once a week, [or] every other week. Sometimes we got attacked and I couldn't use the phones, and sometimes you are just too tired at the end of the day. And there are a lot of things you're not allowed to say on the phone—base location, because we don't know who is listening.

If you can go to Iraq and you can get shot at, and you can put your life on the line, you should be allowed to drink. I don't mean to the extent of being an alcoholic or completely intoxicated all the time, but it is a reasonable thing. We weren't allowed to. We got drug tests all the time over there. We had to pee in a cup all the time. Three or four times I got drug tested. I thought it was ridiculous. There were incidences with alcohol. People had other people send it to them—take Listerine bottles and green food coloring. Sometimes you could even add the mint flavor. The only thing we were allowed were two Budweisers and a shot of Bacardi on the Marine Corps birthday, November 10.

You come back and you get such a sense of accomplishment, something for the rest of your life that you can say you have done. You have achieved, you have accomplished, you served in Iraq—a monumental job. You were there, you did it, you had just as much riding on the line as anyone else did. You made that effort. You did this selflessly. Granted, you might not have wanted to go, but you've signed up to be a marine or army soldier, navy, so you took the initiative to *do* something. Granted they called on you to do it. You honorably served your country and you did your job.

# RUSSELL W. ANDERSON, JR.
### First Sergeant, Army Reserve

Enlisted 1969, deployed age 53
(February 2004–February 2005)
Camp Speicher, Tikrit, Iraq

*A First Sergeant and His Troops*

*Russ Anderson is a divorced father of four, ages 17 to 25, and is himself the third of seven children. He was 53 when he deployed, after being in the Army Reserve for decades. He is now first sergeant and very committed to his troops and training his men and women. "My job was 24/7. Babysitting, counselor, being the evil one, disciplinarian…. I describe my job as the elbow of a sewer pipe that is clogged and flows both ways and stops right there: food, water, safety, gear, training, problems back home." His tour of duty in Iraq was in many ways a career high point, because the unit worked very well and morale was high. His return to civilian life, where he has worked for the FDIC for fifteen years in human services, has been a challenge. He was recruited to do a film for TV entitled "Hidden Wounds" about PTSD and Russ is worried that he has "branded" himself. Despite his symptoms, he feels ready to continue his army career and is due to rotate back to Iraq in June 2007.*

I went into the service in 1969, right after high school. I wasn't going to college, so I could wait and take my chances [with the draft] or enlist. I enlisted in the Army Security Agency—electronic eavesdropping—three years stationed in Ethiopia and Germany. I went back into the Reserves in 1985—retirement [income] would be a good thing to have. A finance clerk, a cargo specialist loading ships out of Boston, then a quartermaster unit, a port detachment unit, and a unit where you instruct soldiers. I went from specialist, sergeant, to staff sergeant, then to sergeant first class, master sergeant, and then first sergeant.

I ended up with the 283rd Transportation Company out of Fairfield, Connecticut—medium truck unit. Depending on what day in December 2003, it had two to eight people in it, [so it was] taking [new] people from all over the country—from 35 states plus Puerto Rico. One hundred and fifty people, male and female, and just about every ethnic group. Between them it was truly representative of America. We went to Fort Drum, did our training in the frozen tundra—[but] you can't train in the snow when you are going to the desert! February 16, 2004, we flew over to Iraq....

I was 53. No, I was not the oldest. The captain was 57, I had another person who was a month older than I was, and the maintenance chief was about two years older. You can be deployed up until age 60. I understand that they are talking about making it 62—I'm 55.

We got there when it started to heat up. We did a few missions hauling fuel, dry goods, food and drinks. We were at FOB [forward operating base] Speicher.... My job was 24/7. Babysitting, counselor, being the evil one, disciplinarian, in charge. I describe my job as the elbow of a sewer pipe that is clogged and flows both ways and stops right there. Food, water, safety, gear, training, problems back home, Red Cross messages.

They're doing the electronic e-mail and webcam now, or phone—"good for morale." I didn't see it that way. What I saw was soldiers being stressed out. With instant communication, now the wife is bitching because she gets lonely taking care of the kids. There isn't another person to help, there's a hole that they've got to fill somehow. The soldier doesn't understand, they're trying to keep alive—and they wouldn't understand each other's stresses. When little Susie hits Billy and the wife says I can't take this anymore, he has to think well, if I was there…. Write it in regular mail! By the time it gets there it's over and done with. It hasn't changed in years—in generations. People love getting mail and packages, not so much e-mail. Mail call is of major importance every day.

E-mail is a major distraction. I had soldiers getting up at three o'clock in the morning for when [their family] would be up, when the kids would be around, then they would go on mission at six. So there is the stress of home and the lack of sleep. The biggest rip-off going—AT&T. To just get on the phone they used up 80 percent of the minutes they had. [*No discounts for soldiers?*] No, not at all, it was *unbelievable*. The VFW [Veterans of Foreign Wars] sends [AT&T phone cards] over, but I told my VFW it's a rip-off.

We had another system called Segovia—the rates were so cheap. You sign up through the computer system. I called my girlfriend twice a week, Tuesday and Friday, and if I happened to miss a day she would get upset, mad. All that back-home stuff with the kids, with my ex, constant bad news. I finally wrote home and said, "I don't want to hear any more bad news unless someone *dies*. I can't do anything about it. Thank you for informing me about my son, his grades, that's fine. But this trouble, that trouble—I don't need it."

⎯

[*Who are the insurgents, terrorists?*] I don't call them terrorists, I call them thugs. They know if they keep blowing things up, people will get tired of it and blame us. Anybody who won't stand and fight can't call themselves a freedom fighter—they're killers as far as I'm concerned. The ones that used to be in power that are not in power anymore. It's like you and I living in a seventeen-bedroom mansion and are told, "Go live in a hut in the desert." You can also rationalize it like, "The foreign soldiers on my soil—I don't care who you are—you don't belong here." "Saddam was bad, we [Iraqis] didn't get blown up a lot, but we could disappear in the night, too." The people in Iraq are just tired of violence—they don't know which way to go. I don't think they're ever going to have a democracy like we have….

The terrorists can hire one person to dig the hole, hire a second person to plant the bomb, a third person to set it off. What I heard, the going rate was a thousand American dollars. Bin Laden is a multi-millionaire—I forget how many hundreds of millions he's worth. [*Who does this?*] I will give you three different people, and they're not even connected with each other. The ones we found out were foreign. They were Syrians, Pakistanis, Jordanians—all [for] the money.

When I first got there we *did* visit a local village once a week on a Friday, just to be friendly. We would have lunch with the elderly. We would bring school supplies to the village. They loved it. They would get soccer balls. They mobbed us. Unfortunately, we were making them beggars. They were almost crushed, crowding around us. Then they would fight over things. Food. But that stopped when things heated up. There were varying ways we were encouraged to be friendly with the Iraqis [but if] there's a potential terrorist or a bomber, our rules of engagement would very much lean towards that....

I was there when they turned it over to sovereignty, and then in January [2005], they had the elections. We were basically shut down for five days during the elections—[except] for essential missions, fuel. The amazing thing about the elections—you have over 70 percent voting. It just shows you: they needed, they wanted a change, and they voted despite death threats and car bombs. We [in the US] are lucky if we get 40 percent on a good day. When that mosque got blown up in Samarra, it [could have] turned into a civil war. That was the perfect time to do it—that was a huge mosque, one of the sacred mosques, really. Well, it didn't erupt into a civil war. I really thought it was going to. ...

[*What about permanent US bases?*] They were building the base up. They were bringing in housing trailers. Speicher was hit pretty bad in the first Gulf War, and then in the initial [part of] this war, so there have to be a lot of repairs to the buildings. It was an air force base so they have to get the runways open. [*Are there other permanent bases?*] They had areas of operations, but I'm not that high up to know. I don't know if it will be permanent or not. I saw repairs being done to make it more comfortable.

[*What were the attitudes of your soldiers?*] A lot were totally confused. "I didn't volunteer for this." "Well, yes you *did*, when you signed the bottom line." Those were the younger ones. "You signed up to do this, whether it was for education or retirement, read the bottom line—'Defend against all enemies of the country'.... You raised your right hand, you're stuck here now. I really don't want to hear it. I'm sorry, but you put on this uniform, you volunteered. No one forces you to wear this uniform."

But the younger people, they *questioned* a lot, they *challenged* a lot compared to my generation, where you say, "Yes" or "No, okay, sergeant." They would get into arguments with you. "I'm lower rank, I shouldn't be doing so and so, a higher rank should."... "No, that's the way the army is." Of course, out on the road everybody does anything—outside the wire—but inside, this is how it goes. They are more educated, a lot of them had college, some had college degrees. They got in—in the first place—to get their college degree. They get pulled out of college, out of their job. The soldiers—they each had their issues and stories about coming over to Iraq.

[*Why did they sign up, apart from the benefits?*] They didn't have a job, it's a part-time job. I had a lot sign up after 9/11. They had never thought about the army, but after 9/11 they had to do something. They were going to school, they were in the Reserves, they had the best of both worlds. "Why are we here—is this really *necessary?*" "I got my life interrupted," that type of thing. They questioned authority....

End of January our replacements came in. February 4, we convoyed down to Kuwait and we stayed until February 22. We were stuck in Kuwait for what seemed like forever and we weren't doing anything—just putting on weight. We got delayed at the Kuwaiti airport. This cargo plane landed near us and then a refrigerated truck backed up to it and they unloaded three American flag-draped coffins. We all looked and said, "Shit, we're going home, these guys aren't." All my soldiers came home alive....

[*What was your reception like coming home?*] They're afraid. You're like a leper—like you're missing a leg. When I came home on leave the only people who shook my hand were TSA [Transportation Security Administration—airport security] agents. No one came up—well, one woman gave me a hug in the middle of the supermarket. Occasionally now I wear a hat that says Iraq on it, people come up and ask. People—I don't know why—are very standoffish. I came back to work, I had a little welcome thing, *muffins, orange juice*. You want to be recognized that you did something. You gave it more than a year's worth of your life. It makes it very difficult. [Veterans] go under the radar because you weren't recognized when you came back. "Okay, I might as well just be quiet."

Plus if anything comes up, like my situation with posttraumatic. I didn't notice it really, it was my girlfriend. All the e-mails back and forth, all the stuff we planned just didn't happen. We went to Vegas, but that was strained. I just withdrew into myself, more angry than usual, I would withdraw from all sorts of emotions, feelings. Basically, she gave me an ultimatum—hit the road or go seek some help! I guess I needed help.

There were fireworks and I knew they were fireworks, but I was jumping. Then I had nightmares until I got on medication. Not about Iraq itself, but a lot of doom, end of the world, nuclear holocaust. Anxiety attacks—unbelievable. Loud noises. I'm a hunter and I was on the gun range with my younger son and these people next to us started firing in rapid succession. I dove under the truck. I was so embarrassed. At least my son didn't see me do it.

Anything can trigger [PTSD]. You [think] you don't have it—you think you're right and everyone else is wrong. I still think that way! You can see how negative I am. You just get dispirited, depressed. They don't have a clue what you're going through, or what you went through. I'm more comfortable with soldiers than I am with civilians. I can talk to a soldier or someone who has had experience. My girlfriend says, "Your whole personality changes, you're more happy, you're more comfortable, you aren't uptight." I thought I would come home changed but I didn't think I would come home like this. I only went on 50 missions. My soldiers went on 200–250 missions. I can't imagine what they are going through. You find out they're getting divorced or they broke up with their girlfriend. They're drinking a lot.

[*What about women in combat?*] [Laughs]. My position? Frankly, they don't belong in the combat zone. Not that they can't *do* it. I had one got caught in an ambush and did a fantastic job. Another one handled a .50 caliber machine gun—they can *do* the job just as well as a man, if not better. Some were outstanding troops, fewer discipline problems. I had nineteen females. But the problem I have to deal with—who is sleeping with who. We had two adulterers and their marriages broke up over it. And quite frankly, sexual-assault-type things. I didn't have any sexual assault in my company, but everyone is worried about that. When you throw men and women together, something is going to happen.

I had four pregnancies when I was there. You've got to get them out of the country in seven days once they find out they were pregnant. My last one thought she was and didn't want to take the test—we only had a month to go in the theater. [*Are they getting pregnant on purpose?*] I would say there is a good percentage of that, absolutely. One of mine did not get pregnant to go home. Two were married, my married couple got pregnant, one went home on leave and got pregnant. The other one was single. [Other soldiers] definitely think it's on purpose. "Isn't it *great* that women can go ahead and do that and be fine, us guys can't?" [But] guys go home and come up with some ailment while on leave—I call them my medical deserters. They had it all planned out what they were going to do. There is a word for that: coward.

They never know how they are going to react under gunfire. I had one soldier, I thought he was going to be one of my better soldiers, he turned out to be a dirt bag. One soldier who was very young and irrational turned out to be a pretty good soldier over there. I had a couple I called John Waynes that I was worried about. They turned out to be pretty good soldiers. I had one kid who as a senior in high school lived in an abandoned warehouse for six months. He got his education through high school in that way. Working-class backgrounds, except for officers.

Soldiers *are* coming back with PTSD—it was one in six, now it's one in three. The VA has got to get money to help them—they just don't have the resources. It took them a year to help me. I had a good quote from a marine who told me, "They only care if you're still giving, not if you gave." The VA is a broke system, just throwing money at it is not going to fix it. My dad was a VA disabled vet—the appointments would be six months apart and then they would postpone them three months more before you could get in. Why do you think it was months before I saw a psychiatrist? I think soldiers need to run through a screening, but they're going to lie to you because they're afraid they're going to have to stay longer. They should say, "We will follow up on you later."

It's a stigma that you're nuts. It's down as a mental illness. And I will tell you the truth, I'm sorry [the film] came out because I'm being treated different. Two people from my home recognized it. [There was] a negative reaction in my army outfit and a negative reaction at work. I told my girlfriend, "Tell people to talk to the people at the VA about it—absolutely—but be quiet about it." Now I have to go through the medical review boards for the Army Reserve to see if I'm fit for duty. Everyone knows I have PTSD and I'm a disabled vet now because of it.

# MICHAEL LAWRENCE
Training Sergeant, Army Reserve

Enlisted 1983, deployed Desert Storm, 1991
Second deployment age 40 (February 2004–March 2005)
Tikrit, Iraq

*A Training Sergeant and His Unit*

*Michael's mother emigrated from Jamaica in the early 1970s, settling in New Haven, Connecticut. She and her children are naturalized American citizens. Michael had planned to go to college without assistance from his mother—not wanting to burden her—but a week after graduation from high school, he was on a plane to Leavenworth, Missouri for boot camp. Michael had his best military experience to date in Iraq—he compared his unit to blades of grass that never break, but bend together in the wind. This was despite the wide age gap typical of a reserve unit, the varied backgrounds of soldiers from 35 states as well as US territories, and some non-citizens, who made up the 150-member team. His view of America as a superpower, inattentive to less-powerful nations, is informed in part by his Caribbean back-ground. He asked at the end of the interview that I leave out his personal political comments (which I have done) because the army is his career. He is married with three children.*

I joined in March of '83 and I have had no break in service since I was eighteen. I joined the Reserves because I wanted to go to college. I went to New Haven State Technical College, where I received an associate's degree in data processing—business. I continued on to Quinnipiac University, pursuing my degree in accounting. I was five classes shy of it when Desert Storm came around and I was deployed. We came back from the war and a lot of us were sick. We didn't know anything about the Desert Storm syndrome. I'm pretty beat up but I'm *rugged*—I'm holding my own.

After I got back from Desert Storm, I tried to go back to college. I'm not saying I lost interest, but in order to readjust to society and all that stuff—it didn't help me much with my focus. I went and got a full-time job at the VA, and I worked there for five years. Then I got on the New Haven Police Department. It didn't agree with me so I decided to go back to active army—my body was attuned to this type of lifestyle, of moving, the getting up, I felt healthier. ...

Then in August of 2003, Captain D. told me, "Hey, you are getting cross-leveled to go with this unit, the 283rd," but then they said the 283rd was reorganizing and disbanding, not going to go to war. In November of '03, they said, "You *are* going, the unit is going."... So we got to Fort Drum January 3, 2004, and February 17 we were in Kuwait. In five days we were sitting in Balad, Iraq and [then] up north to Tikrit, to [FOB] Speicher.

The neat thing about the unit is that from eleven soldiers we grew, in a matter of three weeks, to over 150 strong—35 states, the furthest person was from Hawaii. We had three weeks max to learn each other, know each other, get along with each other. Whatever miracle happened, we became probably one of the tightest units. You would think we were together forever. Some of the active-duty units thought that we were active components and they didn't even realize that we were reserve, the way we carried ourselves, the way we did our missions, the way we were so *on point*. It was one of the best experiences in my military career of coming together like that. We had our tiffs, our fights, but you could not come into that unit and try to break it apart. You would have 150 people jumping down your back—it was so tight-knit. First Sergeant Anderson [see previous narrative by Russell Anderson] could tell you we had our moments. It's funny—we would be playing a role and start yelling and after a while we'll calm down: "Want a Coke?" "Sure." "Sit down. Let's watch a movie."…

This particular day the bombs were coming in. We were playing cards and I looked at Sgt. G. and I said, "Hey, man—something is wrong. Let's go find our soldiers." We were in PT shorts, and we put on our battle gear, grabbed our weapons, locked, and ran across this big gravel field looking for our soldiers and rounding them up and bringing them back to the compound for accountability. We couldn't find one of our soldiers. Maybe from going to Desert Storm my senses are so *heightened*. I can feel when something is wrong.

I looked down on the ground and there was blood. Sergeant M. was with me and he said, "What's wrong, man, what's wrong—you look like you've seen a ghost." "That's Bowser, that's Bowser." And he said, "Man, that's just blood." I said, "No, it's *Bowser*. I don't know how I know it, I don't want to swear to God, but I know it is Bowser." I followed the blood to the tent—the little medical center they had there for medical emergency. "I'm looking for one of my soldiers, Sergeant Bowser." The doctor's face dropped and he said, "He was hit when the missile came in."

They were able to clamp off the main artery, trying to save his leg and save his life. I didn't wait for transportation. I just ran to the hospital and I stayed there four-and-a-half hours while they operated on his leg. They were able to control the bleeding and his artery, but now they were trying to save his leg. And if they couldn't save his leg, they needed to save the upper part of his leg, so if they have to amputate they still have a stub to put a prosthesis on.

Bowser survived, but he lost his leg. They told him they were going to save his leg, but when he went to Germany they told him his leg would never be the same. They could leave it on but he would have to *drag* it, he couldn't walk, he couldn't do anything anymore. So Bowser chose to remove the leg, and learn to do everything with a prosthesis. Now he rides his motorcycle, he is doing real well. [*How old is he?*] By now, he's [in his] early forties.

We had enough young kids to make our job difficult, and we had enough older soldiers to share their experience—the oldest one there had to be 56, the youngest one was seventeen. It was an awesome relationship. [Young soldiers] are very impatient. The first mission, they were, "I'm going to get somebody!" [But] they listened to orders—they were great. One thing we did, we made sure we had *control* of every situation dealing with our young soldiers. We didn't let them run rabid. Some of the other units let these young soldiers run rabid, do whatever they want, they were fairly disobedient. Our soldiers were well groomed for not being like that. They were some of the best soldiers. …

One of my missions, we had to train the 590th, which was a laundry and bath unit, to be gunners. Our mission was a recovery and logistics mission to go down, recover some equipment, pick up some fuel and bring it back. On the way back, me and G., we looked at each other and said, "We're going to get hit." "Yeah." "All right, we're going to run black [without headlights] as long as we can." It was toward the afternoon, the sun was starting to set and it was already getting dark [but] you can still see the road. We ran up on the enemy and the enemy didn't know we were coming, because he was looking for lights. They ambushed the center of the convoy where I was.

The truck in front of me stalled, so my truck got locked in the kill zone. All of a sudden you hear these rounds hitting the truck. Six RPGs came in—it felt like slow motion. The gun truck in front of me started returning fire; these RPGs came right across the front of the truck, and one skipped on the hood. I was shooting at where I saw the rounds coming from. Sergeant H. in the other gun truck, seeing where we were shooting, said, "Your truck looked like a Christmas tree. All I saw was your tracers going in this one bush area." The next day we heard that they pulled four bodies out of there [and] we were counting out how many rounds we expended—well over 3,000 rounds in less than five minutes' firefight. I wasn't scared, I wasn't nervous, I was calm. I guess at one time or another you have to say, "I am prepared. I am ready to go."…

When you read our creed, *"There is no one more professional than I"*—you can see it in us. When it mentions that *"I am the backbone of the army,"* you knew we were the backbone of the army, because we ran it. One of the key things to a successful unit nowadays is mentorship. I think what is going to hurt the future of the army is not having those older soldiers to teach you. That's why I'm such a *survivor.* My instructors came out of Vietnam, Korea, and they taught me how to survive not only in the army but out of the army. To be honest, to me it's harder to survive *in* society because society is a war zone of its own. ...

Well, the unique thing about the 283rd when we were over there, we had women, too. We didn't look at them as *women*, we looked at them as *soldiers*. "B"—I will never forget her. One day I was monitoring the NCS [radio] system and her convoy was hit, an IED, and her truck was the first one to get hit by it. It just missed tearing her face off. It wasn't even inches, let's say *centimeters*. And it went through her roof. She showed me what a *soldier's*—not a *woman's*—what a *soldier's* response to that is. She went into the motor pool the next day, fixed her truck, got a big can of white spray paint and rolled it on. "You missed! Try again." Got in her truck and went and did the other mission.

A lot of people don't realize that post-traumatic stress is realizing that "Hey, I am a human being and I am capable of killing, and I am capable of killing with no remorse." And some of them couldn't deal with reality and the fact that they're dangerous. They're so scared a lot of them end up killing themselves. We had a couple of cases, they shot *themselves*. The thing is, a doctor giving you a bunch of pills so you can hide from the fact that you are a dangerous piece of material that walks on two legs doesn't help you any.

[*Who considers suicide?*] The younger. We only had one older— it bothered her a lot. I was diagnosed with PTSD coming home from Desert Storm. I happened to have a good doctor, so I understood what was going on with [her]. I had a first sergeant in my corner all the time, and he said whatever [the doctor] said, we're going to do it. So we pulled her off the convoy, had her go see the doctor, the medication helped. I don't know if she could even go back and do her [civilian] job anymore.

There was a young lady from the 66th trans[port], we used to see her at the gym—we used to "hi-hi" and talk. And one night she had guard duty and I was teasing her on the radio, and she said, "Oh, yeah, I will see you in the gym tomorrow night." And I said "Why not tomorrow during the day?" "Because I got a convoy," she said. "Okay, I will be on a convoy, too, so tomorrow night is great for me, too." So that day her convoy was hit and she was burned to death. [See narrative by Leslie Ramonas, section IV.] You never knew. I was just awed because I was just sitting here, she was full of life, laughing, talking on the radio, talking about going home on leave.

I had another person there—he was from Jamaica—we were sitting there talking about food. He went up on the road on a convoy and he didn't make it home either. A lot of people didn't make it home. You never knew, so every day you went on that road, it kind of sat in the back of your mind, "Are you ready?" And I admit I'm not afraid of man, I'm just afraid that I'm not going to have my soul right. Man cannot do anything more to me. So much has been done to me already—what more can you do?

I came home with [PTSD] from Desert Storm. People said, "Oh it wasn't that bad, it was a fast war." Oh, they shot at us, they did things to us over there, too—it's just stuff that you don't hear about. We're told that we can't talk about some of this stuff—we understood. But you come home and you're in a different mode. You are in a heightened state. And you come back to a place that they say, "Oh, you're safe"—but for all I know, my neighbor is a mass killer. Being in that combat environment, it makes my senses so heightened. It makes you realize that you're capable of doing so much harm, you have to control it. I had to tell my mom, "Don't ever shake me [awake] from the top. Touch my leg and call my name out." I don't sleep soundly anymore, I sleep lightly—you touch me in any other place, I can react.

[*What is most helpful when you get back?*] Being able to talk to the other soldiers. Believe it or not, being around family is good medicine, but most soldiers can only take it for a short period of time and they start disconnecting and want to be by themselves. And the loved one thinks it's *them*. Sometimes I don't even want to be around my family, I just want to be with my fellow soldiers. I find that talking to other soldiers who have been there with you—you realize that you're feeling the same thing, you don't feel strange about yourself. And you say, "Okay, so I'm not crazy," because that's one of the heavy things. When they're not talking, they're sitting around thinking, "I must be crazy." And they don't realize, "I'm not crazy—somebody else feels this way."…

Iraq is a very diverse place—you have black, white, mulatto. They're understanding that America is diverse in that way. But they also understand that America has a bad history [of] looking down on its minorities and its women. They don't really get mad at the fact that they look down on their women—but the minority *men*. They use it to their advantage. They would come up to the black or Hispanic soldiers and say, "Why are you here? This is not your war." We understand what they're trying to say: because America has treated you so bad—why are you fighting for these people? And we look at them like, "Okay, I know where you're going. Let's leave that alone."...

Do you know what makes this the strongest army in the world? Its diversity. How many different cultures? If I could plop this army in any country, can I find a Spanish-speaking person? Can I find a Chinese-speaking person? French? Korean? That's what makes this a strong army. That's what makes this a strong nation. ...

If you talk to those people over there and you say, "Do you feel safer now than when Saddam was in office?" They say, "When Saddam was in office," because he kept the wolves off their backs. You have so many insurgents there now—you have Syria, Iran, anyone who wants to get a piece of America or England, coming in droves. They're not killing *Americans*, they're killing *Iraqis*. Saddam never tolerated that. You came in that country, he probably would execute you.

If you kill that man [Saddam] now, the civil war would be an uprising and we would have to leave the country. No way you want to do that. All the military minds know that—ethnic cleansing. The people there are tyrants, and I think it takes a bigger tyrant to control a nation of tyrants. I mean—how do you win a war? Do you win a war by making it a political war, where we go over there and discuss this? Or do you win a war by going in there and being the most ruthless person? You win a war by going in there and being ruthless. Because then everyone says, "Well, I don't want him to come in and do that to me, so I'm going to lay my arms down."

We can't go over there and be politicians. I'm sorry, but that's what it looks like we're doing. On the one hand, we're asked to be *soldiers*, on the other hand, they want us to be *politicians*. I am not a politician. I am an ambassador because I represent this country, but I am an ambassador of war. I work for the Department of Defense. My job is to defend my country and our way of life....

No, don't sleep on these people. That's our biggest mistake, as a *superpower*—as a nation of what we call "civilized" people—we *sleep*. Most of these people speak six different languages. They watch more TV than you've ever seen. Matter of fact, their biggest educator is MTV and BET. They know more ghetto slang than I know! Black and Latino culture educates the world—fashion, music. And *of course* they know more about this country than we know. That's why I said, "Do not sleep on them." That is our biggest problem as a nation—we sleep on things. When you sleep on something, you don't recognize that something is there—[if] it's not bothering my favorite TV program. They don't realize that the threat is there. They *sleep*. And someone can come in your country and in four months learn to fly a 747 and crash it into a building and know how to change course, probably disconnect some kind of tracking device. So I really have to say, *"Don't sleep on them."* ...

[Race] is a minor issue. I call it lack of exposure. You have your cliques, you have your barriers. I understand you feel relaxed around different cultures, if you're from a certain global area or a certain state area, you tend to click more with that region. Nothing you couldn't say, "Hey, educate that person... I am not going to tolerate that, zero tolerance for that." Our commander used to tease us—they used to call us the "Jamaica posse." My group consisted of G., who was Jamaican, J. was from Trinidad, one guy was from another one of the West Indies islands, it had Puerto Rico—our group that hung out consisted of two Americans, one Dominican, three or four Puerto Ricans. It was just that our cultures were probably so similar—we gelled. ...

A couple of people are in the process of becoming citizens. It would awe you if you realized that there were a lot of guys and females over there serving and they're not citizens. "I don't want my citizenship when you put me in the ground...." One of the greatest things that came out of the war [was] they were processing the citizenship a lot quicker for those people serving. They got rid of the $350 fees, [but] now that they're home, they don't know how and where to finish it. "Are they going to ask me for the $350 fee now that I'm not over there anymore, am I still waived that...?"

[Iraqis] asked me about the Bible and we sit there and talk. And what is unique about them is that they know their history, but not just the history of their country. They can actually go back to the time of Jesus and further, based on their name. They walk around with their history in their heads. They know their family tree, they know who they're descended from. I just found that fascinating. Here we are, you might as well call us the "lost culture"—we go back as far as we have photos half the time!

I think of the famous Chinese warrior [Sun Tzu]: he said, "Know your enemy. Know how your enemy eats, sleeps. You can't defeat somebody you don't *know*." If you don't try to know him, then you have no understanding of what this person is really fighting for, how much is this person really willing to give up? They have done their homework on us—through MTV, through CNN, through CNBC—they're doing their homework. How much have we done?

Every single one of us that walks into that country says, "You are not changing these people." They have been fighting, they have been arguing, they have been disputing with each other since time began. And when time ends, they are going to be fighting and arguing and disputing. We knew it. We are not going to *change* them....

I would like people to just know a little bit about what we did as a group—a family of soldiers. You end up caring so much about that person. When you're leaving each other, you wonder, how did you ever live without that person as part of your life? That's what I really want them to understand.

# FOUR

## WOMEN IN THE WAR ZONE

# TANYA M. KARST
Petty Officer 2nd Class, Navy

Enlisted 1998–2002, deployed age 22
(July–November 2001)
Persian Gulf

*Launching Tomahawks from Our Destroyer*

*Tanya grew up in New Hampshire in a family in which both grandfathers, her father, sister, and brother-in-law all served in the military. Her brother-in-law counseled her to sign a contract only when she had the job she wanted. "They definitely need people, so they put it in my contract." When her four years in the navy were up, she went to college in Washington state and then to UMass Amherst, studying biology. She expects to graduate in 2008. One of her dreams is to work with tigers in a natural setting. She is pleased that she had an opportunity to see the world, make friends, and do interesting work as a sonar technician in the navy. She was on the boat that fired some of the first Tomahawks at Afghanistan. "That first Tomahawk lit up the whole entire sky, there was just a silhouette of the superstructure. It went off the port side, and it took two hours to get there."*

After high school I took a year off. I wasn't ready for college right away. I didn't want to go—I really had no interest in it. So I enlisted from New Hampshire and went in the navy in August of '98. I went to boot camp in Chicago—the Great Lakes—under the buddy program with a girl who had graduated the year before me in high school. After graduation, I went over to the Naval Training Center. [We] were all sonar technicians (STG) and we all went to San Diego, California. After San Diego, I finally got my orders to Japan, July of '99. I knew people who were there from going to school in San Diego—I was lucky. I was actually really lucky the whole entire time....

Being in Japan, 7th fleet, it's the "Tip of the Spear." You're always the first one out there. You would go in, and you wouldn't even spend a month in port, you would be out and underway already. The ships are doing exercises right outside of the bay or somewhere else. There were plenty of times we had to go off the coast of Korea because North Korea was acting up and we had to make our presence known. They don't tell the crew a lot. They say we're going to go do this, and we're sitting off the coast of whatever piece of land just because that's what we're told to do. You do your daily lives on the ship. Unless something happens, you're never going to know why you're there. We were always miles and miles off the coast. No one really knows we're out there.

Being the "Tip of the Spear," you don't go for six-month deployments like a ship from San Diego or Norfolk. We were out for four because we had to be back. We got to sail with Australian ships and we did many of our qualifications before going to the [Persian] Gulf with the Australian ships. I remember during our qualifications I was the mount captain and I got to shoot the actual gun. We were doing a drill and qualifying people. If we failed these drills, we could not go to the Gulf, so our captain said, "You need to pass because we need to get to the Gulf."

We were doing a practice shoot for the .50 caliber machine guns. The carrier that was with us would send out a plane towing [a] drone target on this big, long cable. You'd wait for the plane to go by and the target to approach and we would have to shoot it. Out of three ships—an Australian and two US ships—I was the only one that shot it. It looks like a little airplane. The qualifiers said I was the only one to hit it. I'm not sure I actually hit it, but they were saying that's what it looked like. "Karst, you did such a good job," so I said, "*Thanks.*" ...

Back to September 11. We were in Port Bahrain. This was our second time, because the first time we weren't allowed to go in town, and the second time we pulled in, they said it was okay—you can go out in town. So it was me and a friend. We needed to stop at the base before returning to the ship. We saw one of the chiefs and he stopped us and he said, "Hey, you need to go direct to the ship, there is a recall. The Twin Towers have just been hit." We thought it was a joke, "You're kidding, ha, ha, funny." And he looks at us, "It is *not* a joke, you need to go back." As we walked down the pier, you could see all the recall flags up on all the ships, "Oh, this is for *real*." He told us that planes had hit, but he didn't say who was behind it. I don't think it was released yet—they didn't even know.

So we went back to the ship, and we're still in our civilian clothes, and we went up to sonar control, and we're getting underway. It was 9:30 at night, we *never* get underway at nighttime. Half the people were drunk, because you're out in the town and you aren't expecting to go back. Everyone was in their civilian clothes, and a lot of people were watching the news. "We are getting underway, get changed right now, go to your stations." I think everyone was still in shock. I know *I* didn't feel any emotion then. It wasn't real—like make-believe.

We're so far way, we're on the other side of the world and you can't believe that this is happening in your own country. But we got underway, we left the actual Gulf, and we went out in the Indian Ocean. We were out circling that ocean for about a week. When exactly a week passed, many wanted to shoot off what we had—obviously we couldn't do it on our own, the president had to tell us. Eventually the CO came over the 1-MC (the PA system) and he said, "Our time has come. We're going to fight back."

It was good news for most and hysteria for others. Some people actually had family in New York that worked in the Towers. I was surprised there weren't a lot of people crying. There were definitely the people that were, but a lot of people, it was too surreal for them to actually cry—it didn't dawn on them. Or it was just like an episode of some show somewhere, so far away, you aren't really thinking about it. Until that day came, we just went about our daily lives—doing circles in the ocean for weeks. What are we doing, no one really knows.

So we were out there just waiting when we got the call. That first shoot—two nights and a day—they allowed everyone to go to the fantail (which is the very back of the ship) to watch the launch. The Tomahawks came out of the *fo'c's'le*, which is the very front of the ship. Everyone had their cameras and their video recorders and we were all back there just waiting. Finally, "All right, five minutes, we're shooting our first Tomahawk." And everyone was cheering, yelling, clapping, singing songs—some of them inappropriate. Finally we heard "one minute" and our attention was back to the mission at hand.

We were off the coast of Pakistan, I'm not sure how many miles. The [missiles] flew over Pakistan and then into Afghanistan. For a while they didn't even tell us what we were shooting at. But we shot at satellite buildings so they could start the air strikes, so they could protect our jets, the fighter jets [which] do the air strikes. The first Tomahawk was really loud, and it is pitch-black out. There is absolutely *nothing*, you have to be careful going outside because you hit something and you're over the side in the ocean.

Everyone had their cameras out, so there was light. That first Tomahawk going up lit up the whole entire sky, there was just a silhouette of the superstructure. It went off the port side and it took two hours to get there. The thing that frustrated so many people: from September 11—the point that it happened—coms [communications] were shut down. We had e-mail capability, and we even had satellite phone, but everything was shut down. We couldn't talk to our families, we couldn't let them know when we were going back because it was a big secret.

We went inside from the Tomahawk shoot, we shot four or five the first night, and it was already on CNN. How can they tell people that we can't tell our families what is going on, because our coms are shut down—yet [CNN] didn't specifically give our name but they said the US had begun its strike. And we were like, "We can't tell our families?" Over a period of weeks we shot thirteen Tomahawks. We were doing circles in the ocean just waiting for future assignments. They let us know when they hit and they let us know what we were aiming at. We even had a few satellite imagery photos of the Tomahawks actually hitting.

[After September 11] I remember watching the news, and you know how they scroll stuff down at the bottom of the screen? It had names of passengers and where they were from. I remember reading the list of names—the plane came out of Boston—there were five people [from] Dover, New Hampshire. Five people from my town on those planes. That was when it really hit home—what if it was one of my friends flying, what if it was someone in my family that was flying? There were thousands of people that were hurt and killed, but there were ones on the plane from my town. So that was an eye-opener, more of a realization of what was going on. Because being in Japan, you're still on the other side of the world.

Before then, I didn't really watch the news because I don't feel that they report on anything good, so that was the first time I really heard of [al-Qaeda] and of bin Laden. I heard the name before—you heard things like bin Laden was trained in the United States. I thought to myself, why are we training these people? It's amazing—information came up about how we are training military officers from all these other countries that aren't necessarily allies with us. I don't understand why we're doing that. You know these people are *enemies*—why are we training them?

When they said they believed it was al-Qaeda, and it was for religion and that the United States was evil, I said to myself, "Who are they to say anything?" Obviously, we don't think the same, we do not have the same rationality as other people. From experiencing other cultures, being in all these other countries, I wasn't surprised. I knew that not everyone had the same views and had the same opinions of the United States. Some places that we pulled into welcomed us and some other places spat on us. That's how the world works—you're not liked by everybody. ...

[*Women in the navy?*] The military either makes you grow up or you stay a child. It's amazing to see how many people stay a child. You can't believe they let these people into the military. I understand that everyone can go in, and they have to fill quotas when you get recruited. But the bitterness, the gossip, and the *fights*, I just wanted to be by myself. I didn't get along with many of the girls. There were two or three girls out of sixty that I got along with—that I would actually call a friend. The rest of my friends were males. Some people would have their TV going all night and they would be loud and obnoxious, and you just have a curtain. A lot of girls slept with these little yellow foamy ear plugs that you can squish down in your ear.

It was just like the first years of high school, "You're looking at my boyfriend." "No, you're looking at *my* boyfriend." It was ridiculous. What I really detested was people not doing their work and then I would have to do their work. People not pulling their own slack. That was very frustrating because everyone has a *lot* of stuff to do. You have to be at quarters at 7:30 in the morning, you're working until taps, which is 10 o'clock. People not doing their job during the day make others do double. I remember saying to my work center sup[erintendent], "Why are you giving me double when they're getting nothing?" He said, "Well, at least I know it's done right the first time." [But] I'm definitely glad I [joined]. I wouldn't take it back for the world. ...

There's a lot of non-citizens in the United States military. Actually, one of my friends who was in my division, she was a Mexican citizen. There's a lot of Filipinos who aren't citizens. There are people from the Dominican Republic, Jamaica, Brazil, and we had one guy that was from Poland. While you are lower-enlisted, E-6 and below, you don't have to become a US citizen. But to become a chief, you have to be a US citizen. A lot of the Filipino people are in engineering and supply. A lot of them can't get a "secret" clearance to do things like cryptology. They can't get that clearance because they're not a US citizen. But then they don't have to pay taxes either—that really upset me. You can be in our military and you don't have to pay taxes? That didn't seem right.

I had some friends that were Filipino. Their language is Tagalog. US military rule is that you can speak a foreign language in the privacy of berthing [sleeping quarters], but out in the work area you have to speak English. They always spoke Tagalog in the workplace. They would be snickering, and laughing and talking Tagalog and they would look at you, and it is very discomforting. It was a big problem with the Tagalog language—no one knows it but them. It had an effect on morale. You can bring it up the chain of command, and ask them to speak English but it's not going to go anywhere....

[*Is harassment a problem for women in the navy?*] I experienced it myself. Verbal harassment, sexual harassment—it's there. I'm very laid back and easygoing, [so] they're lucky they said that to me, not someone else. I thought to myself, "Immature, go home, just get out of my face." That was an officer, and he said, "Hey, Karst, I want to talk to you." I thought it was something to do with work. [*What did he say to you?*] I don't want to repeat it. And he showed me things that I didn't really care to see. And the worst thing is that he had a girlfriend on the boat! I had no idea. I was like, "Oh my goodness, I'm leaving." I'm sure he thought, "If she just walks away, that's it." If he would have grabbed my arm, *that* would have been it. At times I know I should have reported him, but I walked away and I really didn't think twice about it. I don't see it going away because everyone cannot be watched all at one time. So it happens. ...

I moved to Massachusetts after I got out of the military. I wanted to come to UMass but financially it wasn't feasible. You get the Montgomery GI Bill, but you only get so much, and it only goes for so long. Before I got out, they had a $600 bonus. You put in $600 and in turn you get out more. I believe the total now for me is $40,000. Going to UMass full time, that covers two years for out-of-state—which is why I had to leave UMass for a year. It was $20,000 for a year. First of all, I couldn't afford it because you have to pay up front and they reimburse you at the end of the month. The GI Bill only gives you a certain amount of money a month and it doesn't matter how much your tuition was. I hate being in debt. I don't want to do school loans and these days you can't do it *without* school loans....

There is a maximum you can get, if you take 15 credits or 20 credits, if you max out for your money they aren't going to give you any more for your extra credits. You have to use it within ten years or whenever your money runs out, whichever is first. My money is going to run out. You don't exactly have time to get a job that pays well or work enough hours to get a decent paycheck. I have lived off this GI Bill for almost a year and it was extremely hard just living, paying for school, paying for groceries, paying for rent. Here I am, on my own. I don't get anything from my family, paying for school, paying for life, and I get nothing. I [am taking] a year off to become in-state—you don't get the VA benefits unless you are in-state. You have to be a non-student for a year to become in-state....

[*What do you think of Iraq?*] We're not concentrating on Afghanistan anymore. We definitely, as the US, need to have our presence known, but I don't think we need to be over there right now. We had a perfect opportunity to get our troops out with Hurricane Katrina. We needed people *here* to help, help your own country first, and we didn't do that. They didn't find what they were originally looking for, and now they are just digging their nose around in other peoples' business. I think our troops could be used somewhere else in a more efficient, helpful way. I think that the involvement we have is to boost ourselves—I don't think we are really helping anybody out.

We, the US, are just trying to gain power—one of the most powerful countries in the world. Never-ending—I think it is going to be a long, long time before anything is resolved over there. I'd like to think it will be successful. It's going to keep on going. There's always going to be troops over there—eventually it's going to fizzle out.... People tend to believe whatever the news puts out. In the news they kept referring to our involvement as a war, and therefore that is what the majority of Americans believed—that we were at war... before it was actually declared.

# DANIELLE MORIN
Specialist, Army Reserve

Enlisted 2000–2005, deployed age 24
(March-November 2003)
Kuwait; Balad, Iraq

*Men and Women in the Army*

*Danielle is an outgoing and expressive young woman. She developed serious back problems in the military and spent some time dealing with that situation with the VA, and ended her Army Reserve career with a medical discharge. She hopes her medical condition will improve because she would like to work in a veterinarian's office. She recounted her time in Iraq with humorous observations of her fellow soldiers and of Iraqis. She also wondered at the expectations of Americans regarding the war on terror: "You expect the government to be God-like and omnipotently know when everything is going to happen? And at the same time, no one wants to give up their freedoms?" She graduated from Holyoke Community College in 2005.*

*Danielle asked that the following disclaimer accompany her narrative: "The views expressed in this book are those of the author and do not reflect the official policy or position of the Department of Defense, or the US government."*

I enlisted in 2000, pre-September 11, in the Reserves. I walked in and I said I want the bonus and I want my monthly student payment loan and the education kicker—that was what I negotiated for. There was just about nothing that I had excluded from what I could do besides the fact that I was female. "Kicker" is a monthly bonus, not a sign-on bonus. The education kicker is an additional Montgomery GI bill. The recruiters are salesmen and they're just trying to sell the lowest product to you at the highest price.

Then after September 11, everyone called me, my mom, my sister—a complete nut case. "Are you going? Where are you going?" I'm like, "We don't even know who *did* it yet!" I'm not going anywhere. I'm in a small battalion and I just repair radios and secure communications equipment. My unit is so small they don't need us. It did take another month, but in October we were gone! We had less than 72 hours [notice] and I'm like, "Oh my goodness, I thought everybody in the world would get activated before we would." I didn't think we would be the first line of defense. I underestimated my little battalion....

I went to basic training with a girl who had her hairdryer and curling pins. "What the *heck* do you think that's for?" Maybe she thinks, "If I pack it now, as soon as we leave on AIT, we have more flexibility"—she'll be able to use them. "Gosh, it's extra stuff to carry around, just pick it up later—buy it later if you need it that bad." She looks at me and says, "For weekends off." "Weekends off? Whose army did you join?" This poor girl actually thought that she didn't have her first two weekends off, but after that she was going to have Saturday and Sunday off.

I went to Fort Jackson. "If you can, please get me Fort Jackson!"—it's known for [being] "Relaxin' Jackson."... We got activated and went to Fort Bragg. We were told, "You're probably leaving." In 2000, there were not a lot of people of higher rank who had actually ever done anything, so they were all freaked out.... But post-9/11 it was like *everyone* is leaving. It's kind of a shame people in charge were so clueless. A lot of them had only been in basic and AIT. They hadn't had a taste of the real army. At that point they had pinpointed bin Laden, that he was in Afghanistan, and they had labeled the Taliban an evil terrorist group. So we knew it was Afghanistan. We thought we were going—I think our seniors kind of jumped the gun on that. We stayed at Fort Bragg for almost a whole year.

It was at Fort Bragg that I changed my MOS. They said, we're short in intelligence and in CIA agents, which is counter-intelligence. I was an analyst—that's pretty good for me. Attention to detail, menial tasks, putting two and two together. It's time-consuming, you sift through a lot of crap to get some good intel. It's something I am relatively good at. I'm very good at mono-focusing and going straight for putting things together. It felt like it had more of a purpose to piece together the enemy's next step and what your step is, and counteracting. ...

Then we went to Kuwait and advanced to Iraq. We were going to Balad: that's 60 klicks [kilometers] north of Baghdad, an old airport that had been down since Desert Storm. We were trying to repair it, make it useful again. It took two or three days to drive and we got lost in Baghdad. We took the wrong exit off of the highway: we had no clue what the language is, and you put an MP in charge. We're circling around Baghdad. I was freaking out. Because if you drive through a hostile city that's just been overtaken and everybody and their mama has an AK-47 or a small RPG and they're all ticked off—so many people just don't have jobs or a place to live.

It was desert and palm trees in Kuwait and then you cross over into Iraq, it was looking at *National Geographic*—it didn't seem real. I'm looking out the window driving down, I try not to stare, I need to pay attention to where I'm going, but there are little kids with no shoes on the cement. I mean if you dropped a pen, I don't know that it's really worth touching this cement to pick that up because it is *hot*. [Girls wear] a little strap of a dress—that's when it hit me. They don't have roofs! That blew my mind, being from New England. If you have a house, you have to have a roof. Even if you don't have walls—you have to have a roof.

There are still nomads. They travel with their sheep from one place to another, whatever livestock they have. I see that on the Discovery Channel—not in real life. And then you're driving by, there were these kids running up to the vehicle. I'm having a heart attack, I'm going to run them over, but you're not going to stop, *regardless*. You are completely under orders not to stop because you're putting other lives at risk. You're putting everyone behind you at risk—you're separating a convoy. You trained that you do not do it no matter what goes in your way, you keep going. So they [children] are going to run out. Baghdad, that's where they're trying to climb up on the vehicle. They were like ants climbing up your leg. It was almost scary—these are *people*.

I'll never forget when I was hajji-sitting—we had escort detail. This is when Balad became a big, hopping place, we started using that as an airport. When we got there, it was a hole in the wall, we were personally putting up the defenses. This one gentleman, he spoke English very well, he was showing a picture of his wife and she looks *white* to me. I said, "She's really pale." He said, "That is actually prestigious in our country, more exotic." I said, "You are a very educated man. In our culture we don't keep the women in the house. What's the difference?" He smiled and nodded. He said, "I love my wife and she is very busy with our two children. She has so much work to do keeping the house together and the children and raising them correctly and going to school. She is educated and if she wanted to work, if she found a calling, I would never hold her back. But I would not *burden* my wife with working when I can provide for her."

The lower women do work out in the fields. It makes sense that [with] six women, you have one or two guys guarding them with an AK-47. They need to be protected (a) from wildlife that is starving and wants to get at your sheep and (b) who's to say there aren't serial killers out *there*—they're just too busy with other things to label it as a serial killer.... There's no structured system for [Iraqi women] to run away, there's no divorce, there's no WIC [US poverty program for women, infants, and children]. In Baghdad, you saw women that had every inch covered and then you saw another woman in a T-shirt and shorts and she's on her way to the store. There are educated women in suits walking down the street—it's still like old world/new world in Baghdad.

My impression is we definitely saved [Iraqis] from a tremendous evil, it *really* was right up there with Hitler. [Saddam Hussein] hadn't made it as far along, didn't have the resources that

Germany did at that point. He was cut off and isolated. Weapons of mass destruction, we're still looking for them. They could be just hidden underneath the ground, we're not going to find them—you can't go ten feet deep in every bit of sand.

A lot of what we're trying to do now is save our own butt, just making sure we're not getting shot. That to me was an amazing job, the Iraqi police. They're far more courageous than an American would need to be. They have to isolate themselves from their family, they have to be removed from other family members, so they don't know where they are, because they will be tortured to find out where their family member is. Not only are their lives at stake but their entire families. They can't go home without worrying that they are bringing home something. ...

We were getting some good intel off of one family that lived off the base. They told us where people were, a large amount of weapons. It was kind of funny, we even got a tank and a small jet out of those people! We were getting into a fight with another intelligence unit that was saying, "No, those people are bad and we know that they're storing things." And [we] go over there and have dinner with them every Wednesday. We know they've got their AK-47s and there's one RPG in the house, and that's okay by our standards because they need to protect themselves. People say, "Why should you let any of them have an automatic weapon for the household?" Even if you aren't a good guy, you probably need an AK-47 to defend yourself against insurgents even more than we do, because anyone who has money is going to get looted by people that don't have money.

Then we started letting more people on base, letting them on to come fill our sand bags. They were just trying to feed their families and they also take pictures and sell them to people. That was their number-one thing: they saw a female on guard duty, they want us to take off the cover [helmet]. "No, I'm not taking off my helmet for anybody!" They always tried to make the girls take off their hats. I really don't care enough about these people to leave myself exposed, to take off my Kevlar and my vest—are you nuts? They would try to sell things, chunks of watermelon, sunglasses. They are very much traders.

Some guy was trying to sell a howitzer (our soldiers were pretty sure) back to us. It's a large gun, it's larger than an RPG, it's larger than mortar, you're talking about some heavy-duty stuff and the guy was trying to describe it. He simulated lighting it off, and then going over and ducking down, *boom!* He was covering his ears, pretending the explosion went off. He simulated it twice more, this guy is trying to sell to us what he thinks is a howitzer. He said *hawa, hawa*—he was trying to use our word "howitzer" to describe it. Thank goodness one of the guys said, "No, I think he's trying to say something." Oh my God. Our munitions that they stole off the base—they're trying to sell back to us!

Then of course a bunch of [US soldiers] came out, surrounded him, dropped him. He got pulled off, he went to jail, he was going to get the ever-living crap scared out of him. They were trying to find out where he got all this from. But even going to jail was not a bad thing. In the beginning when we got there, they got at least two square meals a day, which is 6,000 calories a day [a high estimate—ed.]—most people didn't get 1,000 calories a day. In effect, people were committing felonies just to get a good meal. The Red Cross comes in, "Oh, they're being tortured, they're being confined, so many people in such a small area." Do you see how they *live*? They live with twenty people in a house, not like we're doing something that is completely against their [culture]. Go ask *them*. Most of them are happy to be in our little jails.

And then the Abu Ghraib thing. That's the main reason we detain people, to try to get some intelligence. So you figure out who are the bad guys from the good guys. You're not going to get any good intelligence from torture. You can't guarantee the kind of intelligence you're going to get from people who are enduring mental torture, stripped naked. There's a whole mentality that I have the power because I am clothed and you don't. It goes back to Egyptian days. Anyone that's on a higher level will be more adorned and have more clothing on. It wouldn't make sense to touch them at that point, to strip them down to their underwear, [but] it's easier to get intelligence out of somebody if they think they're inferior to the one they're talking to. I don't understand it because from a strictly strategic point of view it doesn't even make sense. Above and beyond that, it's morally wrong. You've got to be sick.

But it was an isolated incident, it was happening with a small group of people—it was okayed by a sergeant there. It was an isolated spot, but they made it seem like everybody that had ever been detained by the military was treated that way, that the military okays and condones sexual torture. I think it was the individuals—they tried to blame it that it was army policy. I know someone who was sent to jail for splashing water on an Iraqi, his family. He only splashed *water* on him, he was just trying to take control of the situation. So you're no good as an interrogator if you're not seen as superior to the person you're trying to get information out of. But they tried to blow the whole thing out of proportion.

―

[Being a woman in the army] is very different. That has completely changed my mind on women in the service. I think there does have to be a higher standard for women and it does become a burden sometimes. I was completely gung-ho—women can do anything a man can do. There are certain things like being 5'1", bleeding every month, not being 230 pounds—there are physical differences that need to be recognized. I'm not saying that women don't have a place in the military.

You weren't living in hardened buildings. We had put up our own tents. The wind had blown off part of the top. Some big guy walked by and he's like, "You're going up." "You're not going to be able to throw me up!" It's fifteen feet tall. "How much do you weigh?" And I told him and he said, "Oh, I can bench that, I can definitely throw you up. I bench double you." So I got thrown up on top of this tent. I'm putting that top back together, trying not to fall off.

I think when there's a group of men it's easier to [have] Abu Ghraib be acceptable. I think women tend to think more independently. There's that camaraderie and women do break it up. It took me nine months to become one of the guys. Women are initially labeled—I hate to say this—but it's pretty much a knock on the door, here you go, dyke or a slut, and they're trying to figure out which one. We find ourselves in that spot because you're either going to sleep with them or you're not.

It's definitely different being a woman. It's hard for a woman to change units because you have to establish it all over again. You're new meat on the block. [*Dating?*] It depends on the culture of that unit. In my unit it was a very negative thing, so it just wasn't worth it, at least until you were established. Sometimes there's this, "Well, she slept with one guy, she'll sleep with any guy." And it's different when you're stuck in Iraq. There's no weekend off.

In Iraq every time you went to the bathroom there was no way to not walk into someone on your path. There are some women who even take advantage of it. Personally, I kind of shut down, I couldn't do it. All of my work was so interactive with all the men, it just would not work out. I saw a lot of [females] completely ostracized. They did it to themselves—they can't expect not to face the consequences of what they did. They bring hostility [to other females]. Even if it's a meaningful relationship, you're not one of the guys. If you leave the unit to go elsewhere, you're kind of saying, you're not worth my time but some other guy in another unit is.

I love it when they say [prison guards] flushed a Qur'an down the toilet. This is what kills me about the media. They obviously have exaggerated it because I don't know of any good toilet that can flush a Bible down. If you want to say, "It got thrown in," that would be fine. Maybe it happened, maybe it didn't, but there's no way that it is physically possible to flush a Qur'an down the toilet. Even if you do, you're going to clog the little sucker up. You're not going to get but two pages down there. It is not physically possible. We know that that story has been fabricated. That's what drives me nuts because it makes it sound [like] that's happening everywhere because one idiot did it.

It's so like the American public to say September 11 should never happen again. Society should know, the government should know when we are going to get bombed. Just ask them really nicely, I'm sure the terrorists will tell you! Don't do anything harsh now! Common sense, people! Pick one side or the other. Either be willing to live in a little bit of fear but know that you're treating everybody completely justly, fairly, everybody gets equal treatment. One or the other. Either be okay with fear or be okay with letting the government do their job. You expect the government to be God-like and omnipotently know when everything is going to happen? And at the same time, no one wants to give up their freedoms?

# LYDIA RODRIGUEZ
Specialist, Army National Guard

Enlisted 2001–2007, deployed age 35
(May–December 2003)
Camp Spearhead, Kuwait

*A Mother Goes to War*

*Lydia joined the Army National Guard at age 33 as a mother of three preteen and teen daughters. She was born in Puerto Rico and emigrated when she was eleven. She was a transportation specialist in Kuwait. As an older soldier and a mother, she was particularly aware of how immature and dangerous some young soldiers could be. She was careful who she rode with because she wanted to keep her safety in her own hands. She speaks about her daughters, their pride in her military service, and her own pride in being part of an historic effort. "My kids are proud of me, I know. They're always saying, 'My mom did this, my mom did that.' They want people to know that their mommy wore combat boots—she was out there kicking butt." Lydia graduated from Holyoke Community College in 2006 and hopes to be a writer.*

I joined the military late, I was 33. I was one of the oldest in the company. It was something I always wanted to do. When I was married, my husband was in the navy. I didn't see the time for me to join at the same time because I had kids. Once I got divorced, it was like I needed to do something with my life—something exciting, something challenging, and something fun. And I got interested in the National Guard. Finally, I decided I'm going to do [it]—I joined. To my surprise, I did very well—better than most of the females in the company. But I just joined because I was looking for a challenge, something in my life. And of course two years later I did find a challenge. I got deployed. I didn't want to go, but something inside me—I wanted to. I guess that my kids were the reason I didn't want to go and leave them behind. But there was something inside—I want to go, this is the *action*....

I arrived [at Camp Spearhead, Kuwait] and it was a beautiful night, and I said I cannot wait for morning to see the city. In the morning I got out of my tent and walked outside—and it was an oil-burning facility, they burned oil, sulfur. The light we saw at night was the oil burning, but it looked just like New York City. Exposed to that pollution for nine months—it was bad. There were some days sulfur was so thick you could taste it in your mouth. The sky was black most of the time. I remember I said to [my buddy], "You know what, if the Iraqis don't kill us—this pollution will. In a couple of years, don't be surprised if you go home, you will have some kind of cancer or something." Sometimes I wonder why she passed away when she did.... She had a lot of problems with breathing. Sometimes I wonder if it was related to that. ...

For some reason I always ended up doing security. On one of our missions, one of the trucks broke down. I pulled over with another Humvee from our unit, driven by one of the sergeants. Of course we were in the middle of nowhere on one of the lonely highways of Kuwait—six of us. And maybe 50 feet away, I noticed a van parked, and there were maybe 25, 30 men in civilian clothes. Guns and weapons come out, they hid. So of course we lock and load. We all sat there and waited to see what was going to happen—will we be attacked? I'm scared.

We all dropped and took cover. I didn't realize *where* I dropped. I was taking cover anywhere safe, and the sergeant next to me said, "Do you know where you're lying?" And I looked and there was a big hole for camel spiders, big camel spiders, *huge* camel spiders. These camel spiders can jump ten feet up and they're dangerous, they're fast. I was on top of the hole, but I guess there was nobody home! So of course I freak out and start rolling down the sand. It was a scary experience—thank God nothing happened. We all made it back safe.

On another occasion, I was left behind—everyone was gone and it was me and a guy from my unit. We were driving along the highway and two huge trailers pulled [up]—one on the right and one on the left—and I'm in the middle of these two trailers. One other soldier and two M-16s—that's it for us. I slow down, they slow down, I go fast, they go fast. I mean they did this for about forty minutes and they just wouldn't go. I told the soldier that was with me, "You better lock and load so fast," and he was so scared. He was a short guy—he was more scared than I was. He was saying, "Do you know where we're going?" And I said, "Don't worry, I've been through this before a couple of times. Just have your weapon ready, and if you see something, shoot."

So I'm driving with one hand and in my other hand I have my rifle. I was in a truck (they're five tons), but the trailers were bigger, and of course there were two trailers, two people in each, so four against two. I was smart enough to say, we've got to relax, keep on driving, not shoot, not even look at them, and they'll leave us alone. After a while they went somewhere else. When I got to camp, I was so mad. I said to the sergeant who was supposed to stay with me, "I can't believe you left me up there, do you know what we went through?" He said, "I'm sorry," and I said, "No, you cannot be sorry." He was supposed to be there, too, and he left me behind.

God was on my side every minute that I was there. God was there because there are so many things that happened. The deployment area we used to work on: one day we went to work and they had the whole perimeter covered, they had the MPs. I'm halfway there, and this MP sees me, "You've got to go back." "Why?" "There are mines everywhere in the ground." "You've got to be kidding me! I work here every day, I walk this ground." I mean, I *know* God was on our side because those trucks are heavy, driving around the gravel. I did an about-face and I followed the same steps back that I came [on]. I was scared but I was more *mad* that we were working in the area they're supposed to check—make sure we are safe. Sometimes the military doesn't use common sense. If it makes sense, they don't do it. If it's stupid, I'm sorry to say, they do it. You try telling them why don't we do this instead of this, and of course they don't listen to me because I'm a lower rank. And of course it makes sense that no one listens to me because it has to not make sense for them to do it. It was crazy…!

Some of the guys that were guards were mean. Over there, there was a saying that [their] culture was, "Women were for reproduction and males are for pleasure." Some of the soldiers would see the handholding and the affection between males, and they would hate it and would poke them in the back with their rifles. They were usually the younger kids, trying to show off: "I'm in control, I'm the one with the rifle, I'm the one with the uniform." They used to get out of hand, call them names, they weren't too nice. But the older soldiers were more respectful, they would talk with them, try to make some conversation.

[The] difference between the young and the older soldiers— the older take things more seriously. They do their job. The younger seem to be more irresponsible. Some guys, the minute they have been deployed, "This is my chance to kill somebody." That's what they've been thinking about, "I am going to kill, and kill, and kill." They will mistreat [the Iraqis] and call them names and provoke them, and sometimes they would be driving around and doing something they shouldn't be doing. If I was sitting next to them, I would be like, "You know what? I'm here. Don't you ever put my life in danger like that again." I hate saying it, but how can you put someone else in danger because you're being funny or a show-off? Think about the person that's with you, because what if someone shoots at you and they hit me instead because you did something?

That's why on missions I would want to go with the older people or the people that were younger, but they were mature, because not all of them were like that. Some people—they just didn't care about dying. They would come out and say, "I don't care if I die." And I would not want to go anywhere with them. I would tell the sergeant, "I'm sorry, I don't want to go on mission with him." Why? Because I want to go home. …

There was no privacy. I was very uncomfortable because as a female, I have nowhere to put my personal things. I have a guy here, a guy here, we had women and men in one tent—there was no privacy. We had cots right next to each other—you move and there's his shoulder. They snore, they stink, they don't shower and it was hot. Not to mention when it's time to change, we have trailers that have showers, but they were a walk. Sometimes in the middle of the night you have to get up and get changed. It is like, "Oh my God, I don't want to have to walk all the way down there, because we have five minutes to get dressed." I had brought a big thick blanket, and I would just go under the blanket and change real quick.

But there were some females that would change there with no problem at all. I remember one time I said to them, "Don't you guys care? Don't you have any ethics? Cover yourself! I mean, you don't have to expose yourself." They would take their clothes off like nothing. There was one girl I think was 20, 21—she acted like a 15-year-old kid. She would stand up—she wouldn't even sit while changing, try to hide.

Of course when you're like that, your reputation goes down. But in this particular female, she would do things a ten-year-old would do—immature. I would look at her and think my oldest, my youngest [daughters] wouldn't do that. I look at her and I say, "I'm supposed to count on her?" I'm not saying she wasn't smart— it was the way she acted. She thought we were in the Girl Scouts, selling cookies. And this is *reality*. We're carrying an M-16 and we might get killed—wake up and smell the coffee! Her main thing was boys around the camp....

I ended up going to Germany. I was there for a whole month because I was sick—I had so many tests that had to be done. It's like I was in a battle with myself deciding what I want to do. I wanted to go home and see my kids, but at the same time, there was something telling me that I have to go back... believe it or not, I missed Kuwait. It's crazy to say, but when you spend so much time with people they become family—when I left, it was like leaving family behind. I miss the action and you get used to a routine, doing the same thing every day.

―

I came back and took a bus home. I was shaky and I panicked as we drove home.... I was home for a while and I still couldn't drive.

I could get in my car, know how to do everything, but be shaky, like not knowing what I was supposed to do. It was a weird feeling—like you're driving somewhere where you drive every day, and one day you're kind of confused. It's like your mind isn't there. I was constantly looking to my mirror, watching to see who was following, and my kids would say, "Stop it, it's bothering us." One car was following me one time, he wasn't really following me, but I thought he was because he was going where I was going. I kept looking in my mirror—why is he still right there, what does he want?

I'm home, I'm safe, but still scared that something is going to happen. Sometimes you think out loud and my kids are like, "Mom, are you *okay?*" "I'm fine, I am fine." And they kind of look. I remember my ex-husband called me sometimes and says, "The kids are worried, they are 'are you okay?'" And I said, "Yeah, I am." "They say you've been acting strange, you cry for no reason, you lose your temper—are you okay?" And I say, "Yeah, I'm fine." It was just that my whole personality changed.

I just wasn't myself. I felt like a stranger in my own house. I was there—but I feel out of place. And I feel everywhere I went like I didn't belong there. I had gotten used to the life over there, the routine, how people were, the weather. But the worst thing for me was that I just couldn't sleep. We worked eighteen hours straight and the rest was the free time for sleep. But I couldn't sleep more than three hours. So when I came back, I couldn't sleep either. And the nightmares started and that was worse—why am I going to go to sleep if I'm going to have another nightmare anyway? It was always the same thing—it was always someone following me and following me and I'm trying to hide. Why, why—what am I hiding from?

⌒

I was born in Puerto Rico and I came to the US when I was eleven. Even when I came here I didn't feel the way I felt coming back from Kuwait. I guess it was different because when I first came as a child to the US, I had to learn the language. I still can't pronounce things right—but I don't care. But over there it's different because your life depends on it. If you don't adapt and you don't train yourself and make yourself learn things fast, you're not going to make it.... It was harder to come back home from Kuwait than it was coming here from Puerto Rico.

To know that when my kids have kids and their kids have kids, "My great-grandmother and my grandmother was there," and that makes me feel I am honored. Like when I put on my uniform, I feel proud—not the regular uniform, the class A, the dressy one. I am so proud of who I am, of what I have done, of where I have been. Nobody can take it back. For me, it was just putting it on and having people look at you. And the feeling that my kids are proud of me, I know. They're always saying, "My mom did this, my mom did that." They want people to know that their mommy wore combat boots—she was out there kicking butt.

That makes me feel good. My kids support me. Even though they go, "Mommy, don't go away again," they are proud of me. The picture from the Memorial Day parade in 2005 was put up at my ten-year-old daughter's school on the big board. "This is Alyssa Lopez's mom," and they had a big arrow pointing at me. Of course she was so proud, "Mommy, you were up there, everybody saw you." It's a good feeling. I'm honored, proud not just being in the military but to have served during a time that I know is going to go down in history. People are going to know that Specialist Rodriguez served [in] Operation Iraqi Freedom. So that's something that I can have for the rest of my life and that's a good feeling....

See, America is a free land, you get to pick and choose what you want—I can't tell you that you have to be Catholic. There, in Iraq and Kuwait, it is more like Cuba, they're used to this—this is the way of their living. Even though there are the few that don't like it and want to escape from it, it's just a small number, ten percent would like things to change. The other ninety percent— they get used to it even if it's not what they want. We go over there and we want to change the way they are, but that's the way they want—that's their culture, their way of living. So I think you're never going to change them, they're a different country. If you came to Puerto Rico and said, "You cannot speak Spanish here," *force* people—to us, this is our culture, the way life is supposed to be. The same thing for them. For us to go over there and say we want to change your whole way of living, I don't think that's going to happen. And I think that's why this is going to go on for a while.

# SHANNON KENNEDY
## Sergeant, Army Reserve

Enlisted 1998–2006, deployed age 22
(May 2003–August 2004)
Ramadi, al-Asad Airbase, Iraq; Kuwait

*Making Friends in Iraq*

*Shannon is an empathetic and thoughtful young woman, recently trained as an occupational therapist, now working on her master's degree. She plans to work in psychosocial settings, including using pet therapy because she is a great animal lover. After eight years, she has left the Army Reserve. She joined when she was seventeen, which meant her parents had to sign her contract. She served with the 82nd Airborne, in the 94th MPs, a military police company out of Londonderry, New Hampshire, doing administrative work and also helping her unit train Iraqi police. She made friends with many Iraqis, believing strongly that that was part of her mission. She also was acutely aware of the toll of the war on children: "They would send children up to the gates with 'I'm ticking. I'm ticking.' They had a bomb in their jackets." She had previously been a reservist in Bosnia.*

We shipped out at Easter [2004]. We were in Iraq for a total of fifteen months because we got extended twice while we were over there. We were kind of the forgotten company. We were a reserve company. We saw active-duty components come and go, whereas in the Reserves, we only have a captain as our highest-ranking person, so he can't say much. "Hey, you guys are still here? You still have the equipment, you're going to do this job, you're not going home yet." As a group we never lost a soldier while we were over there, 166 went, 166 came back. We had some injuries, but everyone came home.

We were on the western side of Baghdad, some of us in Ramadi, in Qusay's—one of Saddam Hussein's sons—palace. His palace was all bombed out, the people had taken everything out of it, but that was our base camp. That's where we set up because the walls were still up, so there was good security.... They didn't have enough military police people, so I became one. I did the convoy escorts with them, patrols around Ramadi to make sure everything was going well. Since I was admin, me and this other sergeant would go and pick up the mail for everyone in Baghdad. It's about an hour and 45 minutes to get there.

People were very kind to us when we first got there [May 2003]. They were very polite, always smiling, so everything seemed to be going well. It was towards the end of our stay things started to get worse. We trained Iraqi police officers in an academy. The classes went well and the people were very interested in it, "we want to fix our country" kind of thing. But then we had a graduation, and people are firing on their *own* people because they're associated with the US. Then the people who didn't care for us started to come out, to get bigger and stronger. When we first got there, there weren't any mortars fired at us, there wasn't anything, and then three days afterwards they started to see what they could do— "How far can we push you guys?" It's not everyone, [but] there are those few people who just make it worse for everyone.

[*Were there deaths at your graduation ceremonies?*] Yes. I can't tell you the exact numbers. Some people did end up passing away. But then it just comes with the territory. You get used to it. It's sad to say, but that's how the people are over there. Even children. They would send children up to the gates with, "I'm ticking. I'm ticking." They had a bomb in their jackets. The people who are trying to hurt us don't care about their own people. Then the people who actually *do* want us there *do* care for us. You can tell who they are.

All the kids know some little bit of English. They knew "mister" and some sentences. They knew what MREs [meals ready to eat] were, they knew candy, Skittles, M&Ms—that's what they wanted. They do get television, they get American channels. A lot of them listen to Justin Timberlake, Britney Spears. Those younger girls are like, "Oh, we like Justin Timberlake." I *loved* the kids over there. There was one mother who had two girls; if I had crayons or coloring books, I gave them to the little girls. My mom sent some things. I would give them shoes. [The mother] was a professor at the college, and she lived outside Ramadi but she would bring her two little girls. Those are the people you feel bad [for]... what happened to them? What are they doing now? I always tried to interact with the people over there. I think that's what we *should* be doing.

In the police academy, since I'm a female, all the boys would go, "Can I give you a ring?" I don't want the ring. But I would play thumb wars with them, if you know the thumb war game—just little things, just to make them laugh. And to make them listen, actually. They won't stand in a line, they all crowd, they all want to be first and they all want to come through the door at once. We would pay the people that were working with the Americans. We would bring the money and they would all be crowding the gates— I think it's just their culture. Maybe they never really get anything—it's such a joy to get something. They were so excited about the uniforms, about getting the little piece of paper with their photo on it. They wanted a photograph with the girls [army women]. "Me and her, me and her." Like, "Okay!"...

Some would bring in pictures saying, "This was a friend—this happened." They *would* bring it up, but they would never say how they felt about it. "I lost my wife, I lost this child," but they would never say, "I want to make it better." Or maybe they couldn't relate that to me because they only knew "brother" and showing a picture. All of them would want to talk if you just gave them the time of day, if you just gave them a little bit of common courtesy. I didn't really teach at the police academy. I mostly did their ID badges while we were there....

Our company had a dog over there, which brought up morale—"Mo." The commander said that we could have a dog. So we went and found one, there were a lot of dogs over there. Iraqis do not keep dogs as pets. I have a little picture of my dog in my wallet and it's sitting on a couch in the living room and they go, "In house?" And I go, "Yeah, in house," and they look at you funny.... Saddam, this is what one of the Iraqis told us—I don't know if it's true or not—supposedly if you brought five dead dogs or cats to one of his palaces, he would give you money, because I guess that's what they ate for dinner. [*For dinner?*] Maybe you were supposed to clear the streets of them—that could be an idea, too.

They wouldn't say much about him [Saddam Hussein]. If they see a picture of him, they would say "Saddam no good," because they're with us. Do they really believe that or not, I don't know. There were bumper stickers when we went over there—because they hadn't found him yet—in Arabic saying, "Where is he?" We were there when he was found and all of a sudden all these shots went out in Ramadi, and we were like, "What the heck is going on?" The people were celebrating. At weddings they fire up in the air. All of a sudden, *they* knew before we knew and he was two-and-a-half hours away from us when he was found, so word travels fast. It was like, "What's going to happen now we've caught him?"

His sons were killed when we were over there. Abu Ghraib happened when we were over there. A lot of the people in my company handled prisoners and I don't know if people had to go to such extreme measures. [*What would you say the problem was?*] Actually, it was individual soldiers. The leadership couldn't know the extreme details. The individual soldiers were taking pictures of them in those positions—that's their own doing. I don't feel that anyone was telling them to do it. If someone was telling them to do it, then it was a failure of the leadership. They should have been checking more on the night shift—it was the night shift that was doing that. Because we all went through how to treat people, we all go through that training. And we're all humans... President Bush didn't know everything that was going on. ...

My company being extended twice, we had some very outspoken individuals. We had family members going to the Pentagon to try to get us home because we had been extended twice. We were the longest company overseas.... The sergeant major of the army came to us and told us that we are a good company, "We thank you for your time."

We did not have top-notch equipment. We were a reserve company. When they extended us for the second time, they added up-armored equipment to our Humvees, which just weighed them down and made them operate even worse. We were out on the roads—more so than other companies. Bush—I mean, everyone is kind of upset at first, but it's not him that makes the decisions. That was a huge issue with us—a *huge* issue. A lot of soldiers found a big piece of metal, they stuck it to the Humvee door. There wasn't enough planning involved. There were companies that didn't go out on the road that had up-armored Humvees just driving them around the base camp.... We did have a supply person down in Kuwait. He could get us toilet paper and extra pants and shirts, but not the up-armored equipment or the armored vests. ...

[In Iraq] there's no control, there's no law. Each sheikh has his own little tribe of followers—they have to become one [people]. There is a big power issue, which Saddam installed. You can't just find someone and expect it to happen overnight. And you just hope that the next generation of children that are growing up in the school system over there now are learning more things. Maybe something that one American said to them will hit them and they will say, "You know what, they're trying to help us." Maybe the next generation will be better for the country, but it is definitely not going to happen overnight.

I think they did [Iraqi elections] a little too fast. Even with us training the police, we went in a little too fast. You've got to let them settle from what just happened. Let people kind of process everything, figure out what they're going to do. The first election went poorly, but there *are* educated people over there that can make decisions and can handle things, but they are just outweighed by the few that do dramatic things. Everyone should vote—they have the right to. For them to be holding that ballot, they had an X to show that they had voted, and they were so happy to show it. "I did this." Over here some people think of it as a chore.

The women are treated very differently. In [the] Ramadi area where I was, females were really not seen during the day with their husbands. Their husbands had a friend they were always seen with. We found a book when we were training once with Saddam's picture on it, and inside he showed the female how to bathe, how to wash dishes. It was a book of etiquette of what the female should do. A woman would stand behind her husband and let *him* eat and then she eats. She does most of the farm work outside, the husband goes off into the city to work.

I would have to post security and search the females at the college when we were teaching in the academy, and one female came in—total black over her face, her hands, everything. To search her I felt bad. Other females, they don't touch each other really. She was crying. I felt I was invading her space, but we had to protect ourselves. She understood that, but I don't think she would be continuing to want to come in. She had total black all over her face. I couldn't see her face, but I know she could see me. There are some very educated women, but Saddam just pushed them out of the system.

The sheikhs still have everything. They called all the sheikhs to a meeting at our base camp and I was pulling guard duty at the gate, some of them would smile at me. "I can walk with you in America." They're just trying to get you to come with them. The police chief had a lunch and you don't talk while you're eating. You eat and then you go to a different table to talk. Me, I'm sitting there all smiles, eating my chicken, what have you, and then I tried to talk with them. Little sentences and the interpreter said, "Shannon, you don't talk until *afterwards*." They use one hand for bathroom use and one hand for eating. That's a good thing to know....

I'm a very positive person and there was another sergeant with me who was very positive also. We would play "Sorry!" games—a lot of board games became rituals. We wrote letters. We were there for Christmas. I made wreaths out of mosquito netting, and tied little army bows on them. Me doing things for other people made me happy. Morale is a big, big problem. There were some pretty low lows. A lot of people had families back home, children, wives. For me, it was probably good because I didn't have as much to worry about. But still my mom had ups and downs, I missed my animals. Everyone who wanted leave got leave in our company. Our company would say, your platoon had so many slots, they figure out who is going to get it. Some platoons drew names out of a hat, other platoons said, "Hey you have three kids, I'm single, you go ahead of me." When we got extended for the second time was the time I got to go. I wanted everyone who had families to go home first. It went by so fast and then you're back. While you're away for those two weeks, you miss those people. You worry about those people, what's going on. Because you can't just call them up and say, "Hey, how are you doing? What's happening?"

9/11 happened when I came back from Bosnia and then Iraq happened. It gave me more of a sense of pride. All of a sudden, the military came back into focus again: these people are doing this for us, for this country—American pride. It's sad it happened, it shouldn't have happened, but I think it made us only stronger. And it has made us more as a unit, as a whole. I was very happy serving in the military at that time. I would have [gone] in a heartbeat. It was sad that someone could do such a drastic thing to our country. It affected me in a lot of ways. In Iraq, it kept you more aware of hate, secure information—you shouldn't say, "Oh, I live in Orange, Massachusetts." Some Iraqi would pick that up, maybe they would know something or know a connection. It just keeps you aware. For me, I think it was patriotism. It was just the sense of "I am going to do something good."…

Of 166 of us, there were only 18 women. You have to prove yourself before you gain respect. There are a lot of things you can do to *lose* that respect from your fellow male soldiers. But we're showing over there that we can handle just as much as they can. My height is a *huge* problem. None of those Humvees for me. Say you can't carry something. Well, you do something a little bit extra that day to show that person, hey, I can do this. Some of my bags I would put on a table and then put on me, because if I tried to pick it up, I would be down with the bag. I was always trying to do it myself because some guys are nice and they will want to pick it up for you. But I'm independent, "Let *me* try." I know of a little itty-bitty thing who was a first sergeant. She was the nicest lady, but she knew how to run her company. [*What about sexual orientation?*] We had a female over there that was very short-haired and basically looked like a guy, but she had so much respect from the company….

We had a female who got her weapon taken away from her. She was very bad, went home on leave, came back and she was a lot better. She was afraid because her son was left at home, she and her husband were kind of rocky. It's *so* hard being so lonely. And then having all the added stress of all the mortar attacks, a lot of people have a hard time handling it. She was one of the soldiers who would wear her Kevlar to bed. She would have a hard time sleeping.

I roomed with a lady in her forties. She left four kids at home, one with autism, and she could have chosen to stay home. She chose to go because she had never been activated before and she was almost getting her twenty-year letter. She goes, "You know what, it's just my turn to go." She was a single mother with four kids. I can't imagine being her. The twins went to the grandparents and the other two went to the father. You find other people to take care of them and you set up a family care plan, but she was gone for twenty months. We just *clicked*. We're different in age but [she was] a very kind individual, mature.

## LESLIE RAMONAS
Staff Sergeant, Army Reserve

Enlisted 1977–2005, deployed age 44
(January 2004–March 2005)
Tikrit, Iraq

*Losing Another Woman*

*Leslie Ramonas deployed at age 44 and has now left the Reserves with a disability. She retired from the Salt Lake City Police Department in 2006 and is a part-time student at the University of Utah, pursuing a BA. She grew up in Hispanic Los Angeles, enlisted at seventeen and was an experienced soldier when she went to Iraq after serving in both the Air Force and Marine Reserves. She was a mother figure to a number of young soldiers in Iraq. In a convoy attack, she saw someone she knew burn to death, and was treated for PTSD both in Iraq and since her return. She has maintained a 22-year relationship with her lesbian partner, and they have an adopted 14-year-old son who is talking about becoming a pilot. Leslie wonders at the military attitude toward gays: "I suppose you heard about the gay soldier who was kicked out for being gay? He was an Arab linguist. Are we stupid or what?" Leslie fixes her own Harley Davidson "Fatboy," which she rode to Sturgis, South Dakota, in the summer of 2006. "Psychologically, I am beginning to heal, but am still haunted by the painful memories of Iraq."*

I grew up in Los Angeles in the inner city, a rougher area—East LA. I was just an adventurer and I wanted out of there. I felt like I was going nowhere at home in that neighborhood. It's not like my parents could afford college. I was a senior, and I had one credit that I needed that I didn't get—*one*. So I went into the [air force] and came home on leave and took the GED test.

I married a guy that I had met in Okinawa—I was 21 at that time. Then I got stationed in Korea—I had a great time. Got divorced and got out of the military. I got a job as a police officer. I ended up as a marine reservist, then ended up going Army Reserve, July '03. "Send me, I'll go." I was a truck driver. I got deployed to Iraq January 2, 2004…. [Previously] as a police officer, I went on a "mercenary" gig in Kosovo for the UN and was an investigator over there just after the Kosovo war. So I had been shot at and all that kind of stuff, but nothing, *nothing* compared to Iraq.

[In Iraq] I was a buck sergeant. I kind of took care of the kids—I felt like a mom. They did treat me like a mom—the guys would come to me, I felt like they were my sons. For example, we arrived in Iraq, came in on a C-130—they come in from way up high and they just drop that plane down in the middle of that runway, very unnerving. I wasn't nervous at all, but the guys were nervous and scared….

We were milling around, we were tired, we didn't know where we were. It was dark and we were very disoriented. All of a sudden, there is a firefight right there on the perimeter. We were probably 400 meters from the perimeter, and the soldiers who were guarding that perimeter, up in that tower, started shooting at people that were outside the fence. I guess the bad guys were trying to aggress us. We were just scared to death—especially the kids. All of a sudden, an Apache helicopter shows up and he starts shooting the crap out of stuff—and keep in mind, it's very dark and all this stuff is lighting up. So there are tracers, big booms, and gunfire. Okay, we were kind of nervous, but still interested. "Look at *that*! Oh my gosh! *What* did we get ourselves into?"

The next morning we were cleaning our weapons and this young soldier came to me and sits down beside me, and he said, "I couldn't sleep last night." And I said "Why?" And he said, "Because every time I heard somebody walk by the tent on the rocks [gravel] I thought it was them." And I said, "Who is 'them'?" Because I slept like a rock, I was so tired! "Them—the enemy." Then I realized what he was trying to tell me—that he was scared to death. I'm sure, beyond a shadow of a doubt, that all those other kids were scared to death. That's where I first realized that some of these guys are going to look to me for nurturing, for an arm around the shoulder. And that's exactly how I carried on the rest of the time. …

I volunteered to drive a Warlock truck. This truck had a device that would try to disrupt signals, frequencies that the bad guys or the enemy would use to detonate those roadside bombs. It's a portable device—a lot of this is classified so I can't say too much about it. So we put that in the cab of the truck and we would go with various convoys to help protect part of the convoy…. So I'm with a different unit, called the 498th Transportation Company. They had a regular route from Tikrit to Balad, where they would pick up mail because Balad had an airfield and they could fly in big planes there….

We were number ten in the line of march [convoy trucks]. We have to go through Samarra, which is a very deadly place. So we go over the Samarra bridge—which is frightening—and we make it, and we're heading north back to Tikrit. The third truck in the line of march is a Humvee—and that Humvee was just blown up. Suddenly there's an explosion, and the bomb had napalm in it or jelly fuel. That stuff spread across the road and into the median. And so the roadway was on fire, too. The truck behind that little Humvee also caught fire—finally the fire on their truck burned out.

We went through the smoke and off to our right was a little Humvee on fire, and a soldier on the side of the Humvee on his belly crawling and waving at me with a big bloody arm. His face was bloody, his helmet was off, and it looked like his pants were smoking. He was on his belly crawling—trying to crawl away from the Humvee. We had just had that boy in the back of our truck back in Balad. He chose to drive that Humvee because it had new air conditioning in it.

I can give you the names of those people—it's public knowledge. The name of the soldier on the ground crawling was Specialist Michael Stineman. The driver was Sergeant Jeremy Fischer. The passenger was Sergeant First Class Linda Tarango-Griess. She was their platoon leader. She joined our convoy down in Balad because she needed to get back to Tikrit. She had taken that Humvee down there in a different convoy to get an air conditioner on it—it sits up on top, trying to blow colder air down. It's just so hot in all those trucks.

Specialist F. was my driver and, still to this day, my very good friend and battle buddy. We did a right U-turn and pulled up alongside that bloody soldier. Meanwhile, the Humvee is just ablaze. The other two people are still in the Humvee. We're turned around against traffic—only we're off the road and on the side. The entire convoy except for us just kept going, and they stopped about three or four hundred meters ahead of us and made a box formation. They pulled up side by side of each other, so if they want to get out of the trucks they can be in the middle, protected by their trucks.

We're still three or four hundred meters behind them. Specialist F. jumped out on the Humvee side—the side that the injured soldier was on. Me, I jumped out of my side and began taking fire from buildings and berms that were north and east of us. We began taking small-arms fire. My first instinct was to shoot back, and Specialist F. also shot back. He ran out of ammunition—he had thirty rounds and he shot those off—and he aided Stineman. Because we're getting shot at, it's like, we've got to shoot back or we're all going to die here. What I did is I kept shooting and reloading and shooting and reloading at these people. They were a good distance away, but still we were getting bullets that were hitting the ground around us.

I swear there had to be angels out there because I didn't get hit—I thought for sure I was going to get hit. In fact, I *knew* I was going to get hit. Anyway, I kept shooting. The rear gun truck pulled up. Keep in mind there were six more vehicles behind us. Everybody passed but him, he passed but then he did what we did, the big right-hand U-turn and pulled up alongside of me. He went around the Humvee and was helping Specialist F. aid the soldier. My role: I kept shooting—it's called suppressive fire—and I tried to keep their heads down.

They got Jeremy Fischer, the driver, out of the Humvee, and he just flopped dead on the ground. I've seen a lot of dead people and he was dead. But the soldiers that were helping him didn't know it. I don't think they had never seen anybody that was dead. A minute ago, you're talking to this guy, and the next minute he's flopped on the ground. But they were able to extract him from the

Humvee on the driver's side. The Humvee is burning and burning more. Then the ammunition began to cook off, which means it starts shooting bullets out of it. So now we're getting it from the front and the back—we're getting it from all over. Not one of those things hit us.

Linda is still on the passenger side and nobody could get her out, because it was too hot—so she burned up in there. So she's burning while we're getting shot at and she died. It was just horrible. And I went back around to the front of the truck where I could see her, and we were looking at Jeremy's wounds, and I said, "He's dead, he's dead." Then someone from up in the convoy came back to us and that was Captain A. and his gunner. There were some bad guys behind this berm and there were some bad guys in this building—mud huts. Captain A. got out and said, "Hey, we need to pull Jeremy over behind my truck to protect him and protect us from that Humvee." So they dragged him over for protection and we tried to extinguish the fire with three fire extinguishers. You can't put out burning metal and burning fuel with little tiny fire extinguishers. Why bother.

They're burning up in there, and Captain A. tried CPR on Jeremy, and of course it didn't work. He's got lung tissue hanging out of his right side through a hole—and they're trying to patch that. And someone finally brings us a litter and we get him up in the back of our truck. I'm standing between the guys getting him in the back of the truck and the enemy. I decide to just stand up and try to be his shield. It's like the mother thing. I'm shooting for all it's worth—as fast as I can—changing magazines and trying to be a shield for these guys that are trying to get Jeremy up. And they are all young boys, you know.

I was telling myself as I was shooting that I was going to get hit. I *know* I'm going to get hit because there are all these bullets hitting rocks and hitting dirt all around me. And I told myself this—this was the weirdest mental exercise I have ever had—if it hits me in the leg I will probably fall, but keep shooting. If it hits me in the chest, hopefully my vest will save me. Keep shooting. If it hits me in the head, that's okay because I won't know anything anyway. I was not thinking about home, or family, or my country, or anything. But no matter what pain you feel, keep shooting. It was peak adrenaline, peak survival fight or flight. I was in a fight mode.

[*What about the third person?*] He was the first person they aided. He was *screaming*. I've got to tell you, it was the most hideous, hideous thing, it was just horrible. He was swearing and screaming: "God damn it, ahhhh." *Screaming*. He had a compound fracture of his femur, bone sticking out—a horrible thing. He had shrapnel in his neck which caused all the blood to escape. Oh, man, the thing was horrible. And he's got one arm up in the air—it was a hideous forty minutes.... He did make it. He had a long recovery, but he did make it and he lives in Nebraska. Those three people that were in that Humvee are from the 267th Ordnance Company [National Guard] out of Nebraska....

Linda was just beautiful, beautiful, beautiful, beautiful. She was the first woman to die in a very long time over there. It was strange to have a woman soldier as beautiful as she was dying and I couldn't do anything about it. I go over that in my head. Why didn't I take my M-16 rifle and try to open the door with that? All kinds of mental exercises that I do. I'm even in therapy, not just because of that, but the whole experience over there was just unbelievable. [In therapy] they give you skills to manage. It will never go away, but they also give you medication to help, and help with the jitters: if someone touches me, I jump. I get into these really horrible depressions.

I don't think it's normal to be in that situation for a year or more. It's too long. I believe—and this is something I have learned from the doctors—that your brain, that primitive part of your brain, is meant to get into that fight or flight mode for only a minute or two, to fight a tiger back in the caveman days. That's what it's for. The brain is not meant to go through that for the duration that we go through that. I believe that soldiers should not be in a war zone any longer than six months or three months. The marines go for six months or four months. They rotate a lot. The army just sticks you over there and then they want to extend you even longer. I was there for thirteen months. Way, way, way too long in that environment.

I was nominated for a Bronze Star with Valor, different than just a Bronze Star. It's still pending. It would bring some closure. My commander—after this all happened—called me and Specialist F. into his office and we went over it and he said he was going to nominate us for a Bronze Star with Valor and nominate

F. for a Silver Star, which is *way, way* up there—it is an amazing award. So is the Bronze Star with Valor, so he got us all hyped up and he submitted us for the awards.

Well, the Silver Star got turned down, and then paperwork was lost and I am still to this day trying to get those awards taken care of. I'm out of the army now. We were sorely disappointed, it was very depressing not getting those after we were told that we would. They're [like], "Oh, we lost that." They submitted it way late, and finally it came back and said, "Okay, we will give you a Bronze Star but we find no credible witness to this incident." Wait a minute! There were a lot of people out there—there was an entire convoy of witnesses. I am gathering up witnesses now to have them write their statements and resubmit it. There are these old men from Korea, World War II that are still trying….

It's like validating [that] this nightmare really *did* happen to me. And I think a lot of it is the recognition. Like the government says, "Yes, this did happen to you, you did a good job," pat you on the back. Every application you have for the VA, they want to know what medals you got, which tells them you were in combat. You get a little better benefits. At my VA, it is *fantastic*. The army briefed us on it and they said, "If you have trouble, you need to go to the VA."

When I was in Iraq, I started to have hallucinations after this incident, started having problems, started getting depressed—I just couldn't function properly. So a friend of mine took me into the mental health clinic there, and the doctor took me right in and they put me in an inpatient stress-management thing. So I was being treated in Iraq. They asked me, "Do you want to go home?" and I said, "No, I want to stay with my people."

My leadership in my platoon—there were two or three guys in there that didn't like women. Personally—this is kind of off the record—I believe they were jealous. Of course they had no idea what it was like to go through something like that, so we didn't get that kind of recognition. They didn't like women, you could tell. They were not fair about things. It was just a handful of leaders. The ones that were my age—they were the worst. They didn't think women should be over there in the first place—they wanted to have a boys' club. And their generation never went to war.

I have been in the military for 23 years off and on, I have never been raped, never any of that stuff. You hear a lot about sexual exploitation. I guess that happens—of course it happens. It never happened with any of the young girls in my unit—they were eighteen, nineteen, and twenty. They had the guys wrapped around their little finger, so they could dictate whatever happened. I know this sounds bad, but I believe that women play a big role in what happens to them—in their actions. Then there are asshole guys—no doubt about it. I just happened to be one of those who had good control over myself and I was able to discern danger— I could tell them to buzz off.

—

I believe those people [insurgents], whoever has got the money, whoever can protect them the best—is who they will go with. The people who know that the IED is there, they're not going to come to the soldiers and say, "Hey, there's an IED over here." The insurgents will be their friends. To me, they're *all* insurgents, all of them over there are like that.

I don't even think we should be there at all. Why are we there? We just created a big mess. I believe that Saddam Hussein had them under control, they lived through violence—always have— and here we are sitting watching CNN saying, "Oh, poor people." No, that's how those folks live over there. If they mind their Ps and Qs, they're fine, if they don't try to overthrow the government, then they are fine. The reason Saddam Hussein killed Kurds— he had killed [those] who were trying to overthrow him. What would we do if Texas tried to secede, they had guns, and they were shooting at us? What would we do? That's what Saddam did with the Kurds. The Kurds wanted to expand or be autonomous and he didn't let it happen. Of course his methods were horrible. What would *we* do? So why are we over there?

I *know* why we are over there, but the American public—they don't like to hear it. We are over there purely for economic stability. I call it the big tit—it's the oil. [The administration] is trying to push the American way of life on other people. If you are more like *us*, you'll be a lot better off. That's not necessarily true. [*Will Iraq be a democracy?*] Not in my lifetime. They're tribal people. We're not tribal. We are the West and they are the East and it will never work.

In some ways it was simpler to be in Iraq. Life was simple, it was dangerous, it was scary, but it was simpler. I didn't have to worry about bills, the phone ringing, the day-to-day things that we go through as Americans. I just worked my butt off and went back to my little room, and called it a day, and hoped to God that a mortar didn't land in my lap. That was it. I slept like a baby over there. I could sleep anywhere. Now I'm up at night, pacing the floor, going through some weird stuff. I'm up till 4 o'clock in the morning and then up again at 9 or 10.

I'll tell you, I am lesbian, I have a partner of 22 years. I could never say that in the army. We adopted a son when he was four months old and he will be fourteen the first of September. It's much more difficult than when you are married, straight, and you can express yourself. To keep that all quiet, all I could talk about was my son. We could talk on the phone, we could write letters and occasionally e-mail. I think it was hard on everybody.

[*That part about your partner, do you want that included?*] That's fine because that is my life. I am so tired of trying to hide all that from the government. I suppose you've heard about the gay soldier who was kicked out for being gay? He was an Arab linguist. Are we stupid or *what*? We are so puritanical and it just makes me so mad. It is just unbelievable how puritanical we want to appear.

# FIVE

# WAR'S LASTING IMPACT

# JAIME A. PEREZ
Captain, Army Reserve

Enlisted 1995, deployed age 40
(January–July 2003, October 2005–August 2006)
Baghdad, Rustamiya, Iraq

*Counseling Combat Troops*

*Jaime is in the Army Reserve and has served two tours in Iraq and Kuwait as a mental health professional. He was not himself a combatant, but helped soldiers with the trauma of war in the field. "At one point children became a problem because they were jumping in front of the vehicles. It became like a goat or a deer— sometimes you don't have time to stop." He received his master's in social work in 1995 and answered an advertisement for social workers in the National Guard in Iowa. In 1999 he switched to the Army Reserve when he moved to Massachusetts. He is a counselor in the Vet Center in Springfield, Massachusetts. Jaime is originally from Mayaguez, Puerto Rico. He moved to Louisiana in 1985, where he took his college degree and became a US citizen. His vet center is mentioned in the story in Part VI by Kevin and Joyce Lucey about the last weeks of their son's life. They still wish that they had known about Captain Perez's work with veterans sooner. Jaime is married with two children.*

For many years since Vietnam, Combat Stress Control [CSC] units have been there, but they have never been used to a big extent. We were the first combat stress unit that went into the field on the reserve side, on active duty. I was attached to the Third ID. We went to Kuwait before everything started. It's like another [US] state, everything is very Americanized. I belonged to what is called prevention: we go to the field and we work with the soldiers in order to prevent casualties. And the prevention team at the time was composed of the psychiatrist capable of prescribing medication, a social worker, two NCOs (mental health specialists). We were in a vehicle, we would go after the soldiers, we're available.

We moved with them, we became part of them by being with them 24 hours. Even though they didn't want to come to us, they knew if they needed to talk they were able to find us. We moved from place to place like salesmen. We're going to meet them in camp units, we said who we were, what was our job—no one was coming to knock on the door. If someone was coming saying, I need to talk with you, she or he was going to admit that they were having problems. For any soldier the worst thing that could happen was to lose your weapon, and if you have a mental health issue, especially suicide, that was the first thing that would happen to you.

Our psychiatrist was a brilliant psychiatrist. We were able to accomplish so much because of his leadership by going to the commanders. He being an officer, he went directly to the generals—he started from the top down instead of the bottom to top. Once he saw a one-star general [who then] said to all his troops, "In order for you to get out of the field you need to go through CSC," so suddenly everyone wanted to come to us because they assumed that was a requirement for them to move from Baghdad to the rear. So at one point we were overwhelmed with so many people coming because of this assumption!

We were always following the model of the army—they called it Critical Stress Management. We had a group of eighteen to twenty soldiers and we asked them a set of questions and we encouraged them to answer. We have them engage in a group. By allowing them to talk about whatever they lived through we were able to process that information, and in many occasions it changed from negative cognition to positive cognition. It was the first time that someone gave them an opportunity to talk in a big crowd. For example, they took over one bridge. Everyone was in a different vehicle dealing with a different job, maybe they didn't know everything that happened in the same sequence. But at the end, the majority of them went through the same thoughts, the same things: "I have a problem, I know I have a problem, I'm afraid."

I had one soldier, he was a young soldier, he was so visual that he explained to me he saw a family dying where the big weapon in [his] Bradley fired. The people burned inside the vehicle. He described his worst image of the skin melting, and out of nowhere he said it looked like cheese whiz on top of broccoli. So suddenly, he has a vision full of feeling and he says [it] to the whole group and at the same time they can identify because they saw it. *Now* they're going to a different dimension because they're going to come home and mama is going to give them broccoli and cheese and they're going to lose it.... In Baghdad, I say to them, "It's funny that in our society they teach us so many things, but they don't teach us how to express our feelings." By allowing them to talk about whatever happened to them, hopefully that information is not going to be impregnated in the negative part of [their] "computer."

More powerful than visual is smell. People that smell corpses, it's something that stays there, it's so powerful, anything can trigger that. It's like it's impregnated and you can't get rid of it. People who were exposed to burning bodies—that was common— many of them were never going to be able to go to a barbeque. Even if they don't want to go to a barbeque, if they go to a county fair they're going to have a problem because it's going to come to them. Maybe they're going to be miles away, now it's going to be carried by the wind, the smoke.

I was talking [to soldiers] about working in the hospital. Even though they were in a fight and they saw dying people and destruction of vehicles, for them it was more traumatic working in the Iraqi hospital that was taken over by [the Third ID]. They were having support from physicians and medical personnel from Iraq. This particular soldier was talking about discrimination in treating their own people. If someone came with a different color turban or a different belief, they turned him away even if it was a matter of death or dying. In this particular case, the soldier talked to the [Iraqi] physician and told him, you need to help this lady, and he was talking about what happened to him.

196

I remember working on many traumatic events. They didn't stay in the darkness. They were working to get out of the darkness, they *were* getting out of the darkness…. Some think, "I don't want to go, I don't want to kill, and I'm having a hard time." These individuals are going to have a harder time to be free when they come back home because they didn't want to go in the beginning. There are different personalities. You have the personality that I saw extensively, "Hooah, hooah [an army yell], I'm going to kill. I'm an army soldier, I'm going to do my job, I'm an American."…

I had a client, a soldier I worked with in the field in a group, and we were talking about a fight. The order was we needed to shoot. By shooting, many people think that means to kill everything that moves, even the cats. So everything that was moving in the street needed to go down. But by shooting you don't need to kill. Many people have problems for actions that they took vs. actions that they didn't take and the consequences of not reacting in time. Because if you don't act in time, maybe a bullet will come to you vs. you sending the bullet first, and someone falling dead, the person next to you.

Or, in this case, the soldier, he saw an elderly woman moving from one building to the other and anything moving needed to go down. He knew that if he didn't shoot, someone else was going to shoot. He knew that if he were to shoot, the chances of killing her were going to be very high. So he chose to shoot and he hit her in the butt and he knew that by hitting her in the butt he was not going to kill her, she was going to be wounded. If she was smart enough to be walking in the street he hoped she would be smart enough to get to the medical facility and get help. So he was talking about this in a funny way, but in many cases funny is a face that we hide something else [behind]. His issue was he had to fire, he wasn't trying to kill, he was pretty sure he didn't kill her. Firing on a well-regarded woman—in our society we value our elders.

But again, at one point we learned not to trust anyone. I took a picture of a child and we have many children coming after us for food, money. In this particular case, I was keeping my attention on the children. When I developed the picture I noticed that in the building behind there was a male that you can see only half of his body behind a window or door. So back in the field we learned not to pay attention to the *immediate* thing that we have in front of us because in this case, this person could have been waiting for us to pass with a weapon to fire in our path. The worst that could happen, instead of trust, they're sending the children because they know we love children. At one point children became a problem because they were jumping in front of the vehicles. It became like a goat or a deer in front of the car moving—sometimes you don't have time to stop.

Those soldiers were able to say, I saw something in front of my vehicle but I didn't look, I had to keep going. They were strong enough not to look to the rear mirror to see what was behind— they have an idea, but they're not certain. The majority of them, they knew it was happening but they weren't able to stop. If they stopped, the vehicle behind would push them; they're going to be worried because of the impact. If they were looking, "I don't want to kill him or her," and seeing the process, it was going to be very traumatic....

A story that I have is a very simple story, but for me it has a lot of implications. Water, bottled water—as a society we are getting used to it. For me as a soldier, it had a different meaning, I'm talking about my own experience in the field. They were giving bottles to us of two liters. At one point because everything was rationed, they were giving us only one bottle per day—you needed more, you could go out of your way and find one. But the other thing that happens if you are outside at 10 in the morning, it was 100 degrees. This water was so hot and I was thirsty and dying for some water, it was going to be hot and I am hot already.

When I came back home, Disney[world] had a program giving us admission so I would save money. In Southern Florida in September it's hot and humid and after being in the field for six months where the government was giving me water for free for a two-liter bottle, I didn't feel like paying two dollars for a sixteen-ounce bottle of water. So my wife gets a two-dollar water, she pulls it out of her purse—it was not hot, but not cold like from the freezer. When I had a sip, I lost it because I went back to the field, to my days when I don't have cold water and I lost control because it's hot—too many people around.

Clinically, there's something very different [in] this conflict compared to the first one [Desert Storm]. In this conflict there has been a lot of eye-to-eye contact. I have one soldier that said to me,

"He was going to kill me, he had his weapon. From that point it became him or me and my job is to kill the enemy. He is the enemy. My job is to go back to my family—not to be a casualty." But he was expecting the enemy to become a victim when he stood under his weapon, and with the eye, he was begging for mercy. But we couldn't trust mercy because the one we forgive today is going to be the one that's going to kill me tomorrow. That image of what happened after he pulled the trigger and that slow-moving picture seen by the second, "What if we'd given him a chance? What if....?"

Not even the uniform was safe because the enemy got access to military uniforms and they were dressing as military Americans, and this uniform, their face—you cannot distinguish who is who. In my case, I don't look like a Caucasian—they were looking at me like, "Whoops!" But intelligence learned that something they [imposters] were *not* doing [was] putting their trousers in their boots and that was the only sign they have to identify who was an American soldier and who is not.... Many of them threw away their uniform, they didn't throw away their shoes, so they were dressed as civilians with military shoes, so we were looking for shoes at one point. We could have seen a female, what looked like a female, with military boots, there's something wrong here! The Iraqi men were willing to dress as females.

They were willing to put children in front of the vehicles knowing that we love women and children. Once a vehicle stops, a military vehicle, a Bradley, the weakest point for all these vehicles is in the rear because all the armor is on the top and the front, so they were attacking to the back. Once the convoy stops and they attack, the people in the front need to come back to the rear to protect and by that time, they [the enemy] were going to be taking over.

Even though my contribution is as a social worker, I'm not a soldier, but in a way I felt I was part of it. I was given a very unique opportunity to work with the best, to see the worst with them, to help them. For that time with active duty I would see, act like them, which has been helping me in this phase of my life [as a counselor]. Now I'm helping people adjust from military to civilian.

# DAN MORIARTY
## Lieutenant Colonel, Medical Services Corps, Army Reserve

Enlisted 1983, deployed age 54
(March 2003–February 2004)
Kuwait; Basra, Camp Bucca, Iraq

*Treating Soldiers with PTSD*

*Dan is a social worker at the White River Junction (Vermont) Veterans' Medical Center. He received his master's degree at the Boston College of Social Work and has worked for the VA for 30 years, currently managing eight programs at the center. He lives in New Hampshire and has two sons, 27 and 29. He was deployed at age 54, activated within the space of two days, a single parent who had to suddenly place his disabled son—"an absolute nightmare." He deployed to Kuwait, but also worked in the prison in southern Iraq at Camp Bucca. He arrived during the disorganized first months of the war when it was not clear what his functions as a social worker would be. First he ministered to Iraqis in detention and as displaced persons, and later to American soldiers. As someone with long experience, he believes, "What you have to realize in a war zone is everyone functions differently based on their previous experiences in life. Lots of things that go on in a war zone are very normal reactions to very abnormal situations."*

Lots of the support systems that are set up for reservists are different from where the reservists usually live. As an example, I drill out of Fort Devens, Massachusetts. People came from all over New England to go to Fort Devens, [and] from the Midwest—we have people coming from Florida, or Texas, or California. If you've got a family of a reservist who lives in California, Texas, Michigan, or Florida, it's really difficult for them to get support services out of the unit that is in Massachusetts. For Guardspersons, that's easier because most Guardspersons live close to their armory.

The regular army comes from a base, families are located on the base, they deploy from that base. The wives or significant others who are left behind have a really good support system set up through the active-duty post. But with reservists, that is woefully lacking. That is one mental health perspective people really don't talk much about. It greatly affects your state of mind—when it gets time to get on the bus, you cannot be worried about your family. You have to focus [on] yourself, where you are going, what you're going to be doing. All the nice, wonderful things that nasty people are going to be trying to do to you.

We were activated on February 7, 2003. We spent four weeks at Fort Drum, New York, and we went from -40 degrees F temperature in one day's time in mid-March to 110 degrees. The culture shock and the environmental shock were absolutely incredible. And having to be in what we call MOPP 4, which is all your chemical gear and all your suits on, and the outside temperature was 110, but inside your suit you were a lot hotter than that. This has a dramatic impact, particularly on some older Guardspersons and reservists because they're physically not as up to speed as some of the younger studs—the 18- to 25-year-olds.

Almost everyone arrives in Kuwait. You come in to Camp Wolverine or what was then called Camp Wolf. We arrived one day after the actual war started, on the 22nd. First time I ever flew first class—"Fly first class to war!" We stopped in Germany and we picked up a German flight crew. The German flight crew wanted to be on the ground for about five seconds. Because as soon as we disembarked from the plane, we had to be in MOPP 4—the German crew didn't even have gas masks or anything, so they wanted to be out of there real quick…. We expected, flying in at night, full black-out conditions, but every light in the country was on.

When we first arrived there, there was lots of confusion. We were thrown in with a number of allied forces—Spanish troops, English troops, Dutch troops, and no one seemed to be in control. It was baffling to us because we had sent over an advance team of about eight people who were supposed to coordinate things prior to our arrival so that we could hit the ground running and would have sleeping areas set up and support services. Well, that didn't happen at all. Roughly for the first week we couldn't figure out where the heck we were going to stay. The communications systems and the organizational structure were in such disarray that you couldn't figure out who to contact to get done what you needed to have done....

It became my mission coordinating ongoing mental health services to Iraqi POWs, displaced civilians, former Baath Party members at Camp Bucca. What we would do is, two times a week, drive from Camp Wolf north through Kuwait, cross the border, cross the berm and go to Camp Bucca. It was close to a 150-mile drive one way. Once you cross the border you were dealing with lots of civilians before you get to Bucca. You were dealing with lots of kids who would surround your vehicle and you never knew what was going to happen—their swiping things, their jumping in the vehicle, their tossing things. So that was a harrowing experience, just getting there.

While we were at Bucca, the MPs who were reservists would identify people that they thought needed mental health services. Those were usually individuals who were self-injurious and it was our job to try to figure out whether it was part of their religion, or whether they were in fact suffering from some mental illness, or some emotional disorder. Exclusively men, you did not see displaced women. Who is suicidal, who has some intelligence information that can be used by the US forces or the allied forces to smoke out—say—where Saddam is.

Our job was not to deal with *those* types of individuals, but just to deal with people who were perceived to be having emotional problems. What was difficult to tell was who was who. You very rarely had anybody say, "Oh yeah, I'm a former Baath Party member"—that just wasn't done! You very rarely had anyone say that they were a former soldier because then they were subject to all sorts of interrogation. So everybody was just a displaced person who just happened to be at the wrong place at the wrong time when someone was rounded up.

What was really interesting was that we thought that almost all the people who were rounded up were on Valium. Through interpreters—we used Egyptians, Syrians, some Pakistanis—[we tried] to find out what was going on with each individual. You would ask them a simple question and fifteen minutes later the interpreter would still be talking. "Wait a minute, I think something got lost in the translation!" And then the displaced civilian would respond about a half hour and you would say, "Wait a minute, what's wrong with this!" What we found was that lots of the individuals were on a Valium derivative, the name of which sounded to us to be "Braki sulfate." Individuals would come in and ask for "Braki sulfate." These individuals were reported by the interpreters to have been receiving mental health services with some Iraqi psychiatrist and had been prescribed Valium. They would use it as barter with some of the other people who were detained in their confinement area. [*Pretty soon you would have all of Bucca on Valium.*] No, no we were very *judicious*. We had the MPs helping us out with that.

You had to deal with the cultural aspect. Going over, we were given very little information concerning Iraqi culture and/or their religion. You'd go on the internet, try to look up Islam, Muslim practices and stuff. Try to figure out as best you could what went on with people. You'd also try to figure out religious practices vs. self-injurious behavior. And whether or not someone was hurting himself because of the perception that he should atone for some sins in the past, or whether this was in fact mental health issues. We were always amazed that people could squat for *hours*, sitting on their haunches and not move. We would think to ourselves, that's impossible, how can they actually *do* that—by gosh, our legs would lock up. ...

What happened in about August or September of 2003 was that another unit took over command and control and responsibility for the Bucca area. So my assignment was more in the Kuwait area. Our focus was on trying to assist troops in terms of mental health issues relative to their continued stay in the country. Around that time—July, August, September, October 2003—the Department of Defense said that instead of troops only being on six-month tours, they were going to place people on indefinite tours. So people's orders were changed to these fictitious dates in the future. At that point there were a lot of mental health issues and a lot of distraught individuals who could see no end to their time in the desert.

As a result of that, in November, December 2003 or early 2004, the Department of Defense came out with its one-year "boots on the ground" policy. As soon as troops knew that they had an end date, things began to pick up in terms of mental health. It's easier to cope with things if you have an end date that you can shoot for. Even though you had a one-year "boots on the ground," we would have some units come down to Kuwait, [and] they had turned in all their equipment, they were ready to get on the plane. You could actually see the planes that you were going to lift off [in], and your orders are reversed and they would be sent north again because there was just nobody else to replace them.

I think in terms of active-duty units, those units that are more elite, 82nd Airborne, Tenth Mountain, with high esprit de corps, high morale—those individuals did fairly well. The individuals who had unit leaders that were not very good, not leading by example, not setting good cohesive working mechanisms—those individuals in those units did not do well. And so, lots of times, morale issues were a direct result of individual leaders of those units. People who have had more life experiences, older individuals, seem better than some of the younger kids. The younger kids are more attuned to immediate gratification, not having to work for things over a period of time, having all their amenities, all their electronic devices, instant access to cell phones, instant access to the internet, etc.—those kids had some problems.

The females who were out in the field lived in the same conditions that the guys did—they were given no preferential treatment. The females always had to be attuned to the fact that they were female and that they were living with war fighters. They always had to be aware of where they were, where they were going, go [in] pairs, or keep attuned to the sexual harassment and sexual assault issues.

The primary [mental health issue] was having a definite end date. Hands down, that was the major issue. Lots of people tried to play diagnoses and say people are suffering from PTSD or they're suffering from major depression. What you have to realize in a war zone is everybody functions differently based on their previous experiences in life. Lots of things that go on in a war zone are very normal reactions to very *abnormal* situations. What may seem like really crazy, weird, stupid, totally off-the-wall behavior in a war situation is really normal stuff. And then we constantly have to tell people—especially mental health people—do not under any circumstances initially put a diagnosis on anybody. Wait for a while, see what happens—lots of times people sort things out for themselves.

The issue with PTSD—there has been lots written about doing debriefings with people. Units who lose somebody, or a helicopter crash happens, combat stress control teams are called in for what we call Critical Incident Stress Debriefings (CISD). Right now the use of debriefings is very controversial. There've been some recent studies that show that there's really no difference between people who experience debriefings and people who just sort things out on their own with good support systems—the results seem to be pretty much the same. There's no difference if they had just been working with their own individual guys, their own families, their own support systems, work things out on their own.

Sometimes there is some thought that critical incident stress debriefings will do *harm* rather than help people sort through things and get on with their lives. We call it the buddy system. You always try to take care of your buddy—if you go into a war zone, you always have a buddy. You're looking out for your buddy and he's looking out for you. So if you and your buddy survive a terrible situation, it's natural to just chit-chat about it, see what's going on, share the experience together, versus someone coming in from the outside having you rehash everything. Sometimes the buddy system, and/or the sergeant of a platoon just hashing over stuff, works a lot easier.

There's been a major spike in the number of claims that have been authorized for PTSD recently. We who work in the VA have some concerns, not knowing whether or not it's politicized, and not knowing whether or not they should just let things sort out with people over a period of time and then see what happens. Politicized, in terms of PTSD [being] very much in the news nowadays. It's one of the buzz words in terms of mental health issues with troops coming back. There's a lot of controversy about it because there are some who have worked in the field who say, "Well, this is a major impact of *all* wars and not everybody who comes back from Iraq who has been in firefights has experienced PTSD." We think it's being given too much media coverage and/or people are teaching one another how to come down with PTSD symptoms.

This war is different in terms of its being an all-volunteer force. The troops are being asked to do unbelievable things— particularly units like MP units, civil affairs units, transportation companies, mortuary affairs. There are very few of these units on the active-duty side of the house. The problem is that most of these are in Guard or Reserve units and they are being called on *over* and *over* and *over* again to go back and do it again. Recruitment is down. Somewhere down the line, whether or not people realize it, we're going to have to go back to conscription and the draft.... Not a chance [that we have enough troops to deploy beyond Iraq] and that's the feeling of our troops on the ground, too. They say, "Well, geez, it's just a right-hand turn into Iran." They know once you're on active duty and on orders and you're over there, it's real easy for the Department of Defense to say, "Guess where you're going next?"

# TRAVIS A. JONES
Captain, Army National Guard

Commissioned 1997, deployed age 28
(February 2004–February 2005)
LSA Anaconda, Balad, Iraq

*Counseling Returning Veterans*

*Travis is a social worker who worked as a counselor in a private school until he was deployed to Iraq. On return, he started to work at the White River Junction (Vermont) Vet Center. He is from Kentucky, and graduated from Carson-Newman College, a Southern Baptist college in Jefferson City, Tennessee, where he was on a ROTC scholarship. He also met his wife, a journalist, in college. He transferred to the New Hampshire National Guard in 1999 and was promoted to captain in June 2005. He plans to stay in the National Guard for twenty years. He enjoys working with other veterans, and helping them learn how to handle their symptoms of PTSD. His maxim: "It's not the veteran who has the PTSD—it's the PTSD that has got him."*

Throughout our whole time there, my soldiers and I personally didn't know who the enemy was because over there the enemy has no defined look to them. They could be anybody. We heard reports of where, after major combat operations ceased on May 1, 2003, American soldiers, coalition soldiers thought, "Well, here things are all right." They would talk to the locals, and some kid they thought they could trust would shoot them or throw a grenade at them—kill some soldiers. We heard reports that a soldier wanted to buy a can of Pepsi, so he took his helmet off and someone got behind him and shot him in the head right there. We heard we can't trust anybody, don't talk with anybody, don't interact with them, don't mess with them, because they could be the enemy.

The only Iraqis we had interactions with were those who came into the camp. They would be contract workers and go through a rigorous screening process, have an interpreter with them who was their boss. They would do work such as cleaning up the trash around the camp. They were doing upgrades on the camp like painting the sidewalk or traffic lines that we could probably have done quicker and cheaper—not cheaper, but easier. But it was a way to get the locals some work because they were paid probably a lot more than what they could get outside. There *wasn't* work outside the gate. There were reports of dumpster diving—it would be something like a CD or a magazine. But if they found something like a detailed map of routes we were taking… they could sell the information.

It's a global atmosphere over there. I saw British troops, but that was rare because we were up in Balad, north of Baghdad, and the British troops were in Basra—south. We did have some Australians who worked in the hospital at my base. I saw a small contingent of Albanian troops in the northern section of Iraq. We saw Polish soldiers, Italian soldiers, Japanese, South Korean. At the very beginning there were Spanish soldiers. There were others from South America, I forget which country exactly. I think a lot of them were probably stationed in Kuwait.

My primary job was a convoy commander. I was in charge of receiving the orders where to ship supplies. I was responsible for getting the supplies, delivering them throughout the camp. Also the safety of the men—all soldiers and civilians are attached to convoys for their safety. The whole mission fell on my shoulders for success or failure. The other job I had was serving as an officer in charge of a trailer transfer point. We would have a crew go out there, pick the trailers up, bring them into another yard, and pre-position them. If it's a mission of eight trailers of a certain supply going to Mosul, we would bring in eight trailers of that supply, pre-position them all in a row for the Mosul area and [have] people pick them up.

The women we had in our company, I would say they were all strong. We had a female commander—then she got sent home for medical reasons late in our tour. Her replacement was another woman. I think it was an asset, because in the battalion we were the only company that had a female commander. I think it was a good ice-breaker. A lot of the females we had on our missions in our company were stronger, really more assured because they really wanted to do the job. They wanted to prove themselves more than a guy has to. Many times the females came out better than some of the male soldiers—I saw that from other units.

Different things about this war—the whole convenience thing. Essentially, in the camp where I lived, you want something, you could just go over to the PX and get it. If they didn't have it, you wait a while, you got it. The PX store got a continuous supply of DVDs and magazines and CDs. There's no permitted non-military clothing for soldiers over there, but if you wanted to buy shirts to send home with the name of the camp on it or anything about Iraq, you could do that. Food over there was plentiful. You would never go hungry....

[Our camp] was a place called LSA [Logistics Support Area] Anaconda—it's probably the number one or number two biggest base in Iraq. It would count as a luxury base. Camp Victory—I think the camps around the Green Zone might be more populated or have more services—but definitely, given where Camp Anaconda is, it has a lot of perks. On the internet, you can see all the facilities they have available. With the population it has in it, it has gotten some attention, a documentary or two.

I think of all the conveniences over there. We had a movie theater—they played movies four times a day. You had a softball field and a football field, soccer field and a basketball court, Olympic-sized swimming pool, a track field, a stadium, and a 24-hour gymnasium. All the conveniences of America were pretty much there. The only difference is that you're in a war zone. You meld the two worlds together—a world of danger and a world of convenience. And having the American lifestyle, it makes for a weird mixture.

We had satellite phones. We had ten computers set up initially and an additional ten ports for laptops. Over there the soldier calls home. A lot of soldiers, including myself, had a schedule. Guys would call once a day, once a week, or twice a week. You usually have a certain time because of the eight-hour time difference. Guys liked to call around midday to catch their loved ones in the morning when they just woke up, or they would call early in the morning, call their loved ones before they go to bed at night. My schedule was that I would tell my wife on the phone call when I would call her next or get her on the internet. She always had her cell phone with her. I would always get a hold of her no matter where she was.

It's good, but the disadvantages are that you can always keep tabs on family members. No matter where you are in Iraq, you're near an AT&T phone bank—you know you can get a hold of them. One individual [back home] tried to take a vacation for herself and all of a sudden her husband called her and asked her [where] she was going. She told him. He gave her a guilt trip like, "Why are you going out and having fun? I'm sitting here in Iraq, you need to make sacrifices like I am." She canceled her trip, she felt so guilt-ridden about giving herself a break. I think if there hadn't been communication he probably wouldn't have known about it until the trip was over with. She could have written a letter, or one phone call a week—he would have found out.

Constantly keeping tabs on family members, having cell phones—you're never out of contact with cell phones. The telecommunications over there have very clear signals. The Vietnam veterans told me that they had to wait forever to make a phone call, they might have only one phone call out of their whole tour. Things have changed so much. There were some young children who actually didn't know their father or mother was actually gone. They thought they were somewhere close by or in the United States where they weren't in harm's way. It's controversial if the parent isn't telling them where exactly their own father or mother is.

A lot of the news we got was from the *Stars and Stripes* and armed forces network television. But the TV news—I really didn't pay much attention to it. I usually turned it on to the sports channel or just watched DVDs. Whatever news I would see would not capture all that's going on over here, or it's giving a very small snapshot— an instance like an explosion, or a soldier died. A lot of my attention I paid to anything *American*, news from my wife, or care packages, or sitting down at night and relaxing and watching a movie. That's the American corner I went into. I didn't pay any attention to popularity ratings or protests or political debates. I didn't watch the debates between Kerry and Bush... I found it boring. We had some people who would have political arguments about who was voting for Kerry and who was voting for Bush. I was assigned to be the voting officer, so I had to go around and make sure everybody in the company was a registered voter.

[Leaving], you got ready for your flight order. We all went to Camp Doha, Kuwait. We would sit there and read books, magazines, CDs, if you had a DVD player still, you would watch DVDs with somebody.... The camp was bulging at the seams, troops stopping in to get trained to go up to Iraq, soldiers in there that were waiting to get shipped out from Kuwait to go home.

I worked at my old job for a couple of months and then I started working here at the Vet Center in June [2005]. I wanted to work with the veteran population and not work with children anymore. I'm finding that a lot of vets are having a problem explaining what they went through. They feel that their family members should *know*, and the family members aren't communicating exactly that they don't *want* to know—they don't need to know so much about what happened over there. I've got some veterans who have no one to talk to *at all*.

I have some veterans who want to go back because they felt a sense of belonging over in Iraq—a sense of purpose. Self-esteem issues were eliminated over there. They knew what they needed to do and they had a schedule. Some veterans who were always in trouble—the bad soldiers before they went to Iraq—were great soldiers over there, and now they are back to being the bad soldier again. Veterans really loved it or they really hated it. I think a lot of them loved it just because of the structure of it. Let's say all the younger veterans—they had a structured life over there. Whereas back home they were struggling to keep a job, or they're still in college and they don't know what to do with their lives....

I've seen some soldiers, they just love the army way of life. They had prior active duty and they loved it there, and got back into that rhythm of being in an active-duty lifestyle. They just love being a soldier. There are many of them who have pride in what they did. But they got back home, working a 9-to-5 job at the office, there's no stress there at all, they're just stuck on the computer—they miss that high-octane lifestyle they had over there.

The guys I talked to who hated it hated the personalities over there—they had a lot of personality clashes with other soldiers. Or a lot of them would say leadership just sucked over there, [like] the immediate supervisor or the company commander, the first sergeant, the battalion commander. They were treated *wrong* or nobody was held accountable—or people did wrong and weren't punished for it. Or they didn't like it because of the fact that they were used as a replacement for a unit—taken out of their state National Guard and put into another state. You want to be with the people you trained with and not with a unit where you hardly know anybody and you don't feel welcomed by them.

I met a couple of soldiers who were wearing the Puerto Rico National Guard patch, and they weren't even from Puerto Rico—they were from Chicago. They got transferred to make up for the lack of soldiers for this unit of the Puerto Rico National Guard. All those areas [American territories] have National Guard soldiers—they probably have vet centers in those places as well. They have a vet center in the US Virgin Islands—of all places—because they have a veteran population over there and we get soldiers from that area as well. There were soldiers from other countries who joined for American citizenship. ...

I have learned [PTSD] is a very complex thing, should not be put in one category. I think the word has been used too much. I think people hearing it think somebody is screwed up for life—and that's not the case. It is a diagnosis that can be treated. I'm not going to say it can be totally *cured*—because there is always a chance it can come back—but it can be treated. [My method] is cognitive processing therapy, a structured way of helping the client talk through their trauma. Breaking it down into bits and pieces and exploring the bits and pieces, then try to put it all back together, which lets the client see it in a brand-new way. Like taking a picture and examining the picture piece by piece instead of looking at the whole picture.

A lot of Iraq veterans blame themselves for what happened, "Why did it happen to me?" So you get rid of all the thought distortions that exist, like trying to blame themselves or wonder why they were unlucky, or why it [PTSD] is happening to them. "Why is my buddy—who went through the same thing—not having problems with this and I am? I must be crazy!" Just trying to get those thoughts out of their heads, concentrate on the traumatic event itself. One guy I helped was totally stuck on one event. We just talked about the event itself and afterwards how it affected him during his tour over there. But some people go through multiple traumas over there. I've met a lot of soldiers who said they went through stuff. But some of these stories, it was crazy—I just couldn't believe it. Some of the trauma they have gone through—it was just amazing.

We have a thing: it's not the veteran who has the PTSD—it's the PTSD that has got him. It's something they can overcome and have the tools to combat it.

# ANDREW J. SIMKEWICZ
Sergeant, Army

Enlisted 2002–2006, deployed age 34
(June 2004–June 2005)
Tenth Mountain Division, Baghdad, Iraq

*Helping Veterans Impacted by War*

*Andrew works as a counselor at the Springfield (Massachusetts) Vet Center—a veteran and a social worker. He finds it enlightening to work with veterans because he also learns from them. He has inaugurated programs that involve group discussions, including families. He volunteered for active duty at age 32 because of 9/11, and remains close to the military and to his combat experience. Sgt. "Sim" deployed to both Afghanistan and Iraq, stop-lossed for a final year. He is married with three children and is himself the youngest of four boys. He graduated with a BS in psychology from Springfield College, where he also got his master's in social work in 1996. Andrew has faced the challenge of life after the military, saying, "You almost have to embrace the changes in your life.... You can't come back the same person." He notes that he may write a book some day and in the meantime will be "the best husband and father I can be."*

I started right after 9/11. I was pretty affected by [9/11], so I started talking to a recruiter that month and was in basic training a couple of months after that. It came down to the army or the marines—I was able to help myself a little better with the army. I wanted to do it—but you've got to be careful what you wish for! I made it through safe, so it was a good thing. I was in charge of all the fuel operations in Afghanistan and Iraq for the Tenth Mountain Division. I was in Iraq from June 2004 to June 2005—in Baghdad. I was near the airport at Camp Liberty, and Camp Victory, and Camp Justice. You know, there's a road named "Patriot" [and] I was on "Michigan" once.

I basically pushed fuel, ammunition, food, to different parts of Baghdad. I had six or seven soldiers. We did convoys with 5,000-gallon fuel tankers—we were open twenty hours a day for that. Matter of fact, it was funny when the people came in to replace us. The guy that was taking my job—I told him all the stuff that we do. He seemed disgusted. "This is ridiculous. I only have 24 guys to do this mission." I started laughing and I said, "I think you'll be fine—we only had six."

Because we were active duty—we weren't [in the] Reserves or National Guard—we had guys from everywhere. I had a guy from Puerto Rico, a guy from California, a guy from Micronesia, a guy from Louisiana, a guy from Texas, and one from West Virginia.... Out of all I've done with my life, I've never been able to build bonds with people the way I built them with these guys. Because it is an amazing dynamic to put your life in someone's hands and to go out on a mission, sweating, knowing that the place you're going to has been bombed a few times that day and chances are that you're going to get hit with something. It's a sealing kind of thing—you're almost superstitious about the way you view things.

I did the same thing before every mission. I did checks on everything the same way, made sure that everything was right—spare tires are right, there's plenty of fuel, checking the oil. Making sure that if we were going to get hit, it wasn't because of stupidity, because of the ridiculous mistake of having a flat tire. [Then I would] listen to some of the same songs on my iPod before I left. The things that you do with your weapon, the way you cleaned it before. The similar things you say to yourself. I carried the same photos with me through Afghanistan and Iraq.

I just told my wife the other day—I have the same cross that I was given right before basic training, a St. Christopher's medal. I had it all the way through everything and the other day I got home and it had broken off my neck. So I lost it, and it hurt me a little bit because it was something that I treasured. I was really bummed out about that. That was with me through all my missions, so maybe it was just time for it to go—I don't know.

A lot of people wrote death letters. It's a letter that typically starts, "If you're reading this, things have not gone too well." It's telling the people closest to you how much you love them, sorry that you had to go. I did it in a different way. Before I left, I wrote each of my kids a letter telling them that I love them and what I expect of them in the future. I read it now and it is kind of cheeseball and corny but I think they would have appreciated it.

But I couldn't even deal with writing my wife anything before I left because I was sure I was going to make it home. But when I got there things were so active I ended up writing her a letter, too. I told someone where it was and said, "If need be, make sure you get this to my wife." We have decent accommodations, so it was in a pretty safe spot. But a lot of people carry them in their flak vests, which doesn't make a lot of sense to me because if you get blown up, I'm not sure the letter is going to make it!

I prayed quite a bit when I was there. This is going to sound corny, too, but I made a deal with God. I said basically, "If you're going to kill me, make sure it's in the first few months, because if I've spent twelve months here and then die in my last weeks, I'm going to die a pissed-off individual." You don't want to go through all that and then you think you're going home, and everybody thinks you're going home, and then you don't go home. That happens a lot.

I didn't consider myself afraid too often. When we convoyed in from Kuwait to Baghdad I saw about five trucks—the same ones I was driving, the 5K tankers—blown up on the side of the road, still smoking, some on fire still. I saw five different ones in five different areas when I was driving. I was like, "Oh drat, what am I getting myself into?" I think I was a little afraid at that point. I jokingly told my commander I wouldn't be a bigger target if I wrote "Mohammed is full of crap" on the side of my truck in Arabic.

Concentrating on mortality is definitely a thing, and when you have guys around you, you build this bond that is indescribable. It becomes tighter. In some respects, it's a different family. Even with people you don't care for. There were a couple of guys that I did a lot of missions with that if we were in the regular civilian world I probably would have talked to them once and said, this guy is an idiot. But even those guys, you go on these missions and you have each other's back. And so I think even in those situations there's a closeness that's unbelievable....

It's not like there's an identifiable enemy, where you can shoot at them and they shoot at you and it's traditional war. It's *boom*, and they're gone. There's no one to fire at. They have become more technically and tactically proficient in setting up IEDs and doing their attacks. Before, where they would set it up there would be a wire and there would be a remote guy within a couple of hundred meters. They would wait for the convoy and *boom*, it goes off. Now they can call in things from cell phones—they have remote detonations. I know there are instances in overpasses where there are people up there dropping grenades, someone drives under, *boom* and they blow up. But a lot of these cases it's someone doing vehicle-borne IEDs, or suicide bombers—people that are willing to trade their own lives.

I know when we provided security for the first election, I got really close to an interpreter—he was an Iraqi citizen. I talked to him the day after the election, and I was *amazed* at his experience. He personally had to walk nine-and-a-half miles with a relative of his—I think it was his father. The night before, all these people had got fliers somehow at their front door saying, "If you go vote, you and your family [are] going to be dead." Which still amazes me—it would have been a terrorist note-carrier! Didn't make sense to me. But anyway, he got this flier, so he left his wife and children behind not knowing if he was ever going to see them again.

You get guys from Iran and Syria and Jordan coming in and causing havoc. He got to the election place and one of the defense mechanisms that the Iraqi people were using was talking between themselves, trying to point out if there was a different dialect going on. So they were making conversation with every person around them to make sure that they were Iraqi. Like someone coming from West Virginia—they have a little drawl to their speech, maybe a different dialect. So if they saw that someone had a different dialect, they distanced themselves, because chances are that is a suicide bomber.

Of course one of the people they distanced themselves from *was* a suicide bomber. Everyone had started to go away. This guy panicked and went into the crowd and blew himself up. So he had taken about four or five people with him. [Our interpreter] was there, and he said one of the proudest moments he has ever had as an Iraqi citizen was after that. There were body parts everywhere. He said that everybody got back into line, stepping over body parts so they could go cast their vote.

It was a pretty powerful thing. You know they had over 60 percent turnout with their lives on the line. We as Americans don't have 60 percent—we have 50 percent. Our lives aren't on the line, and we certainly don't have to walk five-ten-fifteen miles to go vote. How many people in America would do that? It really spoke volumes about how motivated they are. You don't hear that on the news here. That's why I rarely watch the news because you don't hear any of the good things that are going on.

There's a *ton* of good things going on over there. These people are so appreciative. It's nothing for people to come up and hug you and say thank you. I think the greatest example is this interpreter. I keep telling stories about him because he's the richest example I have. Throughout his whole life, his family couldn't speak because they were afraid of getting killed, because that's how Saddam worked—undercover investigators everywhere. Anyone who was caught speaking against the government, they were dead within a week. You were either in prison for life or put to death, and he said being in prison for life was really rare.

He had given examples of one time his father and his uncle and two of their best friends were having a conversation. The second in command under Saddam had red hair, he had a blood disorder. His uncle had made a joke that maybe the blood transfusions were going to his head and making his hair red. It was a stupid little joke. Well, someone overheard it, it was said in confidence between four people, and he was dead three days later. *Because of a simple little joke.* This guy murdered his own people all the time.

The fact that they have the freedom to speak now is probably the biggest thing. The fact that they can speak their mind, and talk for and against whatever government they're forming over there, is so appreciated by them—the fact that they *do* have freedoms. Well, they had a good educational system before, and now they have an educational system where they can actually interact. Saddam had a pretty good policy for education—anybody could go to school if they wanted. We're helping the water supply, their electricity is getting better....

You go to Iraq and it's a pretty rich country. There's some nice stuff in Iraq. They have nice roads, they have some pretty good things. My buddy Aladdin—that was his name, that *is* his name— like he says, we should be one of the richest countries in the world. The problem is that Saddam spent all the money on himself, on his palaces, didn't share any of the money with the people. But now, a lot of the revenue is going back to the people, so that is a huge difference from before.

They're going to improve pretty quickly, I think, over the next few years. We have a two-party system and we have trouble agreeing. They have five parties to deal with—so that's their trouble. And the other part is that two of the groups are a lot bigger in size than the other three. You have those three wanting to have the same say as the bigger two. It's just a political mess. I think we've already stepped in as far as we can. At some point, you've got to let them figure it out for themselves. I don't think they want us to step in any more than we have—but that's just from what I've heard and read.

You hear different things. Like my interpreter friend said that the Iraqi people love us, they want us there [and] they are just amazed at how far things have evolved in our time there. Then you hear other people say, we can't wait for you to leave because the insurgency problem probably wouldn't be there if we [US] weren't there. I think the thinking behind it is that the insurgents are there so we won't go to their country next. They would rather have the war at a distance, in Iraq, than in their own land. We would rather keep them busy in Iraq, so they don't come to our country! That's kind of a neat perspective on it. Makes sense to me....

There has never been democracy in the Middle East—it's probably the only region in the world that has never experienced democracy. And to be a part of two beginnings of democracy in the Middle East is a pretty rich thing to contemplate. In Afghanistan we did a really good job and helped build the Afghan army. Then we go to Iraq and we made a big difference there and we were there for the first election. What a privilege that was. I remember I wasn't sure if it was going to be a bloodbath. And the fact that they had such a big turnout and that we provided the security for that turnout—it was really cool. I remember that was one of my proudest days there.

[My unit] all came back together. They're getting ready to deploy again. I wish I could go with them. But at the same time I'm happy I'm getting to stay with my family. I miss the military greatly. I loved it—I loved it. I loved wearing the uniform, I loved the structure, I loved the PT—I loved everything. And I love the camaraderie. I miss my friends a lot. You feel detached from others [when you return], which is a real common thing. You don't talk to them about stuff because, first of all, you don't want to scare the crap out of them. Secondly, they are not going to understand anyway, and that's going to be frustrating to you and them.... I used to have the itch to play baseball in the spring. Now it seems like I have the itch to go back there all the time. I have the itch to put my uniform back on, an itch to do what I was doing before.

Part of my job is to be around veterans, so it definitely helps, but at the same time, there's nothing like wearing that uniform and being over there, testing yourself, and seeing what you're made of. It's an amazing feeling—you're giving of yourself and sacrificing, but at the same time it's an adrenaline thing. You know that you're doing something valuable and *that* is addictive. I think a lot of people struggle with doing something incredibly important over there, [then] coming back to a crappy job over here where they're not happy and don't feel that the level of importance of their job means anything. A lot of people come back to managing stores and doing honest work that they believed was good before, and now they just don't feel that their work is important.

No matter what happens over in Iraq—I hope it goes well—I am going to be proud either way. Because when you sacrifice yourself and represent your country, your family, your friends, and your towns to do something that's bigger than you, I think you have a lot to be proud of.... I don't think this war is ever going to be defined as a win or a loss because we don't really have an enemy, [an] identifiable enemy out there that we can say, "Phew, we won."

I got home right before the 4th of July, and when the fireworks started going off, I thought I was going to die. I was *so* frightened. I don't ever recall being that frightened. I was hiding in my basement. You feel stupid after, but it's real. It's *incredibly* disturbing. Matter of fact, I got pulled over on my way here today, that's why I was ten minutes late. I've been pulled over eight times since I have been back. Not driving *crazy*, just driving different. Speed isn't something you care about, you drive like you stole it. That's been a huge adjustment for me—driving. If you're going through a tight area where everything is kind of consolidated—I *fly* through those areas, there are no stop signs in my world. If I'm going under an overpass, I *fly* through it. Hopefully, I can continue to keep my license. It's amazing—almost every veteran I have—some of them can't drive anymore....

Being in crowded restaurants or in a mall, I always have my back to the corner so I can see everybody, so that if something happens it's going to be the least hassle. So you are hyper-vigilant. You see bad things happen before they happen, if they indeed will happen. It's like the other day was a beautiful day and you see someone with a long winter coat on in a store—it doesn't add up. I'm wearing a T-shirt, and this guy has got a long coat on. That sense of awareness keeps you alive in a war zone. Sometimes it doesn't translate too well into society, [but] I don't know that I totally hate that quality that I have now.

The sleep disturbance—that's one thing that probably affects me most. Sometimes you feel kind of like a freak. You were taught to be paranoid, and then you come back here and you still are paranoid. You know in your head that this is not what you are thinking it is—but you still think it. Those intrusive thoughts are probably the most disturbing. I'm treating other people, I have a [therapy] group that I do now—I get as much out of the group as anybody else does. It is amazing to hear the stories and struggles that people are having and you're like, "Yeah, I can totally relate to that."

The thing I admire so much and love about my job is that everybody I talk to is working so damn hard to try to help themselves. It's hard work. I went to a restaurant last weekend and I sat in the middle of the restaurant. My heart was pounding the whole time. I felt completely uncomfortable, and it was really hard work for me to sit there. And it was hard work for me to stop looking behind me. I would just as soon sit in a closed room where I know everything is all right. It's hard work and a lot of people are doing this hard work and attacking it like some sort of obstacle that they had in the military that they had to overcome. You take your hat off to them....

There comes a point—which I'm getting to—that you almost have to *embrace* the changes in your life and try to appreciate some of the things that you are. Just like this paranoia thing I was telling you about. I thought about it for a while. It's disturbing and upsetting. Now, if something were to happen, I would see it before and be able to protect my family. As disturbing as it is sometimes, sometimes you're almost, "It's not so bad." You can't come back the same person. The anger is a tough one. It's probably the least comfortable of problems to talk about because you never want to be angry anyway, and you certainly don't want people to know if you are angry.

# SCOTT E. PALMER
Sergeant, Army

Enlisted 1999–2004, deployed age 21
(August–October 2003)
Falluja, Iraq

*"It's an Inner Struggle"*

*Scott enlisted in the Massachusetts Army National Guard in 1999 and the active-duty army in 2000. He was deployed to Afghanistan August 2002–January 2003 and later in 2003 to Iraq. He was a fire support specialist and was promoted to sergeant, platoon forward observer. Although his father had a career in the Special Forces, he did not encourage Scott to join the army. At 25, Scott has tried college but currently works as a painting contractor— he spent some weeks in New Orleans working on reconstruction projects. Scott talks about his personal struggles with the aftermath of war. He is feeling better than when he first returned, but acknowledges that he is suffering from PTSD. Scott also discusses the political motivations for the Iraq war, and war generally. He is very critical of the administration's reasons for launching the attack on Iraq. "I thought of the military in use for defensive purposes— acceptable because I knew the world isn't necessarily a safe place. But to send troops preemptively to another country—that's absurd."*

My dad's military—when I was 14, he retired from the Army Special Forces as a major. He actually advised me *not* to join initially, and if I was going to do it—be an officer, not just enlist. He always told me I could do whatever I want. I just wanted to go on an adventure, to experience some kind of reality. I never felt like I was in anything real, meaningful, pertinent. I joined because of media mostly: video games, movies, books, romantic imagery of warfare. When I got to the recruiter I was pretty much the recruiter's dream. "So you can do this job, this job." "No, I want to be in the infantry." "Sure, sign here." Everybody hates their recruiter—they're the person to blame, the gatekeeper, the person who let them in. But there's a very real reason to hate recruiters.

The Bush administration wasn't even in office when I joined the army in '99. [By the time of deployment], I wasn't quite the patriot that I was when I first signed up. I started distrusting my country and what I was doing, my organization—the US Army—and my beliefs about war and killing—a number of moral issues that you have to deal with when you're a soldier. I started to be a little bit rebellious in my attitudes.

When 9/11 happened, it was my mom who called me up. I remember I was walking out to go to the motor pool, all spiffed up in starched uniform and shined boots. All that silliness that you're supposed to wear on Mondays so your superiors know that they have made your life hell. My mom called me on my cell phone and said something about the towers in New York having planes crashing into them. So I said, "Okay, whatever, Mom," and hung up and went back to the barracks. My immediate supervisor was there, and he said, "Palmer, come here, everybody is supposed to stay in the barracks and get by a TV."

So we were sitting in this room and everyone was thinking, "Oh, shit—this is it." We immediately started getting ourselves ready. That evening, our chain of command issued orders to lay out some equipment and make sure everything is all set. We had our duffle bags ready to go just in case, because you never know when the Pentagon is going to make that phone call. Potentially, we could have been deployed within hours, for all we knew.

Some of my platoon were all up and excited. They couldn't wait—none of them had ever seen real combat before. No idea. All they knew was what they saw through TV. I certainly knew that there was a lot more to it than the action movies—GI Joe. I had a lot more empathy and concern for human life than I did as an eighteen-year-old know-it-all. It's funny, because a lot of those guys who were cheering and stuff—excited about the whole deal because they knew there was going to be some retaliation—had completely different opinions after their deployment to Afghanistan and/or Iraq.... There were some guys, macho, "Sweet, sweet, we're going to war," psyched up. Of course they realized how ignorant that was later. *Most* of them. Some of them maintained a completely dumb sense of the world throughout the whole experience.

We knew Afghanistan sucked and we came back with less people than we went there with. We came back with people that got fucked up. We knew Iraq was going to suck. We knew that was going to be the real deal. And nobody, *nobody* wanted to go— not in my platoon. Of the people that had come back from Afghanistan, I'd say maybe only half a dozen from our platoon had any desire to go over there. And for some it was financially motivated because they were in debt.

While we were in Afghanistan, people were talking about how Iraq is going to be next, they're getting ready. Nope, nope, nope, I didn't want to hear it, I'm shutting it out, because I couldn't help it anyways. There were all kinds of opinions on: should we be going? Should we not be going? What's going to be the result of this? Is this going to make more enemies for the US? Some people had that opinion. I was one of them—I thought nothing good was going to come of it. I had a predisposition for negative thinking after Afghanistan.

And in addition to that, it didn't make sense to me that we should be invading a country for possessing chemical or nuclear weapons when we have—and have used—chemical and nuclear weapons ourselves. It didn't seem like we had any right, therefore there had to be ulterior motives. I believe that anything that a politician does is for some kind of political power gain or for monetary gain. I don't think there's any kind of moral structure for what goes on in politics. There are just ways of manipulating people—manipulating opinion. I don't think leaders really believe that they're doing things because of ethical reasons—they're not that dumb—it goes against human nature. It all revolves around business, making money, in what part of the world. How they can make more money by making deals with this person or that person, this corporation and that corporation....

I didn't want to go to Iraq at all. At that point, I was very antiwar. I don't know if there's a neat and tidy word to describe what I believed in at that point. But I knew it definitely was *not* the sending of citizens from one country to another country for the purpose of forcing them into submission at the cost of their lives. I thought of the military in use for defensive purposes—acceptable because I knew the world isn't necessarily a safe place. But to send troops preemptively to another country—that's *absurd*. Something I thought about at that time was if our foreign policy was like our domestic policy: if my neighbor spoke some harsh words to me, and I knew he had a weapon in his house, I could break into his house in the middle of the night and cut his throat. And that would be okay? That's terrible! Isn't that along the same line of thinking that our foreign policy works?

Our foreign policy, our justification for starting wars, is so much more lax than our own civil laws. Violent actions between citizens, between our borders—you can't go over to someone's house and break in and kill them preemptively. Our foreign policy should be an extension of our civil laws. We're much more likely to act out of fear and commit acts of violence in other countries, but [we] don't accept that within our own [borders]. Personally, I think Bush is just a figurehead, a pawn in a much larger game. I think America has been letting these kinds of wars happen for a very long time, where the public is misled and manipulated into letting these wars happen. I would like to say that I am against any war that is anything other than an absolute last resort. Wars like Vietnam, Korea, OIF, and OEF can be considered a last resort? I don't think so. Were other things tried before that?

D. and I were good buddies and [we] were both antiwar. He had a more functional view of the war. His argument with me was, "We're going to help some people out somehow. There has got to be some good that comes of this. At least the dictator Saddam isn't going to be in power any more. At least we can hold on to that, since we don't have any choice in this matter anyways right now." So he had a very intelligent and functional grasp on things.

I was more negative. I was just miserable—pissed off. Still

highly functional. You had to be. There was no slacking or resistance—nothing like that. That's what a lot of people say: once you're in the war, all that matters is you—your survival and your buddy's survival. It doesn't matter what your political views are. You don't act on your antiwar stance so much that you're not going to pull the trigger when someone is shooting at you, when someone is trying to kill you or kill your best friend.

[*When will this war end?*] No more US troops in Iraq, Iraq having some kind of government or puppet government, some kind of sovereignty—I couldn't see that as being more than a decade away. However, this war will cause more wars and more problems. It's just going to escalate because we've pissed off a lot more people. We've made a lot more enemies than we had initially—festering hatred for the American government both inside America and outside. The Arabic world—I don't think the violence is going to stop any time soon. It's all about fear. There's a lot of fear and a lot of hatred and hatred comes from fear. Fear is used as a tool by those that desire power, religious or political. Fear is the most effective way of manipulating a large group of people.

Jihadists and Christian extremists and governments of all Western nations are knee-deep in it now, making it more complicated and less easy to get out of. We're stuck. We're in a bad situation. There has never been a war that didn't leave a US presence for a prolonged period of time afterwards. That's why we still have airbases and army posts all over the world. Every place there has been a war involving the US, they have posts and bases. It's just the way America works.

---

[Our vehicles were not armored], so we ended up getting MRE ration boxes—cardboard boxes—loading them up with rocky sand from the ground and strapping them to the sides, kind of like a moving foxhole. One of those boxes might stop a round from an AK or a rifle, but your body armor was mostly protecting that [area] anyways. What they really did was to slow down the Humvees. You couldn't accelerate very fast, just a lot of excess weight. It was like *placebo* armor. Some of the guys wouldn't put two and two together and figure out that that cardboard box with sand in it is really not going to do shit to help them, but it made them feel better.

I guarded prisoners for a little while. There were three prisoners in this little tent that we were holding until the military intelligence guys were going to pick them up for an interrogation elsewhere. One person would have an axe handle inside of the tent, the other person would be looking through the flap of the tent with his weapon. That way there was no weapon for anybody to grab and try to escape with. First, you really shouldn't have prisoners being held by a platoon, or a company, or a battalion that was involved in direct combat with these guys. They should be processed really quickly—but these guys were around for a week or something.

What we were told was that two of the guys were fairly compliant, and one of the guys was a weapons dealer that was making and selling IEDs in the region. I guess intel ID-ed him and snagged him—just days earlier, [a soldier] had died from an IED. He didn't get treated very well. They would have sandbags over their heads for a good while and then they'd be taken off and they would have to just look at the wall. They would have their hands tied behind their backs and their legs tied so they couldn't run. They had to stand probably four-fifths of the time [out of] 24 hours. Some of the time they were allowed to sit, some of the time they were allowed to sleep, in broken-up sections.

Basically, how I rationalized keeping them awake and yelling at them when they were nodding off was that that wasn't any worse than anything I did in training in the military. They put you through hell in basic training, and I certainly had had more sleep deprivation than these guys. I had been verbally abused more than these guys—and these guys killed somebody. I never killed anybody, so I rationalized that at the time. I mean, it's *bad* because they don't know what's going on. For all they know, we could be sharpening a blade to chop their head off. But they really didn't experience anything worse than what I did.

In one instance I was with this [soldier]—this pissed me off— the kid was a hothead, really arrogant, obnoxious. One of the [detainees] was delirious because we had just woken him up, it was the third day—there was a lot of sleep deprivation. I was there with the axe handle. He starts getting wobbly, he put his hand back and sort of leans on me. I would push him up and he has his hand on my axe handle, not grabbing, but "I can't stand up" kind of deal. And this kid comes up from behind, he jumps him, kicks the back of his knees out, throws him down, kicks him hard in the back of the knees. I thought that was a little excessive, it wasn't called for, [but] there are certainly worse things than getting kicked in the back of the knees. . . .

---

The summer after I got back from Iraq, I started drinking a lot and was in a really bad depressive episode. I was miserable and I narrowly averted disaster. I needed to make my brain chemistry into some sort of logical working. I feel like I lost the person that I used to be. Not only that, but I hate the person I used to be. But in addition to that, I still am, in many ways, the person I used to be. Parts of yourself don't just go away. It's part of who you are, and coming to terms with that can cause anxiety and friction. It can make you really lose it. It can make you lose your mind. You lose sight of who you are, what you are, how you interact with the world around you. . . .

It's an inner struggle. There's this wanting to be in some kind of state that you were in before. You will never, ever, ever be there. You have to come to terms with who you become. Like this army nurse said to me once when I was having a hard time when I got back from Iraq. She noticed that I was crying for no reason, waiting for some test results and blood work, standard stuff on return. She saw from my papers that I just got back. And she said something to me that I will never forget: "It never goes away. But it gets a little better." It makes coming to terms with that really helpful. When you have false expectations of how you're going to perceive reality in the future, you're never going to be where you want to be.

# JON ZAGAMI
Specialist, Army Reserve

Enlisted 2002–2010 (expected), deployed age 18
(April 2003–March 2004)
Combat engineer, Camp Arifjan, Kuwait

*"My Body is Falling Apart"*

*Jon is a student at UMass Amherst, and his three siblings also attended the university. He plans to receive his BA in economics in 2008. He wants to present it to his mother, for whose constant support he is deeply grateful. I heard Jon speak at a meeting about the war, the first time he had spoken in public. A tall, slender young man of 21 years, he was telling the audience that he had had a stroke and was seeking a medical discharge from the army. To date, he has not been able to convince the army that he should be medically discharged, despite extensive medical evaluations. He spent his deployment in Kuwait, feeling underemployed and frustrated that he was close to the war but unable to make a tangible contribution. Jon questions many aspects of the Iraq war, including its rationale— "We never really came up with a reason politically why we were there. They don't issue you a reason." Not least of all, he questions the war's impact on his health, and the limitations of the VA health system.*

Why I joined the military is a good place to start. I was going through high school and the process of looking at colleges, taking SATs—but I was also dealing with the fact that my parents had gotten divorced junior year. My older brother had moved out and I felt that the family structure in my household was falling apart. I wasn't the smartest student—I didn't give my 100 percent at all. I finished high school. I knew I wasn't ready for college because I would rather spend my nights at a pool hall with my friends or at an arcade [rather] than going home and studying.

I liked the idea of the military. I actually did my senior project in school on the military. I researched the marines, navy, army, and the air force, what each had to offer—not only financially, but how they would shape and mold me as a person. I ended up going with the army because of their education benefits. What sold me was that it was the biggest branch, they had the most money, and they seemed to have a lot more opportunities than any other branch. It basically came down to the army and marines, and the marines would give more pride in my eyes—being part of the "few and the proud"—[but] I wanted to be part of the "many and the educated" at college. ...

I went to basic training—Fort Leonard Wood, Missouri. There were people from all over the United States, many that were less privileged than I was—it was like meeting new cultures. We got combat engineering training, explosives training, landmine excavation. We trained with the Seabees. Technically, I'm a carpentry and masonry specialist with the Army Reserve.

I remember I was in my kitchen with my mother and my older sister, and the phone rang. It was an eerie moment—it was like we knew what was going to happen. I picked up the phone. "Specialist Zagami"—this is one of the sergeants at my unit—"I'm calling to let you know that we just received orders—and this one is no joke. You have to have your stuff ready, you will be coming in until we get ready to move." "Okay, no problem," and I remember looking at my mom, she had tears in her eyes. "That's it, Mom, this is real."...

I remember we first drove into Camp Arifjan. It's a very large facility in southeastern Kuwait and there are different satellite camps within. We were looking for where we were supposed to stay. Where is our spot? So we started at a warehouse—we were told we couldn't stay there. Then we're sent to one of the satellite camps. They sent us over to another one, then Camden Yards and Camden Yards wouldn't take us. And then we went to Truckville, and *they* wouldn't take us—we ended up going back to Camden Yards. This went on for hours.

We also heard horror stories. There was a female major that was raped. It was like the women in the unit are your sisters almost. We were very protective of them. Someone has to wait outside the showers while they're in there because when we first got there it was geared towards men. There are a lot more males than females, so we would have to clear it out and post a guard on it for a female to go in and take a shower. In my company, I believe there were five females. Our paralegal was a female. And the other companies had females as well. …

We never saw the leadership. They were doing their thing. We kept hearing about different missions we might have. We were supposed to drive to Haditha Dam in Iraq—we were supposed to go to some city to fortify some bases in Iraq. And it seemed like every mission that came down wasn't happening. We would lose a mission for some reason—another unit is waiting, or some other group would jump all over that. Any mission that came through— they got it before we did. I don't know how true it is, but we heard that our battalion commander fell asleep in a meeting and our punishment was that they were going to keep us in Kuwait, and we were just going to do DPW work in Kuwait. I have nothing bad to say about the guy—I don't even know him.

So, okay, why did we come here? … I went on a recon mission with a small group of guys. We started driving, headed north to see what we could find. We started hitting other state camps—we hit Camp New Jersey, Camp New York, Camp Virginia. At each place it was, "What do you have for us engineers to do here?"…. What are we doing here? Why are we wasting our time, there's nothing going on, there are no missions for us. We can't do anything back in Kuwait because Brown and Root [contractors] contracted everything, even if it's to fill sand bags—they went after that. We were scrounging for missions that really are not helping the war effort. There were guys begging to go to Iraq just to be part of what was going on. If you're going to be part of history, you might as well get up there and do something.

The one mission—our claim to fame—[was] our unit got to

pave a highway from Kuwait into Iraq. Safwon was right over the border, called "sniper city" because the tankers were driving through, the Hemmets [high extended mobility tactical trucks], water trucks and field trucks—they were getting sniped as they were going through the city. It was rough on the roads, they [insurgents] dug out the asphalt—the trucks had to slow down and they were taking casualties. They decided to pave a road right around the city—why go through it—go around it. Our unit got to pave the Safwon bypass, so almost every unit has gone over that now, on our pavement. That was awesome.

When you would go into the city of Safwon, you would have to slow down, and when you did, the children would jump on the vehicles. You weren't allowed to throw candy or anything else because it would make it worse for convoys coming through. They were just orphans whose parents had taken off. These kids are stuck. This plays on the hearts of the soldiers. "That could be my brother, my sister." It tends to be a problem because they crowd on the street, they get hit by a truck.

There are civil affairs units—their job is the hearts and minds. So they would go in and take care. Go out in the field and play soccer, set up orphanages, get stuff from the Red Cross and distribute that to children. Make sure they're getting an education, they're getting a meal, getting water, getting their vaccinations. Our job as engineers is we build stuff, we blow stuff up—we need to drive through, move on. A lot of the kids get on the vehicles. Just keep moving... a bad situation.

You go over and there's a war on. There *must* be all this stuff to do. The fact is that there were so many soldiers with nothing to do. We used to joke that if the taxpayers knew what we are doing over here, there's no way they would allow this. There were thousands of soldiers waiting on work. We were just begging for something to do. Three months flew by. Then they said, "Don't worry, we plan on being out of here in six months." Six months, that's fine, let's get out of here and be done. I think the majority of troops were ready to go. Sunburned all the time and miserable, covered in sand and can't get clean. Everybody stinks, trash burning, the whole place covered in black smoke.

The executive officer [XO] said, "You know, guys, sometimes you've just got to eat a shit sandwich. We're all eating this one together. We're here for a year. I don't want to hear it. Stop your bitching. Get ready and deal with it."... The XO—he was always busy with something—he has that persona, "don't mess with me." It scared people—they were afraid to cross him in any way, shape, or form. I loved our company commander, one of the greatest commanders I've ever seen. He really cared about his troops, he would actually go down to the troops, to the lower levels, "Guys, how are you doing? Tell me what's going on—how is everything back home?"

Our unit made the national news because when they started that leave program, they told us that we weren't going to get it. We had already been shafted on missions, opportunities that we were supposed to have, and we weren't going to take any more. I remember the lieutenant colonel, battalion commander, saying, "You guys aren't going to get leave, sorry." Everybody started writing congressmen, getting hold of the reporters from their home area. We got shafted, we got stuck here, people are ready to blow their brains out—why can't we get leave? Here we are stuck in Kuwait not doing anything. "You're Reserves," was basically the answer we got.

When I was at the hospital during one of my physicals, they said, "At any point in time did you feel suicidal?" I was, "Have you been to theater?" The air force tech sergeant who was doing the physical said, "I haven't been deployed. I've been here the whole time." And I was, "Well, if you ever get deployed you'll feel suicidal, too, because I don't know anyone who has been there that can honestly say they haven't thought about killing themselves. Especially if they've told you that you're going to be there six months and the deployment has taken fourteen months." During the medical review process, every one of the army guys had combat patches on and all the people dealing with us had not been deployed.

I didn't even get two weeks. I got eleven days to come home. Terrible—to go home was *awful*. I love my family more than anything, but to come home was so awkward. You had been living with these guys—you eat with them, sleep with them, you shower with them. They're always there, you're in each other's life all the time, you know everything about their life, their growing up, so much information about these people. They're your family now.... It didn't feel right to be coming home. You had to adjust back into normal society, still pumping like crazy. You're used to living with a bunch of guys. You have a problem, you're used to taking them out to the motor pool—box it out. You've got to come home, be civil. You still feel filthy. You can do whatever you want but it's just for a few days. It is tough.

I hated the stupid questions I got. I think people want to hear gruesome stories. They want to hear that your best friend got shot in the neck and you held him. That's what I got. Shut up. I don't want to hear any of those questions. Stop your questions about who you're killing, who's killing you. It's my eleven days to get away from it all. I'm miserable there. At some point I would probably say the majority of people felt suicidal. There's no easy way to come home and deal with questions: "Were you actually *there?*" It's the middle of winter, and we're sunburned!

While I was there I felt so useless as a person, as a soldier. At the time we weren't part of it and it was so devastating—why am I here? Why am I missing out on everything back home? Why are people missing the birth of their first kid? Why are people missing their kid's graduation? Like my sister was in a pretty severe car accident while I was there—there's nothing you can do. If you're doing nothing there, why can't you come home and see how she is?...

It's funny because people say, "Wow, these guys really didn't really do much!" A lot of your tax dollars are going to pay people that are sitting there, playing video games, football. But when you're sitting there, doing nothing, losing your mind, that's when you get in trouble.... I still hadn't driven a Humvee, so I thought, I want to take the Humvee out and bomb around in the middle of nowhere. We would be jumping berms with Humvees, driving five tons through whatever we could and over whatever we could. We didn't really care, so that was fun for a while.... I guess [another time] someone got killed, fell out of the Humvee and got caught under the tire and got run over and that kind of put a damper on our fun—enough of that.

—

Why were we there, politically? We had our diehard conservatives and we had our bleeding-heart liberals..... We used to debate all the time—why are we here? The easiest answer is we're just here for oil. Why are we here for oil? Because of gas prices, because we consume oil, because of our SUVs? The debate always came down to George W. Bush is trying to finish what his father would have liked to do, but what his father maybe was too smart to do. Or, [Bush] was just trying to get revenge for his father because Saddam Hussein would have killed George H. W. Bush. We debated it *so much*, finally it was like, "Who cares why we're here...?" It would be so cut-and-dried if someone landed on Cape Cod, rolled up on our shores, tried to occupy this country. I would volunteer to go right now.

But over there it was, "*Who* are we fighting for?" I found it pretty hard to say, "Oh, I'm fighting for America." *Are* we fighting for America? I mean, who attacked us from Iraq? I was like, we're fighting for Iraq. We're fighting to free Iraq. But... you're not gaining support by destroying a country. And then even when things are getting destroyed, they told us, "Okay, bomb the hell out of whatever city."...

We had some very educated soldiers. We've got people who have got their masters or going for their Ph.Ds. So we have some very, very intelligent people. The debates were amazing. I was still wet behind the ears—I was only eighteen when I got there. I listened to these conversations—I couldn't keep up with a lot of it, I didn't read enough in high school. That's why I need to get educated because I couldn't even join a conversation. I'm over here because I was told to be and I didn't even question it. They ask me, "Why do you think we're here?" and I was like, "Uhhh... oil." Easy, simple answers. We never really came up with a reason politically why we were there. They don't issue you a reason.

When I first came home, you kind of shut yourself down for a while. I remember I didn't leave my room for a few days—I couldn't deal with being outside. I was on the phone constantly with other guys from the unit, "What's going on?" There are so many choices now, you're on your own now, back on the street, not supposed to worry about anything. "Welcome back. You know why we're there?" I was like, "No, shut up. I don't want to know why you think we were there, because you weren't there." It was ignorance, but it was also me readjusting.

My family understood. When I wanted to talk about what happened, where we were, what we did, I told them. It came out, there was no pressure. No pressure at my house. Now I'm being readjusted to society, being out of the military life. I can listen. I can sit down and say, "What did you read, why do you think we're there?" I can handle that, and I can pose my argument as to why I think [we were there]. But that was one of the hardest things to do coming back.

———

The thing that happened is I got knocked out three times while I was in the theater, non-combat-related [injuries]. I got hit on the head three times and all three times suffered concussions, twice passed out. When you're over there, you're the tough guy, you've got to brush it off. I took some ibuprofen. I went to the medic and she said, "Well, your blood pressure is really high, you should probably monitor this." My mother is a nurse practitioner and so we call her and say, "Mom, my blood pressure is really high," but I wasn't going to tell her I got knocked out three times. My blood pressure is going through the roof and they don't know why it won't go back down.

No MRI ever, no CAT scan, never had anything.... I came home, went to Fort Drum to out-process, went through the medical screening there and said, "I was knocked out three times, is it in the paper work?" "Yes, going to file a claim?" "I feel fine right now, do I need to file a claim?" "No, you don't need to file a claim." "So okay, let's go home." Went home and last February, I had a stroke. I was at UMass, worked out at the gym and I felt like I got stabbed in the head. It hurt *so bad*. I didn't know what happened....

We went to my older sister's house—she was a nursing major—she checked my blood pressure. It was 180/90—out of control. She called my mother and my mother said, "Get him to the hospital right now." The hospital here, we did a scan, but we can't see what's going on. Blood pressure wasn't coming down. Eventually, they said, "How are you doing now?" and I told them I couldn't speak when I first got there.... The pain was terrible. My whole right side was showing the effects. We went to the VA hospital in West Roxbury—they did their own tests. The neurologist came and said, "I'm going to tell you right now, you had a stroke." I said "Okay, whatever." I don't know if it didn't hit me or I didn't know what was going on. My right arm is weaker than my left, and my right leg is weaker than the left.

The doctor said, "I'm going to show you a mirror," and he showed me that the right side of my face is drooping so bad. I remember I said, "Is that going to go back?" And he said, "Oh yes, we'll get it back, don't worry about it, you'll be fine." And I was *devastated*. On my floor are old men and mostly Vietnam vets and they were, "What are *you* doing here—you're a vet?" And I was like, "Yup, I served over in the Middle East." I stayed there at least two weeks. "Look, there's nothing else we can do for you...."

When they released me, I couldn't even walk. My father carried me out of the hospital and put me in the car.... I'm still being seen as a patient now. I still get these headaches—when I get them I can't see. The VA told me, "Oh, that's typical for a migraine headache." I said, "Fine, I've never had a headache like that before." They've got me on medicine to control my blood pressure. I'm 21 years old, I don't know why I should have to be on blood-pressure medication. It's not fatal. They try to keep it low, but as soon as they take me off the meds, it jumps. There's no history of hypertension in my family, or heart conditions. My body is falling apart and I'm only 21 years old.

Other guys in my unit have hypertension, especially those of us who went to work on the Safwon project. There were too many similar cases of health issues in the unit for me to just write it off. Maybe it's fine when they burned the trash—all the smoke is floating into our camp and you couldn't see, there was black smoke everywhere. Maybe it was because we lived on a base where there was a depleted uranium holding field. Now the VA is actually paying for depleted uranium testing with certain servicemen who are having severe health issues, and maybe [it is] something I have to do as part of this process. That would be a good thing to know, but there's nothing you can do about it.

Maybe it was because we were living on an old battlefield from the first war. Maybe there's something in the sand over there. They did all the tests that they thought were necessary to find what was causing this. At the end they just said, "You just got knocked out." Anti-malarial pills, biological weapons pills—we were forced to take them. People watch *Jarhead*—the movie where they're forced to take the pills. People are like, "Well that doesn't happen, does it?" "Yeah [it does], you don't have a choice, they issue it, you have to take it, they watch you take it." Anti-malarial pills and a bottle of pills for biological weapons exposure. I tried to write it down. "Mom, what is this stuff?"

The VA—the doctors are wonderful, you do get good care, but you don't get enough of it. And now with the budget cuts, the hospital closures, over 2,000 [as of September 2007, 3,700—ed.] soldiers have died so far. How many are injured? How many are home with PTSD? How many need healthcare and you're downsizing the VA system? Well, maybe you should downsize the war and increase the VA system.

Now, as a soldier, an injured soldier, the feeling I get is that I'm useless. "Are you ready to re-deploy with us?" The answer from the doctors and from myself is I would be a liability. I wouldn't want someone watching *my* back—I wouldn't want someone in a fighting position with me—that has my health issues. I've been working on a medical discharge since I got out of the hospital, so in February 2007 it will be three years. I have trouble wearing a hat, how am I going to put a Kevlar on? And doctors say, there's no way you can put a Kevlar on because you have an enlarged vessel in your head still, and if that one goes, you're not going to make a near-full recovery. You may not get your leg, your arm, your face back.

Any injury while you were deployed is service-connected. They're trying to say, you had a stroke here for something you did [here]. And my doctor is saying, "No, no, no he had a stroke because he got knocked out in theater, because he had high blood pressure. He didn't have high blood pressure when he went in." I've been given the option of leaving the unit and forfeiting my benefits and I refuse to do that because I didn't choose to have a stroke. I didn't give fourteen months to forfeit my benefits.

If I leave the unit willingly—my choice to walk away—I will lose all my education benefits. I've got to pay back anything beyond the Montgomery GI Bill, including my signing bonus, tuition assistance program (you have to still be in the unit). Reservists— they waive your tuition, but you still have all the fees [non-tuition costs] to pay. I could sign myself out today (on a general discharge) and lose all those benefits. That's not fair, because if I have another stroke I want the VA to pay for that, and if I sign myself out they won't do that. I am going to stay in until they recognize the fact that I was injured due to my service. I will get my disability and I know that I can go to the VA hospital and my issues will be covered. And my education benefits will continue.

The first time I spoke in public they asked, what was it like coming to UMass as a student, a soldier, and I told them. I said you should understand that there are a lot of veterans on this campus and I'm glad we're having this week on the war. But be very careful of what you say because a lot of veterans are in this community and you won't recognize them—they may be out of the service, they may have grown a beard. You may not recognize them, but they are veterans and there are things that you can say that may hurt them—because they fought for your right to be able to say that. The general consensus is that most veterans don't want to speak, they do not feel comfortable talking about their experiences.

There are so many issues that you have to confront about yourself before you can actually go and speak about what you have done, where you have been, where you are going. Like in the classroom, we can be talking about what is going on in the Middle East, and I can raise my hand and say, this is what was going on. And they say, "How do you know, where do you get that information?" Myself. They are citing this or that source. And I'm saying, I have been there and I know. At least it's "shock and awe" that someone has actually done this. A lot of students couldn't care less.

SIX

THE ULTIMATE LOSS

# ALEXANDER ARREDONDO
## Lance Corporal, Marine Corps

Enlisted 2001, deployed age 18
(January–September 2003, May–August 2004)
Nasariya, Najaf, Iraq
KIA August 25, 2004, age 20, awarded Bronze Star with Combat V

*Alex died in Iraq, age 20. His technical high school had its own on-site marine recruiter, building relationships with young students, including Alex. At seventeen, he had his divorced mother sign his enlistment papers. But his father, Carlos, did not know that he had also accepted a $20,000 bonus to join. Soon he and Alex's stepmother, Melida, felt that they, too, were "drafted." Alex was proud to be a marine: "I am starting to feel the basic warrior instinct and pride grow inside." When he was killed in Najaf, his father attacked and burned the marine van in which three servicemen arrived with the devastating news. Alex's death inspired Carlos and Melida to inform families about enlistment and how military recruiters often mislead potential recruits, including non-Americans and people of color. Alex was American-born, but it took his Costa Rican father until 2006 to become an American citizen. The law that gives citizenship to parents of the fallen had been passed two months after Alex died.*

*Alex's letters and e-mails are italicized—spelling and punctuation have not been changed; the letter and email dates are also his. Carlos and Melida tell his—and their—story.*

[*Carlos*:] I told him that I didn't want him to join full-time the marines because I didn't want him to come home in a body bag. And his answer was, "It won't happen, Dad, it won't happen," and I gained confidence from what he was saying…. He was totally involved with the marines. When I found out later, I was a little bit annoyed because I was the father and nobody contacted me. Someone took for granted that we are separated parents, and pretty much went along with his mom and him. I told him how I was feeling, "I want to support you because I love you very much, but I am still very concerned about this." I didn't know at the time that they offered him so much money to join the service. I also learned if he signed up for more years, he will eventually get more money….

He was my love, my older boy, he was my American dream—my boys are my American dream. They were born here. My boy was getting involved more and more with the marines, telling all his friends, all the neighbors, "I'm going to be a marine." One thing always concerned me—the day the car bomb blew up in the dormitories, killed almost 300 marines in Beirut [October 23, 1983]. I even told him, "Can you imagine how each family of these people [felt]?—because it would be devastating."

> *I am starting to feel the basic warrior instinct and pride grow inside. I feel strong and unstoppable with pride. The Crucible [a 54-hour endurance test] is coming close. It's the ultimate task of recruit training that will earn [me] the title United States Marine. I'M PUMPED* [from boot camp]

[*Carlos*:] During the time when he went to war I was worried how he will be taking all these things he was going through, always thinking of post-traumatic stress disorder. Because I know how many other servicemen in wars they can suicide, be drug abuser, be homeless. They are obviously going to kill. I went along with him, I support him…. I remember that I took him to the bus to South Carolina. This kid was so small and was getting so big at the same time.

> *I'll tell you all about the Crucible and Gas Chamber soon [a confidence test]. Thank you for the newspaper clippings. I am going to change my job on Oct. 1st. I want to do an electrical specialty so I might do something where I will*

*work on a ship and be deployed a lot.... P.S. Please send
some info. about Afghanistan, Saudi Arabia, Iran, Iraq. We
get very little amounts of info. down here... But I have
heard some little things here and there about Conflicts, War,
Deployments, etc. THANX. Love you, Alex. September,
2002.*

[*Melida:*] I explained to him there is ROTC. He can go to
college right away, it will pay for his college education—being in
the Reserves. Alex signed into the military early, so he got some
kind of money we didn't know about until we got to know the
marines after Alex had passed.... When he was at boot camp, he
didn't know [he was going to Iraq]. We have one of the letters
which says, "Where's Iraq?" *literally*, and we were like, "Oh my
goodness," because we were listening to the radio every day.

*This seems so unreal to me. I've never seen water this
BLUE before, I've never looked 360 degrees around me
and seen nothing but water, clouds, the sun and a fleet of
battleships surrounding me.... I will also be training a
short time in Kuwait. This is hard for me to comprehend.
It seems like my life changed in an instant. Yesterday I was
in a classroom learning about Trigonometry and History.
I graduated, went to boot camp. Went to school, graduated
as a GRUNT, I was sent across the country to train, now
I'm being sent across the world to fight.*

*Today I am in a class room learning about TACTICAL
URBAN COMBAT and NUCLEAR, BIOLOGICAL,
AND CHEMICAL WARFARE. In the middle of the
Pacific ocean, on my way to experience 1st hand what I am
learning about. I am not afraid of dying. I am more afraid
of what will happen to all the ones that I love if something
happens to me. Soon enough, I will be in the desert, outside
the City of Baghdad, in full combat gear, ready to carry out
my mission. Wondering how this all happened so fast.
Wishing I was back home... taking care of my family.
January, 2003.*

*It's Sunday, Feb. 16th. It's been about one month on ship
now and I am scheduled to get off in Kuwait in less than 2
weeks. By the time you get this I will already be in Iraq
and possibly already kicked off our main assault on*

*Baghdad or the Republican Army. It's probably not as exciting for you as it is for me. Ha. Ha. Don't worry about a thing. We have all been ready mentally and physically for a while now. I have all the knowledge and more that I need going into this situation. February, 2003.*

[*Melida:*] He stayed until late August 2003 [first deployment]. The letters changed. He could see the insurgency starting or at least the change in the attitude around the soldiers. He wrote, "We were surrounded by all these civilians sort of like on top of my vehicle, one of them is going to get himself killed." He didn't want to be the one to do it. He loved them. He had a lot of friends who were Iraqi. He helped train the police force. He enjoyed that.

*I'm still here in Iraq. I'm currently in a large complex in the western outskirts of Baghdad. Myself and my squad have seen just about the most action in my unit, that's cause I'm 1st or 2nd man, 1st team, 1st sqd [squad], 1st plt [platoon], A Co.[company] 1st bn [battalion], 4th Marines. I was one of 18 of the first Marines that entered the city of Baghdad. I am the point man for a lot of Marines and switch sometimes with my buddy York. I got promoted to lance corporal.*

*So much has happened since I've been here I can't focus on writing. Last week we were clearing some buildings in Saddam City when we came under heavy sniper fire. A friend of mine from North Carolina/SOI [school of infantry] was shot and killed [age 20]. His name was Garza he just got married a couple of months ago....It sucks but I understand sacrifices in time of war... At midnight we went out and captured 4 snipers along with a [Navy] Seal [SEAL] team. Later on today we moved 6 tons of explosives (Iraqi) to be destroyed. April 16, 2003.*

[*Melida:*] He was infantry. He chose that—he wanted to see the action. In talking to him, I know why he did it. You get more pay, and more benefits. So he had the best life insurance, okay, so in case something happened to him. He had combat pay. He got injured at one point—you get paid for that—an injury where he can go back. And he couldn't touch any of it in Iraq so when he came home, there was a tidy little fix there.

*Yesterday my unit moved from our complex in Baghdad south about 100 kilometers near Nazirea [Nasariya]. Originally we were supposed to stay here 6 days and then go back to Kuwait for 1 month, then jump back on ship and come back to America but things just changed, now the word is we will stay here for 2 to 30 days, then move to our company strong point at another place in this city, and stay there for 30 to 90 days and no idea after that. It's alright though. I know everyone's probably anxious to see me back home safe and nowhere near combat but I don't mind staying here for the summer. It's not so bad. There's an upside too! Right now I have money going into a bank account and I can't touch it. We are constantly moving so I see all kinds of areas like desert, agricultural areas, low population, mud hut towns, high population inner city Lots of people too! The people who like us, like kids, old men, young beauties in full robe who love American men and the people who don't like us like the ones who throw rocks or shoot at us. April 22, 2003.*

[*Carlos*:] We received letters, e-mails, and phone calls from Alex. When Alex left, when the war was declared, I didn't go to work. I pretty much sat here, with two TVs at the same time, CNN, MSNBC. If I walked to the bathroom, I had a radio, to support me with those news. I was already developing PTSD.

[*Melida*:] I am thinking of calling it something else. I am thinking of calling it "military families stress syndrome." No sleeping—we were insomniacs. Or the opposite, we were narcoleptics…. You know, we had a bad habit: every morning we would welcome the day with a new death. Usually he would wake up first, and I would come out and instead of saying, "Good morning, darling," he would say, "Three more deaths." The morning that Alex was killed I heard that three marines had died in Najaf. It was Carlos's birthday—I didn't know what to tell him.

*I just got your package… with the newspaper clippings…. Right now the clippings are being passed around…. As it looks right now, I'll be in Iraq for a couple more months. We are staying in a date packaging factory in Al Hellah [Hilla] between Baghdad and Najaf. Most of the fighting is pretty much over and we've moved a lot of ammunition and bombs to be destroyed from all over many cities. There were many missiles hidden in schools and other public buildings. Now that's taken care of we are focusing on peacekeeping and humanitarian missions. They're a lot more laid back than combat missions. A lot, a lot!.... We play football (soccer), American football. Rugby, and wall-ball.... Your son–still liberating, April 30, 2003.*

[*Carlos*:] On this day I was traveling—wherever I go, I listen to my radio. I went to the Red Cross to see if they could help me figure out where is my son. I called the US Marines, they told me no news is good news. That day I pull over and started to listen to NPR news. "We've got John Burnett from a town in Iraq," and [Burnett said] "I am in the tobacco factory and with me is Alexander Arredondo...." And then suddenly I listen to my son say he has been traveling in this tank for so many days, with so much noise, the smell of fuel, pounding their asses. It was *unbelievable*. I got out of the car, I jumped and screamed I was so excited. I ended up calling everybody to let everybody know I heard from Alex.

*My unit has broken off again and moved. Now just my platoon is staying inside a police station. We have two weeks to secure a city. We go out every day with the police and do what a beat cop does, patrol the streets. We mostly just deal with shootings and robberies. It's fun to jump in the back of a civilian truck and take off into a packed city. Last night I went into a marketplace to look for a gang and the market was packed with people. We couldn't drive on the street, we got out to patrol and we had to move through the mass of people. It reminded me of right after a basketball game gets out and you try to leave but you can't move forward. I've made a lot of friends in the area that come to the station everyday.... P.S. Oh, yeah. The cops are teaching me Arabic. [signs name in Arabic]. Mid-May, 2003.*

*It looks like I am going to be stuck in Iraq forever. It sucks! It's hot, it smells, I'm quite miserable.... By the way, happy Father's Day Dad. I tried calling that night but the damn AT&T woman wouldn't let me make the call. June 28, 2003.*

[*Carlos:*] When they were asking for help in sending masks, wipes, food, because the supply was behind, I was one of the first ones in line at the post office. And I was there sending boxes. It's not like I made that choice. They pretty much drafted me, too—the government of the United States.

> *I'm in Shomalie, Hillah. I'm sick of all the bullshit these civilians are pulling. It's gonna get one of them shot. It's not just Shomalie, it's all of Hillah, and it's even worse up north. This morning one of our guys almost got hit with what I thought was a knife thrown from some guy on the side of the road. Yesterday one guy started throwing bricks at us and some workers at the city hall during a riot. It started raining bricks and then I noticed the guy, ran out of the gate and kicked his ass all over the street in the[area] of the rioters. He's lucky I didn't shoot him. Besides that it's been normal with exception of our everyday huge explosions and gunfire. I'll take care, you do the same and I'll see you soon. I love you, Your Son, Alex, June 29, 2003.*

[*Melida:*] The first time he was deployed was January 2003. The second time he was deployed he arrived in Kuwait in early June 2004. He ended in Najaf for about three weeks to a month previous to being killed in August. June and July we don't really know. That's part of the reason we want to speak to his friends. Carlos and I are hoping to get to the West Coast to meet the troops that Alex was responsible for.

> *I can't tell you much because of operation security. We've moved to another city to be the main effort. I've been fighting for almost a week now. I'm sure if you watch the news you'll figure it out. I'll contact you as soon as I can. I miss you all and I love you very much. August 9, 2004.*

[*Carlos:*] When the marines showed up at my house, my mother and I were all alone. My mother doesn't speak English. There were two African-American sergeants and a Latino-American Marine. When I first saw them coming over, I thought that was the biggest surprise I can ever have, by having my son on my birthday. I mean, we knew he was fighting in Najaf, his mother *told* me, and the next thing I know they are outside—how could this be *possible*? Where is my boy? They're coming in uniform, I looked for him on my birthday, a surprise—what happened? I asked him, "What you here for? I don't see my boy." And they said, "We're here to see the family." And I said, "I am the homeowner."

Sergeant S. was in charge, "Are you Carlos Arredondo?" and I say, "Yes." And then he said to me, "I'm sorry. We have come to notify you that Alexander Arredondo was killed in combat." And that's what I hear from him. I said nothing. I was looking at him and trying to figure out something. I feel I stopped breathing. I feel like my heart went into the ground. And a lot of things in my head started getting confused. I have to translate English into my Spanish—that process takes a little bit of time in foreign languages.

I just take off running to the back of the yard to meet my mother. She was cutting the grass and I told her, "Mama, the marines are outside—they say Alex was killed." My brother is named Alex also, so my mother was thinking it is her own son. I called my son Brian. I was crying. I said, "Brian, I am so sorry, Brian, the marines are here and they say Alex got killed." He said, "I know that," and when he said, "I know that," from that time everything changed and I said, "What do you mean you know?" and he said, "Because they're here, too, in Bangor, Maine."

"Oh my God, I'm so sorry, Brian. Did they tell you this?" And he said, "No, they didn't tell me. When I saw them pulling over I know already what they was here for." Suddenly I feel something stabbed my chest, I said, "Oh, *no*." I felt a stab, another stab, another stab—I was falling apart right there. He said, "Dad, I've got to go, I've to go find my mother...." I went to meet the marines and I look at them and said, "Oh my God, no, this really didn't happen. It's not happening. It's not happening."

Then I went out and asked the marines to please leave. "I want you to leave. Please, please, I don't want you here no more." I think that maybe I thought if they leave this will not be true. They said, "No, we cannot leave." I want them to leave. I ran into the backyard again, crying for God to help me once again—*please*. And I walk out once again to the garage door.

The marines were still there. They never entered my house. They only came to give the news outside my house. And they stayed there the whole time. At the same time there was a second team in Bangor, Maine—there were four: a chaplain, a navy, and two marines. I found that out later. And I wondered why they never sent a chaplain [to my house]. But anyway, at the time I went to the garage and asked them one more time to leave my house and they said, "We're waiting for your wife. She is on the way here."...

I got my telephone, and I dial a number and I see automatic, Sergeant M. That is the recruiter. And I hit the dial and it ring, this person picked up. "Sergeant M., oh my God, the marines are here, they told me my son got killed, can you please tell me what is going on," and the voice on the other side said, "Sorry, you've got the wrong number." They hung up on me.

I grab a hammer and I walk past the marines to the van. My mother was right there saying, "Don't do that." I hear one of the marines: "Sir, sir, don't do that."... I remember five gallons of gasoline in the garage.... On the way out, I grabbed a propane torch. The next thing I know, my mother's there, trying to take the gasoline away from me. I took the gasoline away from her, the propane torch, this was the marine van which was open. I got the gas and put it on the two front seats.... I remember looking backwards and I seen the marines talking on the phone. I went inside the van and I look around, and I picked up the hammer and I started destroying their computer system, communications. I started grabbing everything from the van and throwing it out the window. And I remember my mother on the driver's side screaming and yelling for help....

I poured gasoline everywhere. The next thing I know, the explosion of fuel, I pretty much went head down, back to the floor, legs up in the air to the door. I could feel the flames, right away—the sensation of being burned.... The sensation, my ear, my face, and when I got off the floor, I just took off running. And then I dived myself into the ground, I rolled back and forth. I used to be a fireman back in Costa Rica and they teach me how to deal with this.

[*Melida:*] I found Alex's last e-mails:

*I'm in Najaf. Do me a favor and check the news online. Save pictures and videos if you can. I'll stay in contact until I move. Let everyone know I love them. Take care. August 11, 2004.*

Alex was killed fourteen days later, on August 25.

# JEFFREY LUCEY
Corporal, Marine Corps

Enlisted 1999, deployed age 21
(January–July 2003)
Nasariya, Basra, Iraq
Committed suicide at home, June 22, 2004, age 23

*Kevin and Joyce Lucey are the parents of Jeffrey Lucey, a marine reservist who served in Iraq. He was never able to recover from the trauma of what he saw and did there. Despite their best efforts to get him help, and due in part to the limitations of the VA, Jeff committed suicide a year after his return. There are suicides in the war zone and there are suicides back in the US, a toll that has not been counted. Jeff died at home after a long battle with PTSD. "Jeff asked whether he could sit in my lap. He was Dad's little boy. That was his last gasp....You had to see his eyes, the listlessness.... It wasn't Jeff. We don't know who was sitting in Jeff's body—but it wasn't Jeff." The Luceys are activists for their son and others like him, lobbying to get the VA to take better care of veterans at risk. They filed a wrongful death lawsuit against the VA and the US government in July 2007. Kevin is a therapist and Joyce is a nurse.*

[*Why did Jeff volunteer?*] [*Joyce:*] I don't think Jeffrey volunteered—I think he was approached by the recruiters. He was eighteen, he was in his first semester of college at HCC [Holyoke Community College]. I believe he was approached at the mall. People ask, why did he join, and to this day we do not have a definite answer. Jeffrey was in college. I think he was probably still floating. They approached him and Jeff was the kind of kid who wouldn't walk away from people. I think that once they saw that he would listen, it was calls on the phone.

I didn't even realize how far gone it was until he said, "I have to sign by December to get the deferred entry into boot camp so I can have my spring semester of college. Then I will go." Then he would go in May, be out by August, back in college in September, which turned out *not* to be true because they said the programs have now all been switched and now you will go to combat training down at Camp Lejeune. So he did not get back into college in September.

[*Kevin:*] One of the most important things is that he is a *reservist*. He is a member of the citizen's army—you cannot treat the reservists in the same way as you can treat regular military. [*Joyce:*] They don't have the support system, they're not in the military culture…. But back to when he said he had to sign by a certain time, "You've got to be kidding, Jeff—why would you even think of it, what would possess you?" He said, "I can get money for college—and the uniform." The ability afterwards to make connections with other marines who are in higher places in jobs—you've got your marine ring, you might get pulled into that company—because it *is* a brotherhood.

[*Kevin:*] And that was also 1999. In 1991 when the first Gulf War occurred, Jeffrey was only ten years old. So then you have all that peacetime, and the way that sold in the media—you're going to have everything, during peace you're going to have tremendous benefits. I remember him talking about the mortgage—because I guess if you're a veteran you qualify for mortgages. So he was looking at his whole life and he was saying, here is my entire future, and never, never *once* did it ever occur—it never occurred to *me*—that he would ever have to experience a war.

[*Joyce:*] It did me—not having any control over what occurred once they signed…. So I said, "Once you're in, you're in." And the other issue was, he believed from what they said that he would come out with $3,500 from boot camp, thirteen weeks. Jeff mentioned this in letters. "They failed to mention that everything that *they* say you need at boot camp you have to buy. I need this uniform, I need these boots, I need a canteen. Everything that they require you to have, they failed to tell me, Mother. It all comes out of *my* money, so I'm going to be lucky if I get out of here with a thousand dollars."

[*Kevin:*] In fact, we helped him with the dress blues. The recruiter never said anything [like], "Oh by the way, out of the money you could be earning, we're going to be taking about fifteen percent or more due to that fact that you have got to pay your own way." [*Joyce:*] They were supposed to get a photo with their dress uniforms. He said "Ma, if you want the picture, send me something—otherwise I don't think I'm going to get these pictures because they want more money, like $200." He's got it in his letters—he was just *so* disappointed in the marines.

They go in when they are young, they believe what they are told—there's no reason not to. The other thing is when he was signed up his recruiter took him to a hotel overnight. He picked him up at our home—my husband and I were getting a little upset—"Jeffrey, do *not* sign." He said, "He just wants to talk with us, Ma." I said okay. He and his friend Paul joined up in the buddy system. I ran into Paul a few weeks ago and I said, "Did you *really* go to a hotel?" And he said, "He took us to a hotel," and then they came back the next morning: "I signed." He was away from his support system.

[*Kevin:*] Regretfully, there is that atmosphere of mistrust that's generated by them. For example, the retention, the re-enlistments—[they say] how they are 125 percent, 117 percent. But what mothers are telling us is happening to their sons is that the officers go up to them in Iraq and they say, "Okay, now you have a choice: you can re-enlist right now for the next four to six years and you'll get a cash bonus. If you're going to stay with us, you're going to be stop-lossed, and you aren't going to get the cash bonus [bonuses paid in theater are not taxed—ed.], but you're still with us—so what would you like to do?"

[*Joyce:*] In Jeff's own words at the time, [Iraq] was a vendetta for [Bush's] dad, and it was oil. He said we shouldn't be going over there and that's *before* he went over there. [*Kevin*:] He wanted to go [to] Afghanistan, [but] he couldn't see any rationale for Iraq. He said, "Afghanistan, that's where bin Laden is, that's where al-Qaeda is." He would have gone there holding the flag. But he just couldn't understand *Iraq*. We kept hearing the testimony—after Jeff died I remember *praying* that they would discover even one weapon of mass destruction. [*Joyce*:] If they had, he would have gone there for a reason. Jeff said, "I have nothing positive to say about our armed deployment." That is not something he came back with, he had it before he left. …

[*Kevin*:] One of the tragedies of all this is when Jeff was recruited, we now say we really should have been more aggressive in trying to convince him. But we felt we did all we could during his first eighteen years—we wanted him to make his own choice. My father was a corporal in the army during WWII. My brother was a LRRP [long-range reconnaissance patrol] in the Vietnam War. And yet—I was in the seminary until age 21—I was a CO [conscientious objector]. So because I was allowed to exercise *my* options, I wanted to give Jeff's *his*. It proved to be lethal. …

[*Kevin*:] In the month of April [2003], he wrote down that he wished he could erase the entire month away from his life. His activity went from Basra up to Nasariya and Baghdad…. [*Joyce*:] He wrote a letter to his girlfriend which said that he had written her a little note one evening because they had heard that the next day they were going with the Marine 24th Division Special-Op Capable into Nasariya, and it was going to be dangerous…. He said all military codes of war were off, shoot anything [that] moved—that's what they were told. They were seeing [Iraqi] troops that were just trying to get back into their home. Jeff said he saw an elderly family shot down—they were just trying to get back into their home.

⁓

They don't sleep, we don't sleep. When you have a man or a woman going through PTSD, you've got to believe that the family is going through PTSD—we're still going through it…. Way back to the Civil War, they called it the irritable heart, [other wars] they called it battle fatigue, combat syndrome, the soldier's heart. In

Jeff's case, my belief is he had a sensitive soul, and all of a sudden he saw sights and had experiences which compromised his humanity. It was totally different from what he was raised with—the values, the beliefs. How do you reconcile it? Some people can and some people can't. It is a traumatic event that has internal impact, and based on what the person is like internally, they can deal with it through counseling. Other people deal with it through substances, alcohol.

[*Joyce:*] Jeffrey—September, October, and November after he returned, he was vomiting every day. It wasn't like it was alcohol, the next morning vomiting. I found out through his girlfriend, Jeff is not at all like he was. He gets up in the morning and all of a sudden he goes to the bathroom. So possibly if Jeff had been picked up at that point he would have been receptive to care. But by the time we got him to the VA, he was so heavily medicating himself with alcohol, he was on Clozapine, he was on Prozac. He had worked himself into a situation where he had not gone to school for a couple of weeks, so he wasn't graduating, he had totaled our car. He was working himself into a hole [wondering], "How do I get out of here? I can't get to work, I'm not studying, I have a relationship problem now with my girlfriend because of all this, and I'm not going to UMass in September because I haven't yet graduated from HCC."

I look at his bank book after he died—$45 dollars left in his account. And he had returned with $14,000. He had helped his older sister, he had helped her boyfriend, he had bought [his sister] Julie's books. Then he found out that the benefits he got from the marines didn't cover certain things in college and now he back-owed them money. When his car got totaled when he first came back, he used money—he had nothing left. He would have to be under stress. We didn't even realize it. ...

[*Kevin:*] We were told so many times by the staff at the VA, your son has to be totally alcohol-free, *then* we will evaluate him for PTSD. And we said, it's only the alcohol that has been holding him together—he's medicating himself. Jeff *told* us he was doing that. And I said, "Now you're going to try to take away the only thing that he has been able to find and then you're saying, bring him back? So after he's dealing with the raw PTSD without any medication, you want us to try to bring him back? It doesn't make sense."

[*Joyce*:] They had good reason with Jeffrey just to assess him—instead they discharged him with alcohol dependency, depression secondary to alcohol. You're looking through the record, he's talking about Iraq to different nurses and they mentioned PTSD—but this is the nurses. When you get to the psychiatrist, it was different.... And they say they can't assess him until he is alcohol-free.

The national policy is a dual diagnostic approach—you treat both at the same time. They didn't even know their own policy. I feel that is partially responsible for Jeff's not being here. You have to take the alcohol away—that I understand—but then they also took away his cigarettes, they also took away his ability to go to Memorial Day services, to go to the bathroom on his own, to shower on his own. Jeff was very humiliated. I understand [it] would have been a liability if he had done something under their watch.

[*Joyce*:] This was someone going through a crisis. There is a small window for some kind of intervention, and there was a one-week period right before he died that he didn't drink. He was by the fireplace, he had tears in his eyes, he was kind of choking up, he said, "I don't know what is wrong with me, I don't know why I feel like this right now." Kevin had the PTSD book and Jeff was looking at it and saying, "I have this"—so intellectually he was there.

[*Joyce*:] From my perspective, all that was happening with Jeffrey, we were in crisis with him, and we didn't know who to turn to, where to get help, where to look up the resources—we didn't know anything. Jeffrey didn't want us to go to the marines, so that was out—we respected that. "Well, maybe he's right, maybe if we do say something and let them know how bad he is...," so we didn't go to the marines. Then we went to the VA only after Kevin called and found out that it wasn't part of the military system, and without Jeff's okay they [the Marines Corps] would find out nothing.

[*Kevin*:] What happened, I called and said, "You've got to help us, we have my son in need, very angry, possibly suicidal," and they said, "Okay." And then I said, "He has also been drinking," and they said, "We can't help you." [*Joyce*:] I even went to the police here and let them know if we're really in trouble, we'll give you a call. We didn't want them to think he's dangerous—he's *not* dangerous, he's falling apart. Maybe had we been able to get him help sooner, known right away that the vet center [in Springfield], existed. At that point Jeffrey was his own person, so it was kind of hard to say, you have to do this or do that.

[*Kevin*:] We think we can change the system a little. Think about it: when these young men and women come home, if they are afflicted with PTSD, you're asking a tormented soul to make rational decisions about their health and about their medical care. Why not have the health proxy presented to them when they have to do their will and their power of attorney? He could be committed, or else the person can say, Yes, he will go into the VA for this period of time. The VA is going to have to change. Do you know we have a system that told us, "Look, the next time he acts up, call the police, lie if you have to. Get him arrested. Or kick him out of the house. Let him hit rock-bottom." It's almost as though they had cut him away from the environment his government had just put him through—and yet this is the VA. ...

[*Joyce*:] And that first night he was suicidal. He had already told his sister that he found a tree out here, which is behind the house, with a rope hanging from it. His girlfriend told the psychiatrist that he was hearing voices that night. He was checking for camel spiders in his room with a flashlight. [*Kevin*:] He could feel people touching him in his room, stroking him. [*Joyce*:] In February, he had a nightmare, and he said, "I was just back in the alleyway and they were coming after me." I know he was having nightmares. His girlfriend said that he was having difficulty sleeping....

This was just a couple of days before he died, and he was really falling apart. We would say, "Jeffrey, where is my little boy?" And he goes, "He's right here." He had taken me for a walk just about a week before he died, down to the brook, and he had the CD player and he wanted me to hear the song "45" by the Shinedown. When he came across those words, "Whatever happened to the young man's heart, swallowed by pain," and it says, "Staring down the barrel of a 45"—that's all he has left.

[*Kevin*:] About ten days before Jeff died, Jeff asked whether he could sit in my lap. He was Dad's little boy. And I had to. I mean, how can you? And then afterwards, that was his last gasp.... You had to see his eyes, the listlessness.... It wasn't Jeff. We don't know who was sitting in Jeff's body, but it wasn't Jeff. It was just like he was back there [in Iraq]. That's the way we experienced it.... The night before Jeff died, we spoke for hours and hours and hours. I told him, make positive out of negative. You have so much knowledge and if you could find the energy you could help us all, maybe get together to try to publish *Jeff's Story*. Not as a book, but as a survival handbook for other kids.

[*Kevin:*] You want to hear a horrible indictment of the VA system? This was after May 28, Memorial Day weekend, involuntary commitment. It was after June 5, we attempted to put him into the VA—no good—and then Joyce called the hospital on June 14, seeing if something could be done. On June 22, the day that Jeff hung himself, the VA sent him a letter stating his follow-up appointment is July 13. We have that letter here.

# CHRONOLOGY OF THE WAR

*(includes references from the narratives)*

## Background to the Iraq War

The paths of Iraq and the US have only recently crossed. Iraq was governed as a British mandate after World War I and the peace treaty of Versailles, becoming self-governing under a royal family, which was then deposed in 1958, after which it became a republic. The Baath Party was established in 1968, and one of its leaders, Saddam Hussein, became president in 1979. The US supported Iraq in its war with Iran from 1980 to 1988, sending envoy Donald Rumsfeld to a 1983 meeting with Saddam Hussein. During that war, Saddam Hussein used chemical weapons against Kurds who were calling for autonomy.

The US and Iraq collided during the Persian Gulf War (1990–1991), with the US Congress voting war powers to the first President George Bush, and the UN authorizing a 32-country coalition because Iraq had invaded the sovereign nation of Kuwait. Saddam Hussein was roundly defeated in Operation Desert Storm—after which the UN conducted weapons inspections, imposed sanctions, and established no-fly zones to keep him from attacking Kurds and Shiites again. In 1993, the US discovered an Iraqi plot to assassinate former President Bush in Kuwait, and launched a cruise-missile retaliation. When Saddam Hussein expelled the UN inspectors in 1998, the US launched Operation Desert Fox—bombing Iraq from the sea. In 2001, President George W. Bush ordered the bombing of Iraq's air defense network when Iraq interfered with US and UK monitoring of the no-fly zones.

After the catastrophic events of September 11, 2001, defeating al-Qaeda and the global war on terror (GWOT) became the focus of President Bush's foreign policy. Operation Enduring Freedom (OEF) was launched in Afghanistan in 2001 to find Osama bin Laden and stop terrorist training. In 2002, the US set up a prison at Guantánamo Bay, Cuba (GITMO), to house hundreds of combatants captured in Afghanistan. President Bush also identified Iraq, Iran, and North Korea as the "axis of evil" and announced his "preemptive strike" doctrine, which he would apply to Iraq. UN inspectors returned to Iraq but did not find weapons of mass destruction (WMD). In October, the US Congress voted to allow President Bush to use force against Iraq. In December, the Pentagon called up reservists, and Secretary of State Colin Powell declared Iraq in breach of UN resolutions.

In 2003, France (openly) and Germany (more discreetly) distanced themselves from the US confrontation with Iraq, prompting Secretary of Defense Rumsfeld to refer to them as "old Europe." US troops were deployed to Turkey and Kuwait and Secretary of State Powell told the UN Security Council—which had refused to sanction the war—that there was evidence of WMDs in Iraq. Major protests were held in the US and overseas in February, challenging the claim that Iraq was linked to global terrorism. President Bush issued an ultimatum on March 17 for Saddam Hussein to leave Iraq in 48 hours. When Hussein rejected the ultimatum on March 19, 2003, the war officially began.

## *"Operation Iraqi Freedom"*

### OIF-2003

| | |
|---|---|
| March 19 | War opens with an effort to bomb Saddam Hussein and his sons |
| March 21 | US, UK ground invasion of Iraq from Kuwait—150,000 US troops and 23,000 coalition troops from 23 countries; oil fields secured |
| March 22 | "Shock and Awe": massive air strikes on Baghdad; navy ships support invasion from Mediterranean and Persian Gulf |
| March 23 | Fighting in Nasariya, "Ambush Alley," capture and recovery of Jessica Lynch |
| April 9 | Coalition forces take Baghdad; Saddam Hussein's statue toppled; looting follows |
| April 21 | Retired General Jay Garner becomes interim civil administrator of Iraq |
| April 22 | In Karbala, first Shia pilgrimage in 25 years |
| April 28 | Secretary of Defense Rumsfeld announces US to withdraw from bases in Saudi Arabia |
| May 1 | Bush declares the "end of major combat operations" (with a sign reading "Mission Accomplished") on the *USS Lincoln* |

| | |
|---|---|
| May | Ambassador L. Paul Bremer III, director of Coalition Provisional Authority (CPA) dissolves Iraqi army, civil service, Baath Party; Green Zone established, with plans for a US embassy compound of 100 acres in middle of Baghdad |
| July 2 | Bush gives "Bring 'em on" speech regarding Iraq insurgency |
| July 13 | US names 25-member Iraqi Governing Council (IGC) |
| July 22 | Saddam Hussein's sons Uday and Qusay killed by US in Mosul |
| August 19 | UN HQ bombed in Baghdad; |
| August | Troop concerns about lack of armor on Humvee vehicles, body armor |
| Aug–Nov | Lieutenant Colonel Allen West, 4th ID, mistreats detainees in Tikrit, is court-martialed, forced to retire from army |
| November 6 | Congress votes $87 billion for reconstruction in Iraq and Afghanistan |
| December 13 | Saddam Hussein is captured near Tikrit |
| December 17 | Lead weapons investigator David Kay leaves Iraq not having found WMDs. Paul Wolfowitz, deputy secretary of defense, announces US can now move its bases from Saudi Arabia to Iraq |

## OIF-2004

| | |
|---|---|
| January 19 | Article 15-6 "Taguba" report (by Major General Taguba) ordered on Abu Ghraib torture of prisoners—report by Major General Antonio Taguba found "criminal abuses." In 2006, General Taguba claims he was forced to retire |
| March 31 | Falluja: Iraqi mob kills four private military contractors, mutilates corpses and hangs two from a bridge |
| April 4 | In "Operation Vigilant Resolve," US launches assault on Falluja in retaliation for killing of contractors and for insurgent attacks on US forces |
| April 18 | Spain pulls its troops out of coalition after a change in government |

| | |
|---|---|
| April 27 | Six soldiers charged with abusing prisoners at Abu Ghraib prison |
| April 29 | Photographs of abuse in Abu Ghraib prison published. From May 2004 to March 2006, ten enlisted men and women are convicted: seven sentenced to one year or less of prison, three sentenced to up to ten years |
| May 17 | President of IGC Ezzedine Salim assassinated |
| May 28 | Iyad Allawi (Shiite) chosen prime minister of interim government |
| June 28 | US occupation authority turns over formal power to interim government |
| July 6 | Specialist Jeffrey Wershow walks into Baghdad University cafeteria for a soda, takes off his helmet and is shot in the head and killed |
| July | Muqtada al-Sadr (whose father was killed by Saddam Hussein) uses Mahdi Army to take control of Baghdad streets; fighting in Baghdad and Najaf increases; peace brokered by Grand Ayatollah al-Sistani. |
| September 6 | 1,000 US soldiers killed in Iraq war to date |
| September | Ohio man with bipolar disorder recruited; parents intervene |
| September | Ahmed Chalabi, Iraqi exile, fails to become leader of interim government |
| October 19 | Saddam Hussein put on trial for 1982 massacre of 148 Shiites from Dujail |
| November 2 | US presidential election: Bush defeats Kerry |
| Nov 8–Dec | Second major US offensive in Falluja: "Operation Phantom Fury" |
| December 8 | In Kuwait, Spec. Wilson asks Sec. Rumsfeld why vehicles are not armored; Rumsfeld answers, "You go to war with the army you have…" |
| December 15 | Parliamentary elections held |
| December | The hunt for biological, chemical, and nuclear weapons in Iraq officially ends |

## OIF-2005

| | |
|---|---|
| January 12 | US calls off search for WMDs |
| January 13 | Election for Iraqi government to draft permanent constitution |
| January 26 | Thirty-one US soldiers detailed for election security killed in helicopter crash |
| January 30 | Iraqis elect 275-seat National Assembly to replace interim government, 58 percent turnout; Sunnis boycott elections |
| February 28 | Suicide bomber kills 115–125 applicants for Iraqi police force, army |
| April 6–7 | Prime Minister Ibrahim al-Jaafari (Shiite) and President Jalal Talabani (Kurd) installed |
| May | $82 billion supplemental appropriations approved by US Congress |
| May 9 | *Newsweek* story regarding flushing Qur'an down toilet in GITMO retracted |
| June 28 | CPA, IGC disbanded as new transitional constitution comes into effect |
| July 16 | Eleven US soldiers charged with abuse of prisoners in Iraq |
| August 6 | Cindy Sheehan sets up antiwar "Camp Casey" in Crawford, TX, to confront President Bush about her son's 2004 death in Iraq; establishes Gold Star [those who have lost a family member] Families for Peace |
| October 15 | Iraqi voters approve new constitution |
| October 26 | 2,000 US soldiers killed in Iraq war to date |
| November 17 | Rep. John Murtha (D-PA), ex-marine, calls for immediate withdrawal of US troops from Iraq |
| November 19 | Twenty-four civilians in Haditha killed by marines after comrade killed by IED |
| December 15 | New National Assembly elected, new constitution to be ratified |
| December 15 | Senator John McCain's anti-torture amendment to defense bill passed |
| December | Fourteen out of 30 countries in coalition have left or reduced troops |

## OIF-2006

| | |
|---|---|
| February 22 | Al-Qaeda bombs al-Askariya (Shiite) Mosque in Samarra |
| February 28 | Zogby poll: 72 percent of US troops in Iraq think US should leave in 2006 |
| March 12 | US soldiers charged with rape and murder in deaths in Mahmudiya |
| March 16 | Congress passes $72 billion emergency war spending package |
| April 13 | Six retired army and marine generals call for Rumsfeld's resignation |
| May 20 | Iraqi Parliament approves coalition government of Prime Minister Nuri al-Maliki (Shiite) and President Jalal Talabani (Kurd) |
| June 8 | Abu Musab al-Zarqawi, al-Qaeda's Iraq leader, killed by US forces |
| November 7 | Democrats win majority in US Congress with Iraq war key issue |
| November 8 | Secretary of Defense Donald Rumsfeld resigns; |
| November | US troops total 140,000; coalition troops total 18,000 |
| December 6 | Bipartisan "Iraq Study Group" publishes its findings that the situation in Iraq is "grave and deteriorating" |
| December 18 | Robert Gates new secretary of defense, replacing Rumsfeld |
| December 30 | Saddam Hussein hanged |
| December 30 | 3,000 US soldiers killed in Iraq war to date |
| December 30 | Different estimates of Iraqi civilian deaths in war since 2003: 34,000 (UN), 57,000 (iraqbodycount.org and Brookings Iraq Index), 150,000 (Iraqi Ministry of Health), or 600,000 (Johns Hopkins School of Public Health, published in *Lancet,* October 11, 2006), out of population of 27 million (or 2.5% of the population) |
| December 31 | $350 billion cost of Iraq war to the US through 2006 |

## OIF-2007 *(January to September)*

| | |
|---|---|
| January 4 | US military leadership shake up: General David Petraeus replaces General George Casey as top commander in Iraq; Admiral William Fallon replaces General John Abizaid as head of Central Command |
| January 10 | President Bush plans US troop "surge" in Baghdad and Anbar province by adding about 28,000 new troops |
| February 11 | US officials claim Iran is supplying new types of weapons to Iraqi insurgents |
| February 16 | US House of Representatives passes nonbinding resolution against troop "surge" and urges phased redeployment of troops by March 2008, but later votes $100 billion for war effort without conditions |
| February 21 | UK announces plans to reduce troop strength at Basra Airbase |
| February 26 | Bomb explodes in Iraqi ministry inside Green Zone |
| March 27 | Iraqi government announces that it will allow return to government of some Baath Party members |
| March 28 | Ryan Crocker replaces Zalmay Khalilzad as US ambassador to Iraq |
| April 12 | Bomber kills eight inside Iraqi Parliament |
| April 24 | Jessica Lynch testifies in congressional hearing that she was not "little girl Rambo," never firing a shot. Lynch claims that the army made her capture and rescue into an heroic tale not based in reality |
| April 27 | Lieutenant Colonel Paul Yingling is first active-duty officer to say US military leaders mishandled war and misinformed Congress |
| April | US military starts building a three-mile, twelve-foot wall between Shiite and Sunni neighborhoods in Baghdad |
| May 9 | Gen. John Batiste, retired major general and ex-commander of First ID in Iraq says US cannot win a sectarian civil war in Iraq |

| | |
|---|---|
| May 15 | Lieutenant General Douglas Lute becomes Iraq "war czar" (coordinator) |
| June | American troop "surge" reaches 30,000 troops, tasked to increase security, reduce sectarian violence, support Iraqi government. American troop level tops 160,000 |
| June 11 | US military announces new strategy to arm Iraqi Sunnis to attack al-Qaeda |
| June 13–16 | Samarra's Shiite Golden Mosque is again attacked and its minarets destroyed; Sunni mosques bombed in retaliation |
| June 17 | General Petraeus speaks of US counterterrorist efforts in Iraq lasting another decade, with a prolonged US military presence there |
| August 24 | US National Intelligence Estimate: Iraqi government has failed to end sectarian violence even with US troop "surge" |
| September 3 | President Bush makes surprise visit to Anbar province to underscore progress in security |
| September 6 | Three supervising marine officers censured for improper performance of duties regarding Haditha killing of 24 civilians in November 2005; most murder charges against perpetrators dropped |
| Sept. 10–11 | Gen. Petraeus, Amb. Crocker tell Congress US is making progress in Iraq but more time is needed |
| September 13 | Abdul al Rishawi, a US Sunni ally against al-Qaeda in Anbar province assassinated |
| September 13 | President Bush says troops will 'return on success'—reducing force level of 168,000 to pre-surge 130,000 by summer 2008 |
| September 16 | Blackwater USA contractors kill 11 Iraqi civilians, Iraqis protest |

# GLOSSARY OF MILITARY TERMS

## Military Ranks from Lower to Upper

**Army**
*Enlisted (E 1–4)*: private/recruit, private, private first class, specialist, corporal;

*Non-commissioned officers (E 4–9)*: sergeant, staff sergeant, sergeant first class, master sergeant, first sergeant, sergeant major, command sergeant major, sergeant major of the army; warrant officers 1–5;

*Commissioned officers (O 1–10)*: second lieutenant, first lieutenant, captain, major, lieutenant colonel, colonel, brigadier general, major general, lieutenant general, general.

**Air Force**
*Enlisted (E 1–4)*: airman basic, airman, senior airman (sergeant);

*Non-commissioned officers (E 5–9)*, staff sergeant, technical sergeant, master sergeant, senior master sergeant, chief master sergeant, chief master sergeant of the AF;

*Commissioned officers (O 1–10)*: second lieutenant through general as in army (above).

**Navy** (uses the term "rates" not "ranks")
*Enlisted (E 1–3)*: seaman recruit, seaman apprentice, seaman;

*Non-commissioned officers (E 4–9)*: petty officer third class; petty officer second class, petty officer first class, chief petty officer, senior chief petty officer, master chief petty officer, master chief petty officer of the navy; chief warrant officers 1–3;

*Commissioned officers (O 1–10)*: ensign, lieutenant junior grade, lieutenant, lieutenant commander, commander, captain, rear admiral (commodore), rear admiral (upper half), vice admiral, admiral.

**Marine Corps**

*Enlisted (E 1–4)*: private, private first class, lance corporal, corporal;

*Non-commissioned officers (E 5–9)*: sergeant, staff sergeant, gunnery sergeant, master sergeant, first sergeant, master gunnery sergeant, sergeant major, sergeant major of the marine corps, chief warrant officers 1–3;

*Commissioned officers (O 1–10)*: second lieutenant through general as in army and air force, commandant of the marine corps.

# Military Units from Smaller to Larger with Approximate Sizes

*Army*: squad (10), platoon (40), company (175), battalion (700), regiment (1,500) brigade (4,500), division (15,000), corps (30,000), army (100,000).

*Air force*: flight (20–100), squadron (100–300), group (300–1,000), wing (1,000–5,000), numbered air force (varies), air force (varies), major command

*Navy*: squadron, wing, naval air force, fleet

*Marine Corps:* team (4), squad (12) platoon (30–60), company (100–200), battalion (600–800), regiment (2,000–3,000), division (10,000), marine expeditionary unit (2,200), marine expeditionary force (50,000)

*Special Forces:* Army Special Forces, Rangers, Delta Force; Navy SEALs; Marine Corps Force Recon

# Military Terms

| | |
|---|---|
| 1-MC | general announcing system, navy shipboard |
| A-team | US Army Special Forces team operating in remote area |
| AAV | amphibious assault vehicle |
| AFB | air force base |
| AK-47 | Russian-made assault rifle prevalent in Iraqi population (also Kalashnikov) |
| AIT | advanced individual training |
| Ammo | ammunition |
| ASVAB | Armed Services Vocational Aptitude Battery (military entrance examination) |
| Bradley | M2, M3 infantry fighting vehicle, armored personnel carrier |
| C-4 | powerful plastic explosive |
| CO | commanding officer |
| CSC | combat stress control |
| Commander in chief | president of the United States |
| Contractors | private firms that contract with the armed forces on site, e.g., Halliburton |
| Court-martial | judicial punishment for members of armed services |
| ECP | entry control point |
| EPW | enemy prisoner of war |
| Firebase | secured (often remote) site |
| FOB | forward operating base |
| GED | General Education Development (alternative to high-school diploma) |
| Hemmet | High extended mobility tactical truck |
| Howitzer | cannon |
| HP4 | shoulder-launched missile |
| Humvee (HMMWV) | high-mobility multipurpose wheeled vehicle |
| HUMINT | human-intelligence collector (interrogator) |
| ID | Infantry Division, as in Third ID |
| IED | improvised explosive device (often used by insurgents on roads) |
| Intel | intelligence information |
| JAG | judge advocate general |

| | |
|---|---|
| Kevlar | resistant fabric used in helmets |
| KIA | killed in action |
| LAR | light-armored reconnaissance (vehicle) |
| LARC | lighter amphibious re-supply cargo |
| LAV | light-armored vehicle |
| LRRP | long-range reconnaissance patrol (Vietnam) |
| LVS | logistics vehicle system |
| M2 | .50 caliber machine gun |
| M-4 | lightweight military assault rifle, useful in close quarters |
| M-16 | lightweight military assault rifle |
| MEF | Marine Expeditionary Force |
| MEU | Marine Expeditionary Unit |
| MEPS | military entrance processing station |
| MIG | Russian-made military airplane |
| MOPP | mission-oriented protective posture (apparel used against NBC attack) |
| Mortar | indirect fire weapon using tube (often used by insurgents) |
| MOS | military occupational specialty |
| MOUT | military operations in urban terrain |
| MRE | meals ready to eat (field rations) |
| NBC | nuclear, biological, chemical (potential attacks) |
| NCO | noncommissioned officer |
| NCS | net control station (radio) |
| NVG | night-vision goggles |
| OEF | Operation Enduring Freedom (Afghanistan 2001–) |
| OIF | Operation Iraqi Freedom (Iraq 2003–) |
| Ops | operations |
| Parris Island | marine training center (boot camp) |
| PTSD | post-traumatic stress disorder |
| PX | Post exchange: military store located on base |
| Rocket | self-propelled projectile (often used by insurgents) |
| Republican Guard | elite Iraqi fighting force |
| ROE | rules of engagement (rules governing action against enemy) |
| ROTC | Reserve Officers' Training Corps |
| RPG | rocket-propelled grenade |

| | |
|---|---|
| SASO | stability and security operations: "winning hearts and minds," supporting nation-building (marines) |
| SEAL | "Sea, air, land" Navy commando team |
| Sniper | rifleman who shoots from concealed position |
| Task Force Tarawa | Second Marine Expeditionary Force (OIF invasion) |
| TCN | third-country nationals (e.g. Filipinos, Pakistanis, Indians working on US bases) |
| Tomahawk | cruise missile fired from ship, land, or aircraft |
| Twentynine Palms | marine desert training, California |
| USMC | US Marine Corps |
| XO | executive officer, second in command |